WHAT PEOPLE SAY...

Steve Nicholas, retired evangelist and data scientist

It's been a joy to read Andy's thoughts and talk them through with him. Part 1 of the book covers the last 2000 years. It inevitably blurs between individual and communal faith and geopolitical powers. Andy's questions for discussion at the end of each section are excellent.

Part 2 covers many themes and sub-themes of the emerging digital global culture, including easily forgotten stresses of the early 21st century such as the Congo, as well as the rise of China with its big data surveillance. It's excellent for bringing up topics for conversation in home groups, at the pub, or wherever. Part 3 has plenty to pick up, reject, argue with. It's not meant to be definitive. It is a structured collection of musings that generate thinking and stimulate wider reading and discussion. It will be best published with white space and wide margins for making notes, ready for lively conversations!

James Behrens, barrister and licensed lay minister

The first part of Andy's book is an amazing account of almost two thousand years. The description of political and economic events are useful in enabling us to see the Christian story in perspective. I was slightly surprised that the second part covering the first twenty five years of this century's was as big as part one. The account of all the various new ideas was very fair.

I liked the third part, 'Being Credible in the Post-Modern World' because it challenges one to think. My response to the question 'Does the Church have a Future' is "Yes, but..."

Richard Knight, retired research scientist

Belief has an ancient history. Christianity has a rather shorter one. In his erudite book, Andy reviews that history largely, though not exclusively, in the Anglican interpretation. He wonders if, with the technological and cultural changes of the 21st century, the conventional church can survive.

Strangely, as an atheist, I am less pessimistic. I was in the West Kennet Long Barrow My brainwaves became synchronised with the three thousand six hundred years of the co-ordinated resonances of the burial chambers. I felt a sunrise penetrate the passages of my mind. As I worshipped, I lay in wonder on a floor of flint.

That wonder will never leave humanity. Whether sensed in organ music, stained glass and ritual, in the acoustic and optic stimuli of an Avebury tomb or the dignity of communion in Salisbury cathedral.

THE CHURCH HAS A PAST HAS IT GOT A FUTURE?

By Rev Andy Roland

Published by
Filament Publishing Ltd
14, Croydon Road, Beddington,
Croydon, Surrey CR0 4PA
+44(0)20 8688 2598
www.filamentpublishing.com

Book design - Ana Celia Silva
Cover design: Daniel Gould

The Church has a past - has it got a future?
by Andy Roland

© 2025 Andy Roland

ISBN 978-1-915465-82-5

All rights reserved
No portion of this work may be copied by any means
without the prior written permission of the publishers

The right to be recognised as the author of this work has
been asserted by Andy Roland in accordance with the
Designs and Copyrights Act 1988

CONTENTS

INTRODUCTION

PART 1
CONTINUING CONVERSATIONS
30 - 2000

PART 2
NEW WORLD / NEW CONSCIOUSNESS
2000 - 2025

PART 3
BEING CREDIBLE IN THE POST
MODERN WORLD

PART 1

CONTINUING CONVERSATIONS
30 - 2000

Foreword - Rt Rev Rob Gillion	13
The Church has a Past has it got a Future? Introduction	15
The First Century	20
The Gentile Religion	25
The Later Roman Empire	28
Barbarians and Norsemen	33
The 12th Century Renaissance	41
The Eastern Roman Empire	46
The Crisis of the 14th and 15th Centuries	51
The Reformation & Counter-Reformation	55
The 18th Century	63
The 19th Century	70
The 20th Century	80

PART 2

NEW WORLD/NEW CONSCIOUSNESS
2000 - 2025

The 21st Century	
Introduction	102
War and Politics	103
Liberalism and International Cooperation	103
Democracy and Autocracy	105
Populism and Autocracy	107
Terrorism	111
War	114
Economics	119
Growth	119
Boom Years	119
The Crash	120
The Rich World	120
China expands	121
Digital Currencies	122
Climate Change and Other Disasters	125
Health	129
Public Health - Pandemics	129
- Other Issues	133
New Medical Science	137
Gene Therapy	137
Microrobots, nanorobots & AI	138
Synthetic Biology	139
The Magic CRISPR	140

Science & Space	143
Graphene	143
Space telescopes	144
Space	145
Archaeology	146
Technology and Communication	148
Computers - the hardware	148
Computers - the software	151
Internet issues: Censorship	154
Cybercrime	154
Pornography	155
AI	157
The history of AI	157
AI applications	158
Large Language Model	159
An AI future	160
Cultural Shifts - Sex	162
Relationships	162
Sexual Practices	164
Surrogacy	165
Sexual Orientation	165
Some Definitions	165
Transgender Issues	171
Gender-fluidity	173
Safeguarding against abuse	174
Women Arising	175
#MeToo	175
Politics	176
BBC	176
Higher positions	177
A Teen Viewpoint	177

Entertainment and Media	178
Social Media	178
Gen Z and Social Media	183
Video Games	185
The Best of the Rest	188
Religion	190
Some Statistics - UK	190
More Statistics - USA	191
Yet More Statistics - the World	192
Sexual abuse in the Church	192
The Makin Review	194
Reacting to the Sexual Revolution	195
The New Atheism	197
Mindfulness	197
A Land of Faiths	199
Islam	202
Church Theology	203
Church Worship	204
Messy Church	205
Food banks	205
Pope Francis	206
New Age Religions	207
So what is the question?	210

PART 3

BEING CREDIBLE IN THE POST-MODERN WORLD

1	Introduction: Who's Listening?	213
2	Good, bad or both? The Natural History of Religion	217
3	Danger! Stories!	222
4	Is 'God' past its sell-by date?	229
5	God in 3D	234
6	The Bible is not the word of God - it is more interesting than that.	241
7	Jesus - the Facts	248
8	Why did Jesus die - according to Jesus?	254
9	Whose Son?	256
10	The Only Way? Faith in a World of Faiths	266
11	What's the Problem? - the Problem of Sin	275
12	What's our Problem? - the Puzzle of Good and Evil	283
13	Sex and Society	291
14	A History of Hell	303

15 Death etc. - The Psychic Realm	313
16 Death etc. - The Realm of Light	317
17 Transformations	327
18 Conclusion: Crisis? What Crisis?	337
Bibliography	347

FOREWORD

BY RT REV ROB GILLION

A daunting task to offer a foreword to a book which is packed full of history and enormous challenges. It is an adventurous journey through the history of the Church and asks important questions for its future.

I would describe Part 1 as a comprehensive map for the journey with some helpful directions and posing some insightful questions at the end of each section.

I suggest this first part might be filling your back pack as you prepare for the journey. Placing in it the tools you need for navigation and rich nourishment to sustain you - which include the stories, often personal, delightfully woven into the historical facts. Plenty of 'Food for Thought'.

The journey then begins in part 2 meeting others on this exciting pilgrimage. A lot of ground is covered, describing a quarter of a century's changes in politics, technology and society. It offers plenty of topics for conversations both christological, ecclesiological and theological.

It is a well crafted and fascinating pilgrimage, stopping often to be refreshed and challenged.

The strength of this pilgrimage is the story-rich journey with many opportunities to contemplate on what has been learnt and to admit there is so much still to be discovered about the future of the Church.

I encourage you to retrace your steps from time to time to time to revisit some of the challenges and questions posed .

Part 3 provides the challenge to discern the credibility of the Church in a post modern world with so many relevant and resonating topics to contemplate and challenge us.

All in all, one is given a bag of tools to help us delve into the history of the Church and a journey with so many great teachers and theologians, including Andy himself!

The book encourages us to find answers, or perhaps to offer a response, to the big questions posed concerning the future of the Church. This book provides a challenge to think critically. It certainly made me think!

Rt Rev Rob Gillion

THE CHURCH HAS A PAST HAS IT GOT A FUTURE?

INTRODUCTION

In the heart of the Sussex woods lies the Monastery of the Holy Trinity. It is home to a small Anglian contemplative community, the Community of the Servants of the Will of God. Its community rule was written in 1966, and starts with this prophetic introduction:

"This rule has come into being within the period of transition between two stages of the Christian era:

"between the age of Christendom, during which the Western nations have been generally conscious of the law of God, even when failing to apply it, and the Church has been normally established, respected and in a position of power;

"and the coming age, when the Church must complete its appointed task of proclaiming the Gospel throughout the world, from within a worldwide, materialistic, and man-centred culture."

This paragraph, over sixty years old, expresses the heart of the question "Does the Church have a future?" By that, I do not mean, "Will the Church survive?" Even if some branches of the worldwide Church wither and die, others will reframe themselves to create new and vibrant communities, even in the Western world.

The question rather is, will the Church survive as a successful sect, something in the manner of the Church of the Latter Day Saints/Mormons in America? Modern Evangelicalism tends towards this pattern. And so, in a different way, does traditional Anglo-Catholicism. Or will the Christian faith reclaim a place in the public square, so that its beliefs and principles command widespread respect in society?

Journey of a Book

This book was not conceived all of a piece, it grew like Topsy. Here is how it developed.

May 2018

On May 2018 I was at a clergy study morning in Kensington on "Sharing Faith" - how we share our faith with others. As the morning progressed I began to feel uneasy about the use of the words "gospel" and "good news", repeated constantly as if their meaning was self-evident. I began to ask myself, "If the gospel is the answer, what's the question?" Perhaps the question is not the same in every society and at every time. During the question and answer session I tried to express my concern, but the bishop said, "That's a statement, I'll only take questions." I felt properly put in my place, but it got me thinking.

I decided to look at the last 2,000 years of Christian history. My central theme was not what the gospel meant or what the Church was saying, but what questions were bubbling up in society to which the Church could make a coherent response.

What sort of questions was I looking for? In 1943 the American psychologist Maslow famously identified a basic five-fold hierarchy of needs:
- physiological needs - food, drink, shelter etc.
- safety needs - health, financial and personal security.
- love and social belonging needs - family, friends, trust.
- esteem needs: - self-respect and respect from others
- self-actualisation needs, including cognitive and aesthetic needs and ultimately spiritual transcendence.

The reality of a hierarchy as such has been questioned, but many find it a useful model. It spotlights the question that I was seeking to look at both historically and today: once you have enough to eat, somewhere to live comfortably, protection from enemies; friends and family around you; work which you feel gives meaning to your life, what then? The question then arises: 'Why do I still feel dissatisfied? What else am I looking for?' How is that question posed in various societies at various times? And how can the Church respond appropriately?

June 2018
When my attention came to the twenty years post-2000 I had a shock. I realised that there were so many and such radical new developments that I needed a completely new approach.

Fortunately God (or the Universe) gave me a helping hand. Just a month after my original idea, I went to a free piano recital at St Bride's Fleet Street. Coming back to Blackfriars I met a young man offering a twelve weekly subscription to the Economist.

I took advantage of the offer and have been a subscriber ever since. It is consistently interesting and from time to time has in-depth articles on special subjects such as Islam and synthetic biology. This has really helped, alongside Wikipedia and other sources of information. I was able to summarise every major new development which has come to fruition in the last twenty or so years, developments which dramatically affect humanity. I have checked what I have written with people who have professional knowledge of these areas. Developments covered include climate change, the internet, social media, AI, euthanasia, synthetic biology, digital currencies, space colonisation and sexual revolutions (several). Normally we think of one of these topics at a time. I hope that in bringing them all together, we can appreciate how new the sea is which Christian churches now have to navigate.

March 2020 - present

By March 2020 most of the first two sections were complete. Then Covid struck! I had no idea what the world would look like after the pandemic. I put the book aside for the time being and wrote something less controversial: 'Jesus the Troublemaker – his last eight days', a historical novel. It seems to me that what we have now is an intensification of previous trends rather than something totally new. The main lines of the future have already been drawn.

STRUCTURE AND SUMMARY

Part 1 - Continuing Converstations

A brief overview of the historical background of western societies over the centuries, together with what religious questions arose to which the Church could give a response.

Part 2 - New World/ New Consciousness

In which all the main developments within politics, science and society over the last quarter of a century are described.

Part 3 - Being Credible in the Post-Modern World

In which the Church is challenged to rethink some of its sacred cows, and secular society is challenged to open its mind to some inconvenient ideas.

PART 1
THE FIRST TWO THOUSAND YEARS

THE FIRST CENTURY

Menorah from the Temple in Jerusalem carried by Roman soldiers. The Arch of Titus, 82 AD

Historical Background

The first century A.D. (Anno Domini) or C.E. (Common Era) was the first hundred years of the 'Pax Romana', the Roman Peace, in which the whole Mediterranean world enjoyed a united economic system and peace. This led to Jewish emigration throughout the empire, from Cadiz to the Crimea. There were eleven synagogues in Rome and over a million Jews in Alexandria and Egypt. The geographical limits of Roman power were decided in the West by the destruction of three Roman legions by Germanic tribes in 9 CE and by the conquest of Britain under the emperor Claudius in 42. There was a period of violence in the 60's - Boudicca's destruction of London in 61, the Jewish revolt in Palestine in 66-70 and destruction of Jerusalem, and the civil war between four imperial claimants in 68. Culturally it was a Greek world, in which almost everyone spoke Greek either as a first or second language. Seneca disparagingly called Rome "Graeca urbs" - "the Greek city". Economically it was a system based on slavery, just as our modern system is based on wage-employment. In Palestine the main economic oppression was the system of absentee landowners, giving the peasant farmers very little security as well as liability to heavy taxation.

Jewish religion

The religious background in the Palestine of Jesus' day was complicated. The Sadducees ruled the Temple in Jerusalem and made up most of the Sanhedrin, the supreme council for Jews. Pharisees were those who were 'zealous' for keeping the Law and were held in high regard by the people. The Essenes lived in monastic communities and were looking forward to God's final liberation of Israel from the rule of the Romans and of the "wicked priest ' in Jerusalem. The Herodians were those who supported Herod the Great's grandsons as providing a limited Jewish autonomy under Rome. In Galilee people were open to a more charismatic form of Judaism, exemplified in the ministry of Jesus.

Jewish questions

Less than two hundred years before the ministry of Jesus, a popular revolt against the Seleucid (Persian) king's attempt to destroy Judaism (e.g. by sacrificing pigs on the altar in the temple at Jerusalem) amazingly defeated the might of the most powerful empire in the Middle East. In Jesus' day those in power were the Romans, with the sons of the tyrannical Herod I and the heartily disliked Temple aristocracy. Perhaps God would deliver Israel again! As Jesus' disciples asked, *"Will God at this time restore the kingdom to Israel?"* Jesus' reply was always, it's none of your business. *"It is not for you to know the times or periods.."* (Acts 1.6,7)

The early church lived in active expectation of the end times, of the final judgement. "(God) has fixed a day when he will have the world judged in righteousness by a man whom he has appointed…" (Acts 17.31) Surely, Jesus' resurrection was the first instalment of the general resurrection which would bring an end to history, wasn't it?

This hope probably began to fade after the destruction of Jerusalem in 68 AD. How come Christianity did not fade along with it? I think it must have been the intense personal experience of being gripped by the Holy Spirit.. So much was this the case that Paul could use language of the end times to describe the normal experience of being a Christian: *"If anyone is in Christ, there is a new creation; everything old has passed away; see, everything has become new!"* And this is something that Gentile Christians shared along with their Jewish brothers and sisters.

But what about ordinary Jewish people?

We are fortunate in knowing what the key question among ordinary Jews was in Jesus' time, because he was asked it twice, both times by non-disciples: *"What must I do to inherit eternal life?"* (Mark 10.17, Luke 10.25). Note that the question was *"What must I do?,"* not *"What must I believe?"*

What was going on here? At that time people's belief about the after-life was the mirror image of today's. Today a once definite belief in life after death is morphing into at best agnosticism, in Jesus' time a faith in which life after death played little or no part (e.g. the Sadducees) was transforming into a belief in God's eternal vindication of those who had stayed faithful, even dying as martyrs, as in the Maccabean revolt 160 years before Jesus' birth.

So the question at the back of the question might have been, "Do I have to die as a martyr - I hope not!" It is clear that the apostles' preaching of Jesus' death and resurrection directly spoke to this issue. The death had been done and the resurrection had already started.

Judaism was a practical religion. You showed your devotion by doing it, living your daily life in accordance with the laws laid down in the first five books of the Bible: Genesis, Exodus, Leviticus, Numbers, Deuteronomy. To do even more than keeping the all the 613 recognised rules was unrealistic, surely?

Jesus responded either by referring to the Ten Commandments (Mark 10.17ff) or by quoting with approval the Shema - the basic Jewish creed: *"Love the Lord your God with all your heart and soul and mind and strength, and love your neighbour as yourself."* (Luke 10.25ff). Or as Paul wrote in Romans 13.9-10: "The commandments, '*You shall not commit adultery; You shall not murder; You shall not steal; You shall not covet*'; *and any other commandment, are summed up in this word, 'Love your neighbour as yourself.' Love does no wrong to a neighbour; therefore, love is the fulfilling of the law."*

What Jesus stressed was the need for a change of heart, (repentance), something that translated into a radical lifestyle which broke down barriers between people. That was how you inherited eternal life, and how you prepared for the coming reign of God.

So what were the questions?
When will God restore the kingdom to Israel?
What must I do to inherit eternal life?

YOUR OWN REFLECTIONS
How would you answer someone who asked 'What must is do to inherit eternal life?'

What is eternal life?

Do you think that the establishment of the state of Israel, and the expulsion of 75% of the Palestinian population is a case of God restoring the kingdom?

THE GENTILE RELIGION

Gentile religion

Religion in the Roman empire was a mixture of traditional worship, religious philosophies, mystery religions and emperor worship.

Augustus (reigned 27 BCE - 14 CE) carried out a vast programme of revival and reform of traditional religion. A classic account of traditional religion in practice comes in Acts, after Paul has healed a cripple: *The crowd shouted in the Lycaonian language, 'The gods have come down to us in human form!' Barnabas they called Zeus, and Paul they called Hermes, because he was the chief speaker. The priest of Zeus, whose temple was just outside the city, brought oxen and garlands to the gates; he and the crowds wanted to offer sacrifice.* (Acts 14.11-13)

Philosophers such as the Stoics argued that people should lead moral lives according to the rational order that governed the universe. Religious debate was a favourite occupation, as seen in the account of Paul's visit to Athens: *Paul argued in the synagogue with the Jews and the devout persons, and also in the market-place every day with those who happened to be there. Some Epicurean and Stoic philosophers debated with Paul. Some said, 'What does this babbler want to say?' Others said, 'He seems to be a proclaimer of foreign divinities.'* (This was because he was telling the good news about Jesus and Resurrection.) *So they took him and brought him to the Areopagus and asked him, 'May we know what this new teaching is that you are presenting? It sounds rather strange to us, so we would like to know what it means.' Now all the Athenians and*

the foreigners living there would spend their time in nothing but telling or hearing something new." (Acts 17.17-21)
In every city there were also a number of Gentiles who were on the fringe of the synagogue, 'God-fearers', attracted by Judaism's monotheism and morality.

The Persian 'mystery' religion of Mithras, with its secret rituals and banquets, though technically illegal, was especially popular among soldiers in the 2nd century.

There is a small Mithras temple outside one of the forts along Hadrian's Wall, with just enough room for the commander of the fort and his senior officers. You can get a taste of this in the Mithraeum opposite Cannon Street station in London.

Augustus had introduced emperor worship at the end of his life, as a ritual 'glue' to hold the empire together. It was particularly strong in the eastern Mediterranean at first, spreading gradually to the west. How this worked in practice is seen in how Pliny, governor of Bithynia (north-east Turkey), writing to emperor Trajan in 112, dealt with those accused and acquitted of being Christians: *"They recited a prayer to the gods at my dictation, made supplication with incense and wine to your statue... and moreover cursed Christ."*

Gentile questions

To the Greeks of that time, both questions which Jews were asking made very little sense. Their world-view assumed that human beings were spirits temporarily enclosed in physical bodies. So what was their question? St Paul tells us. In 1 Corinthians 1.21 Paul says that the Greeks seek God, but that through "wisdom", i.e. philosophy, they failed to know God. In

other words, their question was *"How can I know God?"* Acts 17 reports how Paul's speech in Athens was well received while he stuck to that point, but went down like a lead balloon as soon as he mentioned the resurrection and the last judgement. This concern with the nature of God continued throughout the period of Rome's ascendancy. Around 160 AD Justin, a Christian philosopher, wrote a defence of his faith using the device of a dialogue with a Jew called Trypho. At one point Trypho says, *"Do not the philosophers turn every discourse upon God? and do not questions continually arise abut his unity and providence? Is not this truly the duty of philosophy, to investigate the Deity?"*
(Dialogue 1, from Michael Green, 'Evangelism in the Early Church' p.121)

So what were the questions?
Who or what is God?
and
How can I know God?

YOUR OWN REFLECTIONS
How would you answer someone who asks you 'How can I know God?'

THE LATER ROMAN EMPIRE

*6th century mosaic of Jesus,
Victoria & Albert Museum*

Historical Background

The fourth century was a major turning point in European history. Diocletian was a soldier who rescued the empire from near collapse in the third century. He agreed to the Great Persecution of Christians of 303-311. At a battle in 312 Constantine captured Rome and legalised Christianity the following year, even presiding over a major Church Council, the Council of Nicaea in 325. The Council debated whether Christ was 'of the same substance' or 'of like substance' as God the Father. This divided the Church for the next three centuries.

In 324 Constantine founded Constantinople as the Christian capital of a united Roman Empire. The rest of the century saw vigorous debates between Christians and Roman traditionalists in the West. In the east, the Church became a proletarian movement, inspired by the desert monks who lived in Egypt and Syria. As well as living in hermit communities in the desert, monks worked in city hospitals, in food-supply centres and in burial associations.

They also responded with violence against remaining paganism. In 391 the patriarch of Alexandria called for the destruction of the great temple to Serapis, and was congratulated by the emperor Theodosius. Led by club-wielding monks, mobs terrorised pagan families, culminating in the lynching of the pagan female philosopher Hypatia in Alexandria in 415.

The safe world of the Roman empire was coming to an end. From the 220s it was faced by a hostile and aggressive Persian empire under the Sassanian dynasty. There were constant pressures on the northern frontier from Germanic tribes and in the 5th century those frontiers gave way. In 410 the Visigoths sacked Rome itself, and when Augustine died in Hippo in North Africa in 428, the city was being besieged by the barbarian Vandals.

St Anthony the Great (251-356)

Despite the theological disputes, the key questions that arose in the eastern empire were practical. Evagrius of Pontus (345-399) - a courtier turned priest turned monk turned solitary, identified the Seven Deadly Sins. Anthony was the original pioneer of the move to the desert, after he had given away his wealth at the age of 18.

Abba Poemen asked Abba Anthony,"What should I do?" The old man said, "Do not be confident in your own righteousness, do not worry about a thing once it is done, and control your tongue and your stomach."

St Augustine (354-430)

An invaluable case study of the religious ferment of the fourth century is Augustine, later St Augustine, bishop of Hippo. In his forties, he wrote the first psychological and spiritual autobiography, his "Confessions".

From the age of 19 the young Augustine spent years *"taking seriously the search of wisdom",* (Book 6.11), trying to find the true God and understand the mystery of evil. He did not find the Bible a help. *"The Scriptures...did not appear to me worthy of being compared to the dignity of Marcus Tullius Ciciero."* (Book 3.5).

Above all he wanted to know ultimate truth: *O Truth, Truth, how deeply even then did I sigh and yearn after you in my inmost being." (*Book 3.6*).*

*"Where was I all the time I was looking for you? You were right there before me, but I was running away from myself." (*Book 5.2)
"I kept walking on dark and slippery trails and searching for you outside of myself, while failing to find the God of my own heart." (Confessions, Book 6.1*).*

Augustine left North Africa and settled in Milan, where the celebrated Ambrose was bishop.

"When Mother reached Milan I informed her that while I was not a Christian, neither was I any longer a Manichean. She seemed unimpressed... I was one who now doubted everything, and was convinced that the road that leads to life could not be found." (Book 6.1,2).

What led Augustine towards the Christian faith was clear and sensible teaching on the Bible. *"Now that I heard the Scriptures credibly expounded, I saw that those passages that had struck me as absurd belonged really to the deep mysteries of faith."* (Book 6.5).

"Christ seemed to me to have great authority as a teacher, but of the mystery of "the Word become flesh" I had not the slightest clue... By reading the books of the Platonists I was taught to look for truth as something immaterial and non-physical... Their books fail to reveal the face of devotion, the tears of confession." (Book 7.19, 21).

Augustine went though a very emotional time as he talked with sincere Christians and found his own heart and mind in great agitation. *"A first class uproar now broke out in the house of my inner self... I tugged at my hair and pounded my forehead... weeping in bitter dejection of spirit when I heard a voice coming from the house next door... It was singing over and over in a kind of chant, "Take up and read, take up and read."... I returned quickly to the bench where .. I had left behind a copy of the letters of the Apostle (Paul)... I read silently the first portion of Scripture on which my eye lighted: 'Not in revelling and drunkenness, not in debauchery and licentiousness, not in quarrelling and jealousy. But put on the Lord Jesus Christ, and make no provision for the flesh to gratify its desires.'... Instantly, it seemed, a light of certainty turned on in my heart and all the fog of doubt disappeared."*

(All passages for "The Confessions of Augustine in Modern English, translated and abridged by Sherwood Eliot Wirt,© 1971, published by Lion)

Augustine's moment of conversion is well-known, and is a not uncommon experience in people's lives. The underlying question that drove Augustine forward on his long and tortuous quest was, who is God? What is ultimate truth? The question inspired the other religious movements of the later Roman Empire, such as Manichaeism or Neo-Platonism.

The other point is how the Bible became a reliable spiritual guide to Augustine, which it certainly was not during his early adulthood. Bishop Ambrose was extremely well read, in both Latin and Greek literature. His discussions of the Bible used three levels of interpretation: literal, moral and spiritual. The literal was the straightforward historical meaning. The moral was what meaning could be brought out for people's everyday lives. The spiritual was to show that the wording of texts, not necessarily their literal sense, could be used to point forwards to Christ and the Christian faith. It made sense to Augustine. Does it work today?

So what were his questions?
What is ultimate truth?
How can I know God?

YOUR OWN REFLECTIONS
What would you say to someone who asks you what is ultimate truth?

BARBARIANS AND NORSEMEN

10th century cross at Nevern, Wales, 1845 engraving

Barbarian tribes overran the whole of the western Roman empire in the fifth century. Many of them were converted to Christianity, but to a type of Christianity that the Roman and Eastern Orthodox church considered heretical. There was a resurgence of the empire's power under Justinian in the sixth century, but that collapsed with the renewed invasion of Italy by the Lombards in 569. It must have been rather like New York being taken over by a horde of cowboys - the barbarians were skilful horse-riders. There was gradual conversion of the barbarians in Gaul and Spain, but when, in 597, Pope Gregory sent a monk Augustine (a different person from the bishop of Hippo) to the barbarians in the British Isles they must have seemed quite immune to Christianity. Augustine and his supporting monks *"were appalled at the idea of going to a barbarous fierce and pagan nation, of whose very language they were ignorant"* (Bede). And yet within a century the barbarians in England had embraced the Christian faith and were sending missionaries to convert their Germanic cousins on the continent. What caused the change? What was the question at the heart of their culture which produced such a swift response to the proclamation of the faith? Fortunately, we are told.

Converting the Saxons

The key figure in the conversion of England was King Edwin of Northumbria. About 623 Edwin was in exile and in serious danger from an enemy. One night he saw a stranger who asked what reward he would give to the man who arranged for his fortunes to turn around. *"If the man who can truthfully foretell such good fortune can also give you better and wiser guidance for your life and salvation than anything known to your parents and kinsfolk, will you promise to obey him and follow his advice?"* Of course Edwin said yes, but when he had become king, he got cold feet.

About 627 he summoned a council of his wise men at York. At this council one of the king's chief men said, *"Your Majesty, when we compare the present life of man on earth with that time of which we have no knowledge, it seems to me like the swift flight of a single sparrow through the banqueting-hall where you are sitting at dinner on a winter's day with your thanes and councillors. In the midst there is a comforting fire to warm the hall; outside the storms of winter rain and snow are raging. The sparrow flies swiftly in through one door of the hall, and out through another. While he is inside, he is safe from the winter storms; but after a few moments of comfort, he vanishes from sight into the wintry world from which he came. Even so, man appears on earth for a little while; but of what went before this life or of what follows we know nothing.*

Therefore if this new teaching has brought any more certain knowledge, it seems only right that we should follow it."

At the high priest's suggestion, Paulinus the missionary was asked to explain in more detail the church's teaching. The assembly was convinced and the pagan high priest led the way to destroy the pagan temples at what is now Goodmanham.
(From Bede, 673-735: 'A History of the English Church and People', trans © Leo Sherley-Price, Penguin)

Monks and Monarchs

All six Anglo-Saxon kingdoms in what is now England adopted the new faith within a century. This meant that the kings of each kingdom had been baptised, mostly by monks sent from Rome. And at the Synod of Whitby in 664 King Oswy of Northumbria opted to accept the authority of the Roman church over the date of Easter. It linked the Anglos-Saxons to the wider culture of Europe. It did not mean the kingdoms stopped fighting each other, however.

But kings were only part of the story. The humility and zeal of monks, both Celtic and Roman, genuinely persuaded people so that by the end of the century Anglo-Saxon missionaries had preached to and been martyred by their kinsfolk in present day Netherlands and Germany. At home many ordinary folk established small family prayer communities, especially along the Thames valley. Some became hermits. Many made pilgrimage to Rome. Reading and writing became important.

Latin became known while Anglo-Saxon literature and Bible translations flourished. All this was decimated through the Viking attacks which began with the destruction of the monastery of Lindisfarne in 793.

What were the Anglo-Saxons converted to? Essentially to Christ the Victor. The cross was seen not so much a solution to the problem of sin (that came five hundred years later), as a victory over the powers of evil. The earliest Anglo-Saxon poem, 'The Dream of the Rood (or Cross)', c. 8th century, includes these lines:

> *He stripped himself then, the young hero - that was God almighty -*
> *strong and resolute; he ascended on the high gallows, brave in the sight of many, when he wanted to ransom mankind...*

Historical background - Norsemen/Vikings

The great age of Norse piracy was from 793 to 1066. For the first hundred years Norsemen from Scandinavia, raided, plundered, killed and enslaved people all over Europe, from Lindisfarne to Seville. They then settled in Ukraine/Russia, formed the emperor's bodyguard in Byzantium and created settlements in Iceland, Greenland and, briefly, Newfoundland. At first they were bitterly opposed to Christianity, having seen the forced conversion of the continental Saxons under Charlemagne, and had no compunction in killing unarmed monks.

In 865 a Danish army started the conquest of the Saxon kingdoms of Britain, seizing Northumbria, Mercia and East Anglia. The Great Heathen Army was defeated by Alfred of Wessex at the battle of Ethandun/Edington in 878. The leader Guthrum was baptised, and a boundary between Northumbria, East Anglia and eastern Mercia (Danelaw) and southern and western England was agreed. Danish attacks continued sporadically for twenty years, after which the Norsemen turned their attention to France.

The 10th and 11th centuries was the great age of Norwegian and Danish conquests, from Normandy (911), to Ireland, (Dublin 853-902, 914-1014), to England (1013, 1066), to South Italy, Sicily and Malta (1046-1139). The Norsemen were also great traders and settlers, ranging down through the Volga and Dnieper rivers and getting as far as Baghdad. Dublin was the biggest slave port in Europe.

Power and persuasion
The Norsemen were primarily turned Christian by their kings, largely in the 11th century; but perhaps for political reasons as much as spiritual. Both Danish kings Guthrum and Harald Bluetooth were baptised after defeat in battle. The Christian God was clearly more powerful than Thor or Odin at least at times. And the Church was the entry point into the whole culture of the Later Roman Empire. The Norse kings were perhaps not so much baptised into Christ as baptised into Christendom. Here is the story of how two of the Norse societies adopted Christianity.

Norway
The conversion of Norway was started by Harald Haraldson, nicknamed the Good (reigned 934 - 961). As a teenager he was sent to the English court of Athelstan, where he was baptised. Subsequently he followed both the Christian and the old pagan religions, being buried in a pagan burial mound.

He was killed in battle with the sons of Eric Blood-axe, his predecessor. One of the sons was Harald Greycloak, who became king as Harald II. He had been baptised in Northumbria. He was forced into exile when the Danish king, Harald Bluetooth, took over control. Harald Bluetooth sent two chiefs to persuade people to turn Christian.

Over thirty years later, Olaf Tryggevason invaded Norway and overturned Danish rule. He had led a stormy life, including many years as a slave, then as a pirate raiding settlements and ports. At the Scilly Isles he met a seer who told him *"Thou wilt become a renowned king, and do celebrated deeds. Many men wilt thou bring to faith and baptism, both to thy own and others' good."* As the seer prophesied, he was sorely wounded in a fight but survived and accepted baptism. He was king of Norway for just five years from 995. He built the first church in Norway and founded Trondheim. He baptised the explorer Leif Ericsson, who took a priest with him on his expedition to Greenland. Olaf routinely used force to compel conversion to Christianity, including execution and torture of those who refused. He died in a sea battle with Swedish and Danish ships in 1000.

Fifteen years later Olaf Haraldson, son of a local chief, invaded and became king of Norway. He had lived as a soldier and plunderer, but had been baptised in Rouen in Normandy under the auspices of Duke Robert II, a devout Christian. Olaf destroyed heathen temples, built churches and established a network of priests. Many chieftains feared that Christianisation would rob them of their power and freedom, and in 1028 Olaf was forced into exile by the (Christian) Danish king Cnut (Canute). In 1030 Olaf returned and the two sides met in battle at Stiklestad where Olav was *'killed by his own people'.* (Anglo-Saxon Chronicle). A year later his body was recovered, and found to be uncorrupted. It was reburied in Trondheim, where healing miracles began to take place. This dramatically changed the popular feeling and the Norwegians accepted the Christian faith. The Bishop of Nidaros/Trondheim declared Olaf a saint. Sagas were quickly written which extolled him as a holy king. He is still patron saint of Norway.

Iceland

Iceland has a unique history, because they had no king. Instead in 930 the ruling chiefs organised an annual 'allthing' - a two day affair where a third of the laws of the community were read out each year.

Christian missionaries started coming in 981, sword in hand, but had no great success. The Icelandic Stefnir Thorgilsson was declared an outlaw and expelled after he had destroyed a number of heathen shrines. Then the king of Norway, Olaf Tryggevason closed his harbours to Icelandic ships and threatened to kill hostages. At an allthing in 1000 civil war seemed likely, until both sides accepted the pagan law-speaker, Thorgeir Thorkelsson, as an arbitrator. Thorgeir *'lay down and spread his cloak over himself, and rested all that day and the following night, and did not speak a word. And the next morning, he got up and sent word that people should go to the Law Rock.'*

There Thorgeir made his speech:
"It now seems advisable to me that we do not let those who most wish to oppose each other prevail, and let us arbitrate between them, so that each side has its own way in something, and let us all have the same law and the same religion. It will prove true that if we tear apart the law, we will also tear apart the peace."

He announced that Iceland would become Christian on condition that infanticide by exposure and eating of horseflesh continue and private pagan worship be permitted. People abided by decision and were baptised. The concessions to pagan practices were banned by the king Olaf Haraldson of Norway fifteen years later.

So what were the questions?
This story from Bede tells us the two questions these Anglo-Saxon warriors had in their minds, questions which led to the rapid conversion of the kingdoms:

How can I get sound guidance for my life, better than the sagas our fathers have handed down?
What happens after death, or before birth?

The main question which had to be thrashed out in the Scandinavian kingdoms was,
What should be the basis of society?

YOUR OWN REFLECTIONS
What would you say to someone who asks you what is the best story they should model their life on?

What happens after death? Or before birth?

What are the fundamental principles of a law-abiding society?

How important are miracles?

THE 12TH CENTURY RENAISSANCE

*Ivory Crucifixion from Venice c.1180, from the Musée de Cluny.
Photo by Maryann 6/3/2006 Joconde 000SC002818*

Historical background

In 632 the prophet Mohammed died at Mecca. Following his death Arab Muslim armies captured Egypt, Palestine, Syria, Persia and over the next century the whole of North Africa and southern Spain. The ancient Christian centres of Jerusalem, Antioch and Alexandria were now in Muslim hands. The Mediterranean was no longer a safe space for trade, leading to division between the western and eastern halves of the former Roman empire.

For over three centuries the Christian countries of Europe were constantly being attacked by enemies on all sides. The Abbey of Luxeuil, Burgundy, in the very heart of Western Europe, was sacked four times: by Saracens from the south in 737 and again around 870, by Vikings from the west in 886, and by Hungarians from the east in 917.

The turning point came in 955 when the German king Otto decisively defeated the Magyars or Hungarians at the battle of Lechfeld. Within a hundred years the Viking kingdoms had largely accepted Christianity, and between 1061 and 1091 the Normans conquered Muslim Sicily. At last there was reasonable security and people could start rebuilding a Christian civilisation.

Reason and faith

There was a new emphasis on reason and argument. The first universities were created, in Bologna (1088), Paris (c.1150) and Oxford (1167), and major philosophers began to write, Anselm (1033 - 1107), Abelard (1079 - 1142) and Thomas Aquinas (1225 - 1274). There was a new atmosphere of rigorous thinking. For example:

"Of all the things that exist, there is one nature that is supreme. It alone is self-sufficient in its eternal happiness, yet through its all-powerful goodness it creates and gives to all other things their very existence and their goodness. Now, take someone who either has never heard of, or does not believe in, and so does not know this... I think that they can, even if of average ability, convince themselves of the truth of these beliefs, simply by reason alone." Anselm, Monolgion ch.1

"The key to wisdom is this - constant and frequent questioning, for by doubting we are led to question and by questioning we arrive at the truth." Abelard

"It seems that God does not exist. For if of two contraries one were infinite, the other would be altogether absent. Now the name God means infinite goodness. If he existed, there would be no evil discoverable in the world. But there is evil discoverable in the world.

Therefore God does not exist. Furthermore, it is superfluous to assume two or more causes where one or a few are sufficient. Now everything we experience can be traced back to nature or to human will. It is therefore not necessary to assume God's existence." Thomas Aquinas, Summa Theologiae

The last quotation shows that even at the height of the Ages of Faith people were not blind to possible criticisms of Christianity. In fact it is a much more elegant argument for atheism than anything Bertrand Russell or Richard Dawkins wrote. Thomas Aquinas goes on to his five proofs of God. These all follow the same pattern. Everything we know has a cause. If we press that far enough, we come to a First Cause, Prime Mover etc. In my view these don't really work as a proof of God so much as a challenge to the logical coherence of atheism.

Religious Emotion

However, there is more to being human than reason. There was a new emphasis on feelings. Troubadours were found in every court, singing their songs of courtly love particularly between 1180 and 1220. Images of the crucifixion became more realistic, with an emphasis on the physical sufferings of Christ to move the feelings of the beholder.

Above all, thousands of men and women all over Europe made decisions to abandon their possessions and society and devote themselves to a life of prayer and service.

"Religion in the Middle Ages was usually taken to be synonymous with monasticism. If a man were said to have been 'converted to religion' the meaning was not that he had been baptised but that he had become a monk; and the amazing thing is that in this sense one might almost talk of the 'conversion' of Europe in the eleventh and twelfth centuries."
(R.H.C.Davis - A History of Mediaeval Europe p. 260)

The Big Question

What was the question in people's hearts which led to this movement? It was the call to know God's love and respond to it. Bernard of Clairvaux (1090 - 1153) was a great leader of this movement and the most famous preacher of his time. He and his fellow-Cistercians stressed constantly the overwhelming importance of love.

"You want me to tell you why God is to be loved and how much. I answer, the reason for loving God is God Himself; and the measure of love due to Him is immeasurable love...
And first, of His title to our love. Could any title be greater than this, that He gave Himself for us unworthy wretches? And being God, what better gift could He offer than Himself? Hence, if one seeks for God's claim upon our love here is the chiefest: Because He first loved us."   (On Loving God, chapter 1)

It did not only lead to joining monasteries. All over Europe lay communities of passionate Christians sprang up, in response to the inner question, "How can I fall in love with Jesus?" Falling in love with Jesus meant giving oneself in a radical way. A fine example is Marie d'Oignies and those who followed her.

Marie was a devout girl living just south of Brussels. In 1190, at the age of 14, her parents arranged for her to be married to Jean, a wealthy neighbour. But Marie was made of stern stuff. She did not want to live a wealthy lifestyle and she persuaded her husband to give away all his wealth and to join her in caring for lepers in the nearby town of Willhelmbroux, cleaning their wounds, and working with their hands to support themselves. Soon other women joined them. This became a mass movement of lay religious called Beguines. Soon there were thousands of

women in lay communities all over the Low Countries, Germany and northern France. They helped the poor, they preached, they prayed, they read the Bible in their own languages. All to express their heartfelt love for Jesus:
"Jesus, dearest Lover of mine, let me approach you... with deep love for you in my heart, and let me never grow cold, so that I constantly feel your intense love in my heart and in my soul and in my five senses and in my members. Then I can never grow cold."
(Mechthilde of Magdeburg)

"Beloved, if I love a beloved, be you, Love, my Beloved; you gave yourself as Love for your loved one's sake, and thus you, Love, uplifted me, your loved one, with you! O Love, if I were but love, and could I but love you, Love, with love! O Love, for love's sake, grant that I, having become love, may know Love wholly as Love!"
(Hadewijch of Brabant)

So what was the question?
What was the inner question, that led to such a powerful movement of self-giving?
Was it?
How can I fall in love with Jesus?

YOUR OWN REFLECTIONS
What advice would you give to someone who says they want to have Jesus at the centre of their heart?

What question are people more likely to ask these days?

THE EASTERN ROMAN EMPIRE

6th c. icon of Christ Pantocrator, Sinai

A Christian empire

The founding of Constantinople on the site of the fishing village of Byzantium was a game-changer for world history. For the next 1,000 years the Byzantine empire would dominate the eastern Mediterranean through triumph and disaster. While the Western Roman Empire dissolved into separate barbarian kingdoms, the Eastern Roman Empire remained intact and even reconquered Italy and North Africa for a time until Italy was invaded by a new barbarian group, the Lombards.

The seventh and eighth centuries were disastrous, with the Arab conquest of Palestine, Egypt, Cyprus and North Africa, and the Slav conquest of much of mainland Greece.

During this period the iconoclastic controversy (726-843) tore at the internal unity of the church and empire. This controversy was about whether images - pictures and statues - were permitted in church. It was finally settled in 843 at the council of Constantinople which reaffirmed the pronouncement of the earlier Council of Nicaea (787) that "veneration of honour" was permitted but that "true adoration" belonged to God alone. Since then painted icons have been a key aspect of Orthodox prayer and worship. The 'Restoration of the Images' is celebrated on the first Sunday of Lent each year as 'the Triumph of Orthodoxy'.

Mission

The ninth and tenth centuries saw the revival of Byzantine self-confidence and influence. In the 9th century Cyril and Methodius, known as the Apostles to the Slavs, devised the alphabet for translating the Bible and liturgical books into old Church Slavonic. Boris I, also called Boris the Baptiser, created the independent Bulgarian Orthodox Church in 864.

A century later Vladimir, Prince of Kiev had sent out envoys to find out what was the best religion to adopt. The envoys returned and reported, *"the Greeks led us to the edifices where they worship their God, and we knew not whether we were in heaven or on earth. For on earth there is no such splendour or such beauty, and we are at a loss how to describe it. We know only that God dwells there among men, and their service is fairer than the ceremonies of other nations. For we cannot forget that beauty."*

So in the 980s Kievan Rus became part of the Orthodox family Churches.

East and West

In the eleventh century the western and eastern churches split, partly over the phrase 'and the Son', (Filioque in Latin), which the Western Church had added to the phrase about the Holy Spirit in the Nicene Creed, *"who proceeds from the Father..."*. Despite several attempts, there has not yet been reunification. Eastern Catholic Churches keep Orthodox church traditions but accept papal supremacy.

Disaster

The eleventh and twelfth centuries were disasters for Byzantium. Through the defeats of Manzikert (1071) and Myriokephalon (1176), the whole of Anantolia, inland Turkey, was lost to Turkish tribes, and Constantinople lost its bread basket. In response to a personal appeal by the Byzantine emperor, the Pope announced a crusade.

Frankish armies conquered Palestine and Jerusalem (1099), but were roundly defeated in 1187. Then in 1204 crusaders, egged on by the Venetians, carried out the dreadful sack of Constantinople. The empire fell into separate states, some ruled by Franks, some by Greeks. Constantinople was recaptured in 1261, but was fatally weakened. The Ottoman Empire gradually expanded until Constantinople finally fell in 1453.

There followed four hundred years of intermittent persecution in Greece and Bulgaria followed by almost a century of intense persecution in Russia. What enabled Orthodox Christianity to survive? Was it that at its heart was a spirituality that didn't depend on power or security? A graffiti that the author saw on a visit to Mount Athos simply said, *'Orthodoxy or death.'*

The Prayer of Quiet

The heart of Eastern Orthodox spirituality is the prayer of quiet, in Greek 'hesychia' or stillness. It is rooted in the prayer life of the Desert Fathers, monks living in the Egyptian desert in the fourth century. It meant both the solitary life as a hermit, and *'the practice of inner prayer, aiming at union with God on a level beyond images, concepts and language.'* (Kallistos Ware). A classic approach to this day is the constant repetition of the 'Jesus Prayer' until it takes root in the heart: *"Jesus, Son of God, have mercy on me a sinner."*

The actual experience of grace is vital. St Symeon the New Theologian (960-1022) said, *"If anyone claims that all believers have received and possessed the Holy Spirit without having consciousness of experience of Him, he blasphemes, by treating as a falsehood the words of Christ who says that the Spirit is 'a well of water springing up into eternal life...'"*

Gregory Palamas

The spiritual crisis of Eastern Orthodoxy came in 1336 through an exchange of letters between Barlaam, a priest and humanist philosopher in Constantinople, and Gregory Palamas, a monk of Mount Athos. Barlaam had attacked the phrase 'and the Son', but in a way that Gregory thought dangerously rationalist. Palamas wrote nine treatises on defending 'those who practice Sacred Quietude.' In particular he defended the goal of the prayer of quiet as being an experience of the Uncreated Light, asserting that we are capable of knowing the uncreated energies of God in this life and the life beyond.

"There is an unknowing that is higher than all knowledge, a darkness that is supremely bright; and in this dazzling darkness divine things are given to the saints."

Barlaam vigorously attacked the practices of hesychia, but he was finally condemned by a synod in 1351 and became a Roman Catholic. Gregory's victory is celebrated each year on the Second Sunday of Great Lent.

What was the question?
What is greater than this world, greater than life or death?

YOUR OWN REFLECTIONS
What resource do I have to help me stand firm in the difficult and dangerous situations?

THE CRISIS OF THE 14TH & 15TH CENTURIES

Life-size crucifix, Italian c. 1250
(Victoria and Albert Museum)

Historical background

Europe had become steadily more prosperous in the 13th century. The 14th century saw a series of disasters. There was the great famine of 1315 - 1317; plagues such as the Black Death of 1348 which killed 45% - 50% of the population, with further plagues in 1361, 1371, 1400 etc. The Italian poet Petrarch (1304-1374) wrote: "Will posterity credit that there as a time when… houses were emptied, cities abandoned, countrysides untilled, fields heaped with corpses, dreadful solitude over all the world?"

The Hundred Years' War (1337-1453) devastated France, as well as the economy of Europe. In 1330 the great banking houses of Florence maintained the credit of trade all over Europe, led by the Bardi and Peruzzi banks. When Edward III of England reneged on his war debts in 1345, the entire banking system collapsed. Two hundred years later, at the height of the Renaissance, the credit of the Fugger's bank, the largest at the time, had only a quarter of the credit of either of the two main Florentine banks on their own.

Politically, almost every other English king ended up deposed and killed: Edward II, Richard II, Henry VI, Edward V, Richard III. And in the Catholic Church between 1316 and 1455 there were thirteen Popes and eight Anti-Popes.

Religious responses

The response of serious Christians was to withdraw even more from the world, but in an interior way. The 14th century saw some of the most enduring Christian writers: Julian of Norwich, Walter Hilton, the author of the Cloud of Unknowing, Meister Eckhart, Henry of Suso and many others. They give instruction on how to achieve contemplation, to shut the mind from earthly concerns and open one's heart in *"the dark cloud of unknowing"* to the direct though hidden presence of God. But this was for the spiritual elite.

"I charge thee and beseech thee... that thou neither read it, nor write it, not speak it... to any but if it be to such one, that by thy supposing purposed him to be a perfect follower of Christ not only in active living but in the sovereignest point of contemplative living... (The Cloud of Unknowing, the Prologue, edited)

How did ordinary people react when they thought about the Christian faith? Sebastian Brant (1457-1521), a university jurist, wrote a popular poem, the Ship of Fools:

A fool is he who has forsook
his faith in Writ and Holy Book
and thinks that he can live as well
without a God, without a hell...
The Lord doth verily proclaim:
who sins on earth, in hell finds shame,
and who on earth in prudence lives,
to him eternal praise God gives.

The best "Good News" that Brant can offer is for people to fear hell and live prudently.

A major problem was corruption within the church. The great scholar Erasmus wrote in 1509: *"The whole tribe (of clergy) is so universally loathed that even a chance encounter is thought to be ill-omened - and yet they are gloriously self-satisfied... They believe it is the highest form of piety to be so uneducated that they cannot even read..."* (In Praise of Folly).

A major response for serious Christians was the so-called "Devotio Moderna" - Modern Devotion - a reform movement aimed at encouraging a serious Christian life for lay and clergy alike. It stressed inner devotion and short periods of meditation. The most famous exponent was Thomas à Kempis, the writer of "The Imitation of Christ" (c.1418) which instantly became popular and is still the most widely read devotional book after the Bible.

"He who follows me can never walk in darkness, says the Lord. By these words, Christ urges us to mould our lives and characters in the image of his, if we wish to be truly enlightened and freed from all blindness of heart." (Start of chapter 1.1)

"No one has a harder struggle than the man who is striving to overcome himself; and it should be our business... every day to get the upper hand over our old natures and to show some progress and improvement." (From chapter 1.3)

"If we were utterly dead to self, and if our hearts were stripped of encumbrance, then we could get a glimpse of the things of God, and experience something of heavenly contempla (From chapter 1.11)

"Be a man and make an effort - only a good habit can defeat an evil one." (Chapter 1.21)

So what was the question?
It seems to me that the background question in all this was
How can I live a good life?
Together with the accompanying question,
How can I be acceptable to God?
The fundamental answer was, *"Look at the example of Jesus and try harder."* This may have been good news to some, but to a certain German Augustinian monk and theology professor called Martin Luther, it was very bad news indeed.

YOUR OWN REFLECTIONS
What would you say to someone who wants to live a good life but is struggling with their conscience and getting depressed?

THE REFORMATION & COUNTER-REFORMATION

Martin Luther's Rose 1530

War and politics - 16th century

The 16th century began with politics as normal. The Protestant Reformation changed all that. The fissiparous nature of the Holy Roman Empire allowed Protestant churches to survive in the quasi-independent German principalities. The Peace of Augsburg (1555) declared the principle 'Cuius regio eius religio', - each political region could now decide on its own religion. England and the Scandinavian kingdoms adopted Protestantism.

In 1531-32 Henry VIII declared himself head of the Church in England and between 1535 and 1538 dissolved all the monasteries, releasing something like 33% of the entire land area of the country.. Lively reformed churches in France, Poland and Italy were eventually suppressed. The eighty year war (1568-1648) between Dutch Protestants and Spain ended with the southern half of the Spanish Netherlands remaining Roman Catholic, while the Netherlands or United Provinces adopted the Calvinist Reformed Church. An offshoot was 'The Great Enterprise', Spain's attempt to invade England in 1588 and the ensuing war which lasted till 1604.

Meanwhile the Ottoman threat hung over Europe. Suleyman the Magnificent, who reigned 1520 - 1566, conquered almost the whole of Hungary in the Battle of Mohacs 1526, besieged Vienna in 1529, captured Baghdad in 1535 and almost seized Malta in 1565. The conflict between the Ottomans and European powers even reached the Philippines. The Battle of Lepanto in 1571 wrested control of the Mediterranean back from Ottoman control.

War and politics - 17th century

In the 17th century protestantism led to popular political movements, culminating in the English Civil War (1641-1647). The Thirty Years War (1618-1648) devastated Germany and checked the ambitions of the Austrian Habsburg emperors. In 1685 Louis XIV of France announced the Revocation of the Edict of Nantes, putting an end to almost a century of partial religious toleration; hundreds of thousands of Protestants became refugees. He undertook aggressive wars of expansion, conquering Alsace and Lorraine but failed in his larger ambitions. In 1683 the Ottomans again besieged Vienna but were defeated by the Polish king John III Sobieski. In the ensuing war the Habsburgs recaptured almost the whole of Hungary.

New worlds

The world itself doubled in size. Columbus discovered the American continent by mistake in 1492. In 1493 Pope Alexander VI partitioned the entire continent. Brazil was given to Portugal, the rest of the continent to Spain. The conquests of Mexico and Peru were brutal, fuelled by the conquistadores' lust for gold. Spain became a superpower on the back of South American gold. It also took over Portugal and the Portuguese empire along the coasts of Africa and India through a dynastic union from 1580 to 1640.

The most devastating effect on non-European peoples were the illnesses the Spanish brought with them, as well as the wars and massacres, which together virtually destroyed the native population. The need for African labour to replace the native population was the start of the trans-Atlantic slave trade.

England and France created settlements on the seaboards of North America from New Orleans to Newfoundland, some of them founded by people seeking greater religious freedom than that which they found in their own countries. These became permanent and came under more direct rule from European capitals in the 17th century. The United Provinces/the Netherlands created their own overseas empire in the West Indies and particularly in the East Indies, known as the Spice Islands.

Religion

Martin Luther was born in 1483 near Saxony. He was a student of law, but after a frightening experience in a thunderstorm, he gave up law and became a monk. He was awarded Doctor of Theology in 1512. But he was deeply troubled over how to become acceptable to God. Thirty years later he wrote,

"I had conceived a burning desire to understand what Paul meant in his Letter to the Romans, but thus far there had stood in my way ... that one phrase which is in chapter one: 'The righteousness of God is revealed in it.'... I hated this righteous God who punishes sinners... I meditated night and day on these words until at last, by the mercy of God,... I began to understand that in this verse the righteousness of God is that by which the righteous man lives by the gift of God, in other words by faith.... This immediately made me feel as if I had been born again and entered through open gates into paradise itself."
(The European Reformations Source Book p.26).

Note: Luther's breakthrough moment makes better sense in Latin, because the word 'iustitia' means both justice and righteousness as does 'δικαιοσύνη' in Greek. So the Justice of God which condemns sinners became the Righteousness of God which is given to sinners.

The great engine which changed this insight from just a different theological approach to a religious revolution was the invention of printing, particularly the printing of the Bible. Now everyone who could read was able to check for themselves if Luther's message was properly grounded or not. In 1516 Erasmus, the foremost scholar of his day, had rushed his Greek version of the New Testament into print. He wrote in 'Paraclesis' (1516):

"I am totally against those who do not want the Holy Scripture to be read by the laity in their vernacular, as if Christ taught so obscurely that he can hardly be understood even by a few theologians... I desire that everyone including women read the gospels and the Pauline letters. These ought to be translated into all languages so that not only the Scots and the Irish but also

the Turks and the Saracens could read and understand them... Thus I would like the farmer to sing the Scripture as he ploughs, the weaver to hum it as he weaves... let the conversation of all Christians therefore relate to Scripture."
(The European Reformations Source Book p.48)

What ensued from this was a radical democratisation of society, a response to the key question, *"How can I work out the truth for myself?"*
Luther was aware that the Bible could be misused. He wrote in 1521:
"Be sure, moreover, that you do not make Christ into a Moses ... as if the gospel were simply a textbook of teachings or laws. Therefore you should grasp Christ, his words, works and sufferings in a twofold manner. First as an example that is presented to you, which you should follow and imitate... However, this is the smallest part of the gospel, on the basis of which it cannot yet even be called a gospel... The chief article and foundation of the gospel is that before you take Christ as an example, you accept and recognise him as a gift... This is the great fire of the love of God for us, whereby the heart and conscience become happy, secure and content... So you see that the gospel is really not a book of laws and commandments which require deeds of us, but a book of divine promises in which God promises, offers, and gives us all his possessions and benefits in Christ."
(From 'A Brief Instruction on What to Look For and Expect in the Gospels', 1521, the European Reformations Source Book p.49)

Luther's revolutionary message was truly Good News to those who struggled with the question, 'How can I be freed from church-induced guilt?'

It may be that it was this question which fuelled the violence against images and shrines that so disfigured the Protestant Reformation. Faith in God's grace was transmuted into hatred of all the church apparatus which had been a barrier in the past. For instance, this is Geneva in 1535:

"The entire multitude... hurried through the convent to the rooms of the friars, breaking and destroying all that they found, statues, books and breviaries... Like enraged wolves, they began to break these statues, especially a marvellously beautiful blessed crucifix and a statue of Our Lady, with large axes and hammers. They did not leave one statue intact..."

(From Jeanne de Jussie - Calvinist Germs or the Beginning of Heresy in Geneva, the European Reformations Source Book p.168)

Very quickly this new and anarchic freedom had morphed into a new orthodoxy, especially in Calvin's Geneva. Note that it is the ordinary secular authorities who make the decisions:

"In the name of Almighty God, we, the Syndics, the Small and the Great Council... have ordained and established in our city and territory the observation and maintenance of the ecclesiastical polity which follows, since we see that it is taken from the Gospel of Jesus Christ.

"First, there are four orders of offices which our Lord has instituted for the government of His Church, namely: the pastors, secondly, the doctors, then the elders, otherwise called those delegated by the Seigneury, and, fourthly, the deacons..."

(The European Reformations Source Book p.170)

How the church should be governed became the key dispute between the Church of England and those who wanted a presbyterian form of government, the Puritans.

This led directly to the English Civil war of 1641-1645 and to the beheading of Charles I outside the Banqueting Hall of Whitehall. It is sobering to reflect on how quickly the question, *"How can I be right with God"* became *"How can I be right?"*

The other big dispute within the reformed churches, following Calvin's lead, was over predestination. In 1562 the English bishops produced 39 articles to set in stone the beliefs of the English reformed church. Article XVII - the longest one - was on Predestination and Election:
"Predestination to Life is the everlasting purpose of God, whereby... he hath constantly decreed by his counsel secret to us, to deliver from curse and damnation those whom he hath chosen in Christ out of mankind... As the godly consideration of Predestination and our Election in Christ, is full of sweet, pleasant, and unspeakable comfort to godly persons... so for curious and carnal persons, lacking the Spirit of Christ, to have continually before their eyes the sentence of God's Predestination, is a most dangerous downfall, whereby the Devil doth thrust them either into desperation, or into wretchlessness of most unclean living..."

Not much Good News there!

The Roman Catholic Church had of course had centuries of experience of being right, and that was not about to change, e.g.:
"If anyone says that the sinner is justified by faith alone in the sense that nothing is required by way of cooperation in order to obtain the grace of justification, and that it is not at all necessary that he should be prepared and dispose by the movement of his will, anathema sit. (Let him be accursed). (Canon 9 on Justification, Council of Trent 1547)

So what were the questions?
How can I be right with God?
How important is it to have right beliefs?

YOUR OWN REFLECTIONS
What would you say to someone who asked how they could relate to God without feeling fear or guilt? Is this possible?

And equally, what would you say to someone in any religious discussion who simply says, 'I know I'm right?' Does it make a difference if they go on to say, 'In any case, I know my holy book is right.'

THE 18TH CENTURY

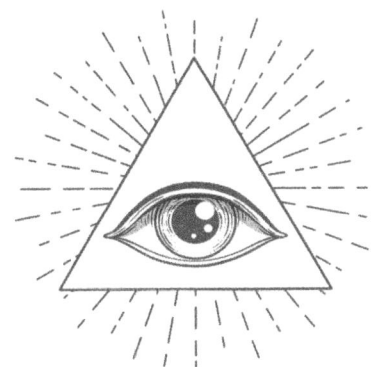

The Eye of Providence

War and politics

The 18th century could almost be called the French century. It was dominated by France's quest to be a world power. At the start England and the Netherlands defeated Louis XIV's ambitions in Europe. In India in the 1740s the French governor Dupleix tried to create a large territorial empire but was defeated by Clive. The French were the first to colonise the seaboard of Canada from 1605 but were conquered by the British in 1760. In 1860 French Canadians were still the majority in the Province of Canada.

France did have a success in the American War of Independence, or the American Revolutionary War, (1775-1783) France was an active ally with the Continental Army and significantly contributed to the victory of the American revolutionaries. The national debt which burdened France thereafter was a significant factor leading to their own revolution 1789-1794.

In the ensuing wars France controlled the whole of Europe from Sweden to Spain and Italy and almost conquered Russia. 1803 Napoleon agreed to the Louisiana Purchase, by which the United States took over the vast French territories in the mid-West, allowing the United States of America to fulfil their 'manifest destiny' *"from sea to shining sea".*

Britain meanwhile was enjoying a century of peaceful if vitriolic politics. The 'Glorious Revolution' of 1688, in which William and Mary became monarchs in place of the unpopular James II, signalled the triumph of the landed classes over an influential but ultimately powerless monarchy.

By 1780 the need for electoral reform to take account of the growth of cities was evident, but after the start of the wars with revolutionary France this was sidelined for 40 years.

Society and economics
The Industrial Revolution, c. 1760-1820, has been called the most important event in the history of humanity since the domestication of animals and plants. Using inventions like Cartwright's power loom, factories replaced homes in textile production, making great Britain the world's first economic superpower. Transport links were improved through canal building 1760-1810. Improved steam engines for pumping out water allowed deeper mines and greater production of coal and iron.

The agricultural revolution of better breeding of sheep and cattle and of ways to improve agricultural yields meant that for the first time famine was not a regular occurrence. The population of England grew from just over 5 million to just over 8 million. London' population rose from about 600,000 to 1 million. As cities grew bigger so did their problems. The 'Gin Craze' of 1695-1735 saw 8,000 gin shops spring up in the capital, with all the social ills portrayed by the artist Hogarth. The first police force was created around 1754, the Bow Street Runners.

The slave trade, bringing people from Africa to work in colonies in the West Indies and America was a major driver in the enrichment of the landed class in Britain and in the affluence of cities like Bristol. Up to the Abolition of the Slave Trade Act in 1807 over 2,500,000 Africans were transported to the West Indies and America in British ships, 41% of the total of individuals so transported - not counting those who died on the way.

Smallpox was a leading cause of death, killing some 400,000 Europeans a year. In late 18th century London over a fifth of men age 15-34 were being teated for the disease.

In 1796 Edward Jenner discovered that inoculation with cowpox could prevent the much more deadly disease, since when by 1975 inoculation had eradicated the disease globally.

Deism

After the shameful episodes of the religious wars that devastated Germany (1618-1648), the fifteen year Puritan dictatorship in England (1645-1660), the persecution of the French and Italian Protestants and the Inquisition, deism became the favourite belief system of literate society. Deism accepted that God set the universe in motion, but denied him any influence thereafter.

The belief in God who does not intervene became the implied position of much of the Church of England. As Dr Johnson said to a lady, *"My dear, you must believe in God, whatever the clergy tell you."* (Citation needed)

The mood of the time is described by Bishop Butler in the Prologue of his "Analogy of Religion Natural and Revealed" (1736).

"It is come, I know not how, to be taken for granted, by many persons, that Christianity is not so much as a subject of enquiry; but that it is now, at length, discovered to be fictitious. And accordingly they treat it, as if, in the present age, this were an agreed point among all people of discernment; and nothing remained, but to set it up as a principal subject of mirth and ridicule, as it were by way of reprisals, for its having so long interrupted the pleasures of the world."

Bishop Butler's book became the main Anglican defence of Christianity for over a hundred years. Rather then trying to provide proofs, he appealed to a series of patterns, "analogies", in nature and human affairs which made the truth of Christianity probable. But what is remarkable is the need of such a work, and the sea of scepticism in which the Anglican church swam.

Pietism

But a new spirit was abroad. In 1675 a German Lutheran pastor, Philipp Spener, wrote a book, 'Earnest Desire for a Reform of the True Evangelical Church;' the name Pietism, which became the name of this movement, came from a corruption of the two opening Latin words of the title, Pia Desideria. Among his proposals for renewing the church were: Bible study in private meetings (little churches within the church); lay people to share in church government; more emphasis on devotional life in theological teaching; and preaching designed to implant Christianity in the inner man. What the Pietists expected was a change of heart and consequent holiness of life. Worldly amusement s such as theatre and dancing were frowned on; social evils were addressed, for example by the new orphanage at Halle; and Protestant missions went abroad to the Caribbean, India and elsewhere. The new movement attracted wholehearted supporters and opponents, but by 1750 it was well established throughout Middle and North Germany.

Two zealous young Anglican clergymen, John and Charles Wesley, were deeply affected by the spirituality they saw in Moravian pietists, both in America and England. It was at one of their meetings in Aldersgate that in 1738 John found his heart "strangely warmed" on hearing Luther's Preface to the Epistle to the Romans read, and counted that day as his conversion. The following year he followed his friend George Whitefield's example of preaching in the open air to thousands of working men and women. From that was born the world-wide Methodist Church.

What did people who heard John Wesley preach respond to? Here is one man, John Nelson, who heard John Wesley preach in 1739 at the Foundry, Moorfields.

"Oh! That was a blessed morning for my soul! As soon as he got up on the stand, he stroked back his hair and turned his face towards where I stood, and I thought he fixed his eyes upon me. His countenance struck such an awful dread upon me before I heard him speak, that it made my heart beat like the pendulum of a clock, and when he did speak, I thought his whole discourse was aimed at me. When he had done, I said, 'This man can tell the

secrets of my heart." (Quoted in John Wesley - Contemporary Perspectives p.184)

The religion which both the Pietist and Wesleyan movements offered was a not a religion of the intellect but a religion of the heart. Emotion and feeling had at last a recognised place in the Christian life. And it was a place accessible to all, whatever their station in life. 'How can I feel the presence of God in my life?" might have been the question in the minds of those who went to hear John Wesley preach.

It was John's brother Charles Wesley who in his hymns provided both a response and a vehicle which could transform emotion into worship, as in this well-known hymn, written about 1747:

Love divine, all loves excelling,
Joy of heaven to earth come down;
Fix in us thy humble dwelling;
All thy faithful mercies crown!

Jesus, Thou art all compassion,
Pure unbounded love Thou art;
Visit us with Thy salvation;
Enter every trembling heart.

It was not an attitude with which the rationalist Bishop Butler could sympathise, as he said to the Wesleys: *"Sir, the pretending to extraordinary revelations and gifts of the Holy Ghost is a horrid thing, a very horrid thing."*

So what were the questions?

George III (1738-1820) was quite pious and rarely missed church services. For him the key question was expressed in a

letter to his son Augustus, Duke of Cumberland, *"It is with great satisfaction I perceive by your letters that your mind is impressed with those sentiments of duty to our Great Creator which alone can preserve you from the snares of this world or make you with comfort either look forward to a future state or pass your life with satisfaction; besides, no real confidence can be placed in any one whose intentions are not known to be guided by a due observance of the Laws of God, for any other tie is so weak that it must break when evil advice or any inclinations pull against it."* So for him, the key question was:
"How can I live a moral life?"

On 24th May 1738 A young serious clergyman, John Wesley, went "very unwillingly" to a society at Aldersgate. *"About a quarter before nine, while (a reading from Luther) was describing the change which God works in the heart through faith in Christ, I felt my heart strangely warmed. I felt I did trust in Christ, Christ alone for salvation, and an assurance was given me that he had taken away my sins, even mine, and saved me from the law of sin and death."* For John Wesley however, the question was,
How can I experience God at work in my heart?

This difference between formal and personal religion has characterised the church ever since.

YOUR OWN REFLECTIONS
Which, for you, is the most important, feelings, beliefs or actions?

THE 19TH CENTURY

The Light of the World by Holman Hunt, pastiche, 1866.

A century of change

The 19th century was a time of enormous change. So many changes in fact that the easiest way to grasp them is to list them.

- **Population.** The population of the UK grew from 10.5 million to 40 million and that of London from 1 million to 6.7 million.

- **Transport and Time.** Steam railways revolutionised travel as well as the notion of time - Bristol no longer set its clocks 13 minutes earlier than London.

- **Lighting.** In 1815 the Westminster GasLight and Coke Company was founded, and gas-lighting quickly spread through the towns and cities of Britain and indeed globally. It meant that factories could work much longer hours, especially in winter.

- **Social Unrest.** Discontent and collective action grew among industrial workers. Karl Marx wrote 'The Communist Manifesto' in 1848, the same year that a wave of middle class revolutions swept Europe. These were by and large contained or defeated.

- **USA.** The United States expanded from the 13 East Coast states in 1800 to conquer the width of the continent by 1850, followed by the devastating Civil War 1861-1865.

- **British Empire.** The British Empire, from having just part of the West Indies and trading posts in India and Africa in 1800, by 1900 had become the greatest empire the world had ever seen.

- **Slavery.** Slavery was abolished throughout the West (Britain in 1833, France in 1848, United States in 1865), and in its place came the economic servitude of Asia and Africa, fuelled by the triumph of industrial production in Europe and America.

- **Peace and war.** Europe had virtual peace for a century apart from the Crimean war, but the Prussian wars against Austria and France (1866 and 1870) cemented the Prussian dominance of Germany and made the First World War all but inevitable.

- **Democracy**. The right to vote for governing bodies was originally restricted to property-owning men. In the 1840's the USA extended to the right to vote to most white men. France enacted universal male suffrage (the right to vote) in 1848. In the UK various Reform Acts increased the size of the male electorate, from 13% in 1832 to 35% in 1878, 60% in 1884 and 100% in 1918.

- **Women's suffrage.** The movement for women to have the right to vote began in 1850 in the USA and 1870 in the UK. Full voting rights were won between 1918 and 1928.

- **Evolution**. In the world of ideas, Darwin's book 'On the Origin of Species by Means of Natural Selection, or the Preservation of Favoured Races in the Struggle for Life' (1859) was a revolution in itself, placing human beings firmly within the animal kingdom and subject to 'the survival of the fittest'.

Churches in Britain

In 1800 the church in England pursued its comfortable way, with a vigorous evangelical movement advocating both heartfelt faith and social action.

Over 1,650 British missionaries from the Church Missionary Society (founded 1799) went all over the world, and of course missionaries went from other churches. This was 100 years after the Lutherans and 250 years after the Jesuits.

Following the great Reform Act of 1832 there was a wholesale onslaught on the comfortable corruption of the established church, such as nepotism, sinecures and plurality of livings (being rectors of multiple parishes).

At the same time a group of young Anglican clergy, calling themselves Anglo-Catholics, called for a return to catholic church tradition and ritual.

"Should it ever happen... that the Apostolical Church should be forsaken degraded, nay trampled and despoiled by the State and people of England...the Church would, first of all, be constant in intercession. Secondly remonstrance - calm, distinct and persevering, in public and in private ... is the unequivocal duty of every Christian.

Finally... to resign himself more thoroughly... to the daily and hourly duties of piety, purity, charity and justice." Rev John Keble, the Assize Sermon at Oxford 1833.

There was a mighty upsurge in church building, with different denominations competing for members. Organs, instead of church bands, became the norm in parish churches.

In 1829 the Roman Catholic Relief Act was the culmination of fifty years of gradual catholic emancipation from the penal laws; in 1850 the Pope established a full hierarchy of Roman Catholic dioceses and parishes, to the fury of the Church of England. This followed the immigration of a million Irish men and women (all Catholic) fleeing the Great Famine of 1845 - 1849.

In 1865 William Booth started the organisation which was to become, in 1878, the Salvation Army, working among London's poor. *"The three 'S's' best expressed the way in which the Army administered to the 'down and outs': first, soup; second, soap; and finally, salvation."*

The 1851 census recorded that out of a population of 18 million, 11 million were in church: 5.3 million Anglicans, 4.5 million other Protestants and 400,000 Roman Catholics. (Figures have been rounded), i.e. 60% of the country.

In 1914 the figure for adult church membership (not church attendance) was 27%.

Churches elsewhere

France: After the devastation of the French Revolution, Napoleon made a Concordat with the Pope by which church life was re-instated, with the clergy being paid by the state and bishops appointed by the government. The Third Republic (1871-1940) vigorously combatted the influence of the Catholic Church; in 1862 religious instruction in schools was forbidden and in 1882 all schools were made state schools.

Italy: Italy continued as an overwhelmingly Catholic country. In 1860 the Papacy lost the political power it had held in central Italy for 1300 years. Ten years later it compensated for this in the First Vatican Council by declaring that when the Pope spoke officially, 'ex cathedra', he was infallible.

United States: Following the Great Awakenings of the first and second halves of the century, the Evangelical churches in America flourished, and large evangelistic meetings, such as those of Moody and Sankey in the 1870's, became part of the church culture.

Germany: The Lutheran Church was happy with Prussian dominance of Germany and became effectively the established church. Meanwhile biblical scholars in the University of Tübingen, such as Strauss and Feuerbach followed by

Wellhausen etc., examined the biblical texts sifting out what they regarded as unhistorical. Two seminal books were Strauss's 'Life of Jesus' (1846) and Feuerbach's 'The Essence of Christianity' (1854).

The Higher Criticism, emanating from German universities cut the umbilical cord between the Bible and faith. In 1860 seven Anglicans disseminated these opinions in 'Essays and Reviews,' leading to a five year heresy trial which ended in their acquittal.

What people thought

Those are the bare facts. What were people actually thinking? It was perhaps poets who came nearest to calibrating the movement of opinions, rather like seismographers tracking the force of distant earthquakes.

> *The Sea of Faith*
> *Was once, too, at the full, and round earth's shore*
> *Lay like the folds of a bright girdle furled.*
> *But now I only hear*
> *Its melancholy, long, withdrawing roar,*
> *Retreating, to the breath*
> *Of the night-wind, down the vast edges drear*
> *And naked shingles of the world.*
>
> *Ah, love, let us be true*
> *To one another! for the world, which seems*
> *To lie before us like a land of dreams,*
> *So various, so beautiful, so new,*
> *hath really neither joy, not love, nor light,*
> *Nor certitude, nor peace, nor help for pain;*
> *And we are here as on a darkling plain*
> *Swept with confused alarms of struggle and flight,*
> *Where ignorant armies clash by night.*

This bleak vision was written by Matthew Arnold on his honeymoon in 1851, the same year that 60% of the population went to church.

The working classes were least churched. In the same year (the year of the Great Exhibition) Henry Mayhew published his *"London Labour and the London Poor"*. He asked one labourer in south London if he knew what St Paul's Cathedral was. *"A church, sir, so I've heard,"* was the reply.

But what were the respectable middle classes thinking as they sat in their rented pews?

> *Ah, make the most of what we yet may spend,*
> *Before we too into the Dust descend;*
> *Dust into Dust, and under Dust to lie,*
> *Sans wine, sans Song, sans Singer, and - sans End!*

This is the last verse of perhaps the most popular Victorian poem, Edward Fitzgerald's translation of 'The Rubaiyat of Omar Khayyam' (1859, popular from 1872 onwards)

In the same year as the above poem, Matthew Arnold wrote: *"Never let us deny to this story power and pathos, or treat with hostility ideas which have entered so deep into the life of Christendom. But the story is not true; it never really happened..."*

Elsewhere, he gave the following definition: *"Religion is morality touched by emotion."*

And then there is 'The Mikado' (Gilbert and Sullivan,1875): *"I'm really very sorry for you all, but it's an unjust world, and virtue is triumphant only in theatrical performances."*

The Church's Response

The Church was faced with two possible responses, as it had been from the very beginning of Christianity: preach the gospel without regard to the surrounding culture, or enter into a dialogue with the culture.

Evangelicalism took the first avenue, a warm faith which appealed directly to the heart. A prime exponent was Charles Spurgeon (1834-1892). A Baptist from Essex, converted at 15, he moved at the age of 19 to the largest Baptist Chapel in London. In 1861 he built the Metropolitan Tabernacle with seating for 5,000. He preached over 3,600 sermons. Here he is talking about free grace (in a rural Essex accent): *"The proud heart says, I do not understand this. The proud heart does not understand it, because it does not like it."*

Meanwhile ordinary parish life continued up and down the country. This is a description of the Surrey parish of Beddington in 1860. A well-known Evangelical clergyman had just become rector at the age of 85

"My father found the Parish in excellent order. Clothing and coal clubs, the dispensary, and district visiting societies, with Sunday and Day Schools had been established, and each had a share in his interest and attention. He attended with pastoral care to the accounts of the state of the poor given by the ladies who visited the districts of the Parish, at the monthly meeting of the Society at the Rectory; and he always concluded with an affectionate address and a prayer. Each Saturday afternoon some time was devoted to the study of the Bible with his Curates; and a Saturday evening meeting was established in the Rectory."

But a sense of underlying malaise can seen in these extracts from a sermon of Bishop Yeatman (1845-1922) the suffragan Bishop of Southwark when he opened a new 'iron church' at the industrial end of the above parish in 1893:

"There is a thought which presses on us on such an occasion as this; it is a thought which holds not with the most faithful but with the less faithful. As I wander from place to place, among the suffering and degraded men and women on the South bank of the Thames, seeing their needs, seeing their degradedness, knowing the necessity of money to them in the ills of today, we ask then, what right have we when our wealth, as God has blessed it, is so necessary for the whole body of Christ's Church in a thousand ways, what right have we to build churches?...

"Christianity is fast losing its hold upon certain ranks, unless we missionarize - if our Church is to be this Missionary Church there are two things necessary. The one is example, the other is work... Therefore we must present a solid front. Not turned by contrary influences, but united in the bonds of love."

It all sounds a bit desperate. And the corner was not about to be turned any time soon.

So what was the question?
No one posed the question more perceptively than Karl Marx (1813-1883). In 1843 he wrote (in German) the introduction to 'A Contribution to the Critique of Hegel's Philosophy of Right' - published in 1844.

"Religion is the sigh of the oppressed creature, the heart of a heartless world, and the soul of soulless conditions. It is the opium of the people".

Note: Opium was not then illegal. In today's world a better term would be Valium, i.e. religion is the anti-depressant of the people.

The quotation pinpoints why religion retained its importance to the majority of the population. It provided the heart in an increasingly heartless industrial world. In other words:
How can I retain my humanity in an age of industrial capitalism?

YOUR OWN REFLECTIONS
Does it make sense to call society godless, soulless or heartless? If so, what is the remedy?

THE 20TH CENTURY

Christ - Salvador Dali
by AnnieLouise55 on DeviantArt
deviantart.com

The 20th century was a time of enormous turmoil and war, of gigantic technological progress and bewildering cultural change. Again, an overview is only possible through a series of bullet points.

War and Turmoil

- Population. World population rose from 1.6 billion in 1900 to 6 billion (6,000,000,000) in 2000.
- WW1. The First World War (1914-1918) destroyed the optimistic culture that preceded it. 20 million people died, 9.7 million in the armed forces, and 10 million civilians.
- Peace? The Treaty of Versailles in 1919 redrew the map of Europe by dismembering the Austro-Hungarian empire.

- The old monarchies were dissolved; this led to fascist dictatorships in Hungary, Italy, Germany and Spain.

- USSR. The Bolshevik Revolution in Russia and consequent Civil War (1917-1922) caused 10 million deaths, including 8 million civilians, and led to the brutal dictatorship of Stalin.

- Suffragettes. Emmeline Pankhurst founded the Women's Social and Political Union in 1903, which turned to militant action in 1912. In the UK property-owning women over 30 were given the vote in 1918 and all women in 1928. Women in the USA got the right to vote in 1920.

- The Great Crash. Post-war prosperity in the U.S. came to an end in the Great Crash of 1929. The stock market lost a third of its value in six days and 3,000 banks failed. A worldwide depression followed which continued up to the Second World War.

- WW2. The Second World War (1939-1945) was the most destructive war ever. 80 million people died, including 50-55 million civilians: 20-27 million in the Soviet Union, 15-20 million in China, Germany/Austria 7 million, Jews 6 million, Poland up to 6 million, UK 450,000.

- Nuclear Weapons. The first atomic bomb was dropped on Hiroshima 6th August 1945, which ended the war against Japan. In 1949 the Soviet Union exploded their first atomic bomb. In 1951 the US tested a hydrogen bomb with 1,000 more destructive power. This led to a policy of deterrence or "Mutually Assured Destruction," MAD.

- UN. The United Nations was founded in 1945 with 51 members. Today it has 193.

- Cold War. The Cold War defined relations between the Soviet Union with the Warsaw Pact countries versus the United States and Western Europe (North Atlantic Treaty Organisation or NATO) between 1947 and 1991, with the permanent risk of nuclear war. Though there was no war in Europe, there were many proxy wars as in Cuba, Vietnam, and Afghanistan. 1967-70 saw the high-point of protests against the Vietnam war, forcing President Johnson not to seek re-election. The protests were global, such as the Grosvenor Square demonstration, London, of March 1968.

- Palestine/Israel. The state of Israel was created out of the Jewish-Arab war of 1948. 750,000 Palestinians, 85% of population were made refugees and 418 villages razed. In 1967, following a pre-emptive strike by the Israeli air force, Israel captured the whole of what had been Palestine. A further 300,000 Palestinians became refugees.

- China. The People's Republic of China was established in 1949 under Mao Zedong (1893-1976). During the 'Great leap Forward" (1958-1963) 52 million Chinese died from famine. Great numbers died (400,000 - 3 million) or had their lives destroyed during the Cultural Revolution (1966 - 1969/76). Following Mao's death the Party moved towards a market economy bringing with it 30 years of explosive growth.

- Colonies. After the WW2 Britain, France, Belgium and Portugal dismantled their colonial empires: Vietnam

(1945), India and Pakistan (1947), Malaya (1957), Ghana (1957), Algeria (1958), Nigeria. (1960), Congo (1960), Cyprus (1960), Jamaica (1962). Angola (1975) etc.

- The Vietnam War. Lasted from 1955 to 1975 with up to 200,000 US troops involved in 1965. The last U.S. troops withdrew in 1973.

- Assassinations. The century started whist the assassination of Archduke Franz Ferdinand in Sarajevo which sparked off the First World War. In 1948 Gandhi was shot by a Hindu nationalist In the U.S. J F Kennedy (1963), Martin Luther King (1968) and Robert Kennedy (1968) were assassinated. The brief window of hope for a real peace between Israel and Palestinians following the Oslo accords came to a virtual end with the assassination of the Israeli Prime Minister Yitzhak Rabin in 1995.

Hope

- In November 1989 the Berlin Wall (or Anti-Fascist Protection Rampart as it was known in East Germany) came down after 28 years separating the two parts of Germany.

- In 1991 the Soviet Union collapsed with the fifteen federal republics, e.g. Ukraine, Lithuania, Georgia, Kazakhstan etc., becoming independent states.

- In 1994 apartheid ended in South Africa after 46 years with the democratic election of Nelson Mandela as President.

- *"The end of history"?* This was the headline of an article by a State Department official Francis Fukuyama in the magazine "The National Interest" 1989.

Technological Change

- Electricity. The first a/c power stations were operating in the 1890's. The UK National Grid was established in 1933. Electricity is essential to all aspects of modern life

- Transport. The four-stroke petrol engine was invented by Rudolph Otto in 1880. In 1913 The Ford Model T was the first mass-produced car ('Any customer can have a car painted any colour that he wants so long as it is black.'). By 1980 87% of Americans owned at least one car.

- Aeroplanes. 1903 saw the Wright brothers making the first heavier-than-air powered flight. Planes were developed in the First World War, the Royal Air Force being formed in 1918. 1958 saw the first commercial transatlantic service. In 1970 over 310 million passengers were carried worldwide.

- Telephone. Telephones were invented in 1876. In 1902 the first London telephone exchange opened. From 1980 the first generations of mobile phones were developed. By 2000 over 43 million mobile phones were in use in the UK.

- Skyscrapers and tower blocks. The first steel-framed tall building was in Chicago in 1885. A move to a tubular structure in the 1960's allowed skyscrapers all over the world to ignore height and straight lines. Tower blocks were introduced in the UK in 1951 and many were built up to 1980 to cope with the housing crisis.

- Computers. The first single-chip microprocessor was Intel 4004 in 1971. In 1975 George E. Pake, the head of research at Xerox, wrote an article on 'The Office of the Future'. He predicted *"a revolution... over the next 20 years"*, involving a television display terminal sitting on his desk. *"I'll be able to call up documents from my files on the screen, or by pressing a button. I can get my mail or any messages. I don't know how much hard copy I'll want in this world. It will change our daily life, and this could be kind of scary."*

- Space. The first space flight with a human was with Yuri Gagarin in 1961. Telstar, an active, direct relay communications satellite was launched in 1962. The first moon landing took place by NASA in 1969.

- Nuclear power. The first full-scale nuclear power station was in Calder Hall, UK in 1956.

- Medical advances. 1946 chemotherapy was introduced as a treatment for cancer. In 1967 Dr Christian Barnard performed the world's first human heart transplant in Cape Town.

- DNA. In 1953 Francis Crick announced to the lunchtime regulars at the Eagle pub in Cambridge that he and James Watson *"had discovered the secret of life."* This was the double helix structure of DNA (DeoxyriboNucleic Acid). It led to the Human Genome Project, which, from 1990 to 2003, mapped all the genes of the human genome - all the genetic information of human beings.

- Global warming. *"What we are now doing to the world... is new in the experience of the Earth. It is mankind and his activities that are changing the environment of our planet in damaging and dangerous ways. The result is that change in future is likely to be more fundamental and more widespread than anything we have known hitherto.*

Change to the sea around us, change to the atmosphere above, leading in turn to change in the world's climate, which could alter the way we live in the most fundamental way of all."
(Margaret Thatcher, speech to the United Nations 1989).

Cultural change

Art: Up to 1900 all Western art had been representational. From 1910 artists in Paris like Braque and Picasso started deconstructing the visible world in Cubist art. After the Second World War America led the vanguard with Abstract Expressionism with artist such as Jackson Pollock and Mark Rothko.

"At a certain moment the canvas began to appear to one American painter after another as an arena in which to act. What was to go on the canvas was not a picture but an event." - Harold Rosenberg, art critic.

Music: Four centuries of music based on the major and minor keys of the 8-note octave were challenged by composers stretching the boundaries of tonality, e.g. by Stravinsky's ballet "The Rite of Spring" which caused a near-riot at its first performance in Paris in 1913: *"a laborious and puerile barbarity"* according to the critic of Le Figaro. The second challenge was from the Austrian composer Arnold Schoenberg who in 1921 abandoned tonality entirely in favour of a strict scheme of using all twelve semi-tones of the normal octave, with concomitant ideas of serialism and tone-rows.

Much more popular in the 1920's was the explosion of jazz into popular culture, creating "the Jazz Age" with dances like the Charleston, the Black Bottom and the Lindy Hop.

Rock and roll was born in 1955/6 with 'Rock around the Clock' and 'Heartbreak Hotel'. The Beatles were together as a group from 1960 to 1970, selling over 800 million albums, and mobbed by screaming fans, a phenomenon described as 'Beatlemania'. In an interview in 1966 John Lennon said, *"We're more popular than Jesus now. I don't know which will go first— rock 'n' roll or Christianity."*

In 1967 there was a "Summer of Love" when 100,000 young people converged on San Francisco to celebrate hippie culture. High school and college students abandoned their eduction for a summer of sex, drugs and rock and roll. As Timothy Leary, advocate for LSD to expand the mind, then put it, *"Turn on, tune in, drop out."*

Britain had its first rock festival 'Barbeque 67' in Spalding, Lincolnshire

Psychoanalysis: Sigmund Freud (1856-1939) created the technique of psychoanalysis based on theories of the unconscious, infantile sexuality and transference. Key books were "The Interpretation of Dreams" (1899), and "Introductory Lectures on Psycho-Analysis", (1915-1917).

"To us he is no more a person now but a whole climate of opinion under whom we conduct our different lives"
            From 'In Memory of Sigmund Freud' by W H Auden.

Politics: The Labour Party eclipsed the Liberal Party in 1922 and briefly formed a government two years later. Also in 1922 the Transport and General Worker's Union was formed with 900,000 members, the largest trade union in the world. In 1945 The Labour Party formed the government, and created the National Health Service and nationalised coal, steel, railways and the Bank of England.

Cinema: On December 28th 1895 the Lumière brothers made the first commercial public screening of a film, the same year that Léon Gaumont started the Gaumont Film Company. From 1897 large cinemas started being built in all major cities. The first 'talkie', 'The Jazz Singer', was a smash hit in 1927. The high point of cinema going was after the Second World War. In 1946 there were 1,635 million admissions, i.e. 36 tickets per year for every adult in the country. All in black-and-white. Colour only became common in the 1950's. In the 1980's ticket sales dropped to 2 per person per year.

Radio and Television: The BBC (British Broadcasting Corporation) was created in 1922. Television became available in the UK in the 1950's with colour arriving in the 1960's. ITV was launched in 1955. Sky, a subscription television company, was formed in 1990. The Internet The number of users of the internet rose from 40 million people 1995 to 413 million in 2000 and 1 billion in 2005. We became a connected world.

Restaurants: Richard and Mary McDonald started their first restaurant in 1940. Through franchising, there are now over 40,000 outlets worldwide. Indian restaurants in Britain mushroomed, from 6 in 1939 to 3,500 in 1982. Pizza Express opened its first restaurant in 1965; there are now 370 in the UK and Ireland

The Pill: The contraceptive pill was approved in the US and UK in 1960/1961. This dramatically redefined women's expectations of life.

Reforming legislation: In 1967 homosexual acts between consenting adults were decriminalised. The 1973 Matrimonial Causes Act replaced the former requirement to prove adultery with simply irretrievable breakdown, based on several possible grounds.

Drug use: Due to international control structures, between 1906 and 2006 opium use declined from 1.5% to 0.25% of the global population, while cocaine and amphetamines rose from 0.1% to 0.37%. Cannabis is the most widely used drug.

Religion

A new church Surprisingly, the 20th century opened with a radical new type of Christianity - Pentecostalism. Early instances broke out in Topeka, Kansas in 1901, in the Welsh Revival in 1904-5, at Azusa St, Los Angeles in 1906, and at All Saints Monkwearmouth, Sunderland, UK in September 1907. When the fire of the Lord fell it burned up the debt'. The Pentecostal churches developed out of the Evangelical Holiness Movement and emphasise "speaking in tongues" as a consequence of being baptised by the Holy Spirit. By 2011 Pentecostal churches worldwide had 500 million adherents.
"The most amazing thing about the runaway divisiveness in the young pentecostal movement is that ... the more the pentecostals fought, the more they multiplied."
(Harvey Cox - Fire from Heaven, 1995)

Popular Perceptions

1910. Henry Scott Holland preached a sermon after the death of Edward VII, in which he looked at various responses to death and spoke of the Christian hope. What he set out as a blind alley has become enshrined in popular culture:

"Death is nothing at all. It does not count. I have only slipped away into the next room."

1914-1918 The Great War. All soldiers were given a pocket New Testament, but the churches were shocked at the depth of disbelief they discovered among the troops. Some chaplains were popular, others were not:

> *"Our padre were a solemn bloke,*
> *We called 'im 'dismal Jim'.*
> *It fairly gave ye t'bloomin' creeps,*
> *To sit and 'ark at 'im.*
> *When 'e ere on wi' Judgement Day,*
> *Abaht that great white throne,*
> *And 'ow each chap would 'ave to stand*
> *And answer on 'is own,*
> *And if 'e tried to charnce 'is arm,*
> *And 'ide a single sin,*
> *There'd be the angel Gabriel,*
> *Wi' books to do 'im in..."*

From 'Well?' by G Studdert Kennedy, 'Woodbine Willie',
1883-1929

However, 'Abide with me' was hugely popular in the trenches. It was then first sung at the Cup Final of 1927, and has been sung every year except one since.

A Character in E M Forster's novel 'A Passage to India' makes the cutting remark: *"Poor, talkative, little, Christianity",*

Statistics
Here are some church statistics:

	1927	1957	1970
Church of England	2,660,000	2,354,000	1,804,000
Roman Catholics	2,660,000	4,064,000	4,829,000
Nonconformists	2,019,000	1,641,000	1,328,000
Scottish Presbyterians	1,308,000	1,348,000	1,179,000

(www.brin.ac.uk)

Church of England numbers fell from 2,515,000 in 1939 to 1,944,000 in 1947. Numbers recovered up to 2,354,000 in 1957, then dropped markedly from 1962. Roman Catholic numbers grew strongly and consistently up to 1969. Nonconformists showed a slow but steady decline from 1927.

The percentage of the population attending church at least once a month within the Church of England was 21.2% in 1991. In 2001, after the Decade of Evangelism, this percentage had dropped to 16.3%.

Speaking Out

1941- 44 Two influential Christian apologias were the radio play by Dorothy Sayers 'The Man Born to be King' and three radio talks by C.S.Lewis later published as 'Mere Christianity', which has sold 3.5 million copies in English since 2001.

"Quarrelling means trying to show that the other man is in the wrong. And there would be no sense in trying to do that unless you and he had some sort of agreement as to what Right and Wrong are." (Mere Christianity, chapter 1)

1942 Archbishop William Temple (1881-1944) set out a vision for a just post-war order in 'Christianity and the Social Order'.

"The Church is the only society that exists for the benefit of those who are not its members."

In the 1950's American evangelists started broadcasting service regularly on television, through their own television stations. Names like Oral Roberts, Jerry Falwell and Pat Robertson became household names.

"Someone needs to say this plainly: The faith healers and health-and-wealth preachers who dominate religious television are shameless frauds. Their message is not the true Gospel of Jesus Christ. There is nothing spiritual or miraculous about their on-stage chicanery. It is all a devious ruse designed to take advantage of desperate people."
(John MacArthur Jr., Pastor of Grace Community Church, California)

1955 The American evangelist Billy Graham led the Greater London Crusade at Haringey Arena, which attracted two million people.

"This is a holy moment and a sacred moment, for which we have long prayed. There are many hungry hearts here tonight — people who have been disillusioned with life, confused and mixed up, and before you leave this building tonight you can find the greatest peace and joy and inward satisfaction you have ever known."

In 1963 Bishop John Robinson wrote 'Honest to God'. 'The Observer (Sunday newspaper) ran this headline in their review section' **Our Image of God Must Go.** The initial print run of the book was 6,000. Partly as a result of the Observer article it has sold over a million copies since. This is from Bishop Robinson's preface:

"If our defence of the Faith is limited to (a restating of traditional orthodoxy in modern terms), we shall find in all likelihood that we have lost out to all but a tiny religious remnant. A much more radical recasting , I would judge, is demanded, in the process of which the most fundamental categories of our theology - of God, of the supernatural, and of religion itself - must go into the melting pot."

An amusing reaction to Robinson's recasting of God as 'the ground of our being' comes in a modern retranslation of Mark 8.29 (unattributed): *"Jesus said to them "But whom say ye that I am?". And Peter answereth and saith unto him, 'Thou art the eschatological manifestation of the ground of our being, in the kerygma of which we find the ultimate meaning in our interpersonal relationships."*

('Ship of Fools' website)

In 1981 the Alpha course developed as an introduction to the Christian faith in ten sessions. This grew from four courses at Holy Trinity Brompton to 10,500 courses worldwide in 1998 (its peak). Charismatic experience is a central feature. By 2011 the course book 'Questions of Life' had sold over 1.5 million copies worldwide.

New Things

1961: A radically new translation of the New Testament was published, the New English Bible. The Old Testament was published in 1970. It included this marvellous translation of Hebrews 11.31-32:
'By faith Rahab the prostitute ... gave the spies a friendly welcome. Need I say more?'

1962 - 1965: The Second Vatican Council was called by Pope John XXIII to *"open the windows [of the Church] and let in some fresh air."* The Council allowed the mass to be celebrated in the language of the people instead of Latin, greater lay participation in worship, and commended *"that sweet and living love of sacred Scripture".*

1980: 'The Alternative Service Book', a modern liturgy for the Church of England, replaced the Book of Common Prayer (1662) in most parishes. This ended a decade of experimentation. Once when the Bishop of Kensington was celebrating communion, he started by proclaiming, *"The Lord is here,"* only to have the vicar murmur, *"No he isn't. This is Series 2."*

1985: A Church of England report 'Faith in the City' criticised Conservative policies on social welfare and funded social programmes in Urban Priority Areas.

Around 1960 a second pentecostal wave started in California and travelled worldwide as the charismatic movement, bringing pentecostal experiences into the traditional mainstream churches, including, in 1968, the Roman Catholic Church: *"At the heart of a world imbued with a rationalistic skepticism, a new experience of the Holy Spirit suddenly burst forth. And, since then, that experience has assumed a breadth of a worldwide Renewal movement."* (From the preface to a 1983 book by Cardinal Suenens)

A third wave of Pentecostal churches were founded, such as the Association of Vineyard Churches led by John Wimber from 1982. His theology was based on Jesus' example in the gospels, majoring on evangelism, healing (signs and wonders) and social action. There were about 2,000 Vineyard churches by 2000.

The extraordinary spread of Pentecostalism needs to be appreciated.

"(Pentecostalism) has succeeded because it has spoken to the spiritual emptiness of our time by reaching... into what might be called 'primal spirituality', that largely unprocessed nucleus of the psyche in which the unending struggle for a sense of purpose and significance goes on." (Harvey Cox, Fire from Heaven, p. 81)

Mega-churches blossomed world-wide. Hillsong in Sydney Australia grew from 45 members in 1983 to 20,000 at the end of the century. There are four mega churches in Lagos, Nigeria, founded around the mid-70s, each now with a membership of around 50,000. The Yoido Full Gospel Church in South Korea reached 200,000 members in 1981 and now claims 480,000. (Wikipedia).

When the Roman Catholic Church declared 2000 a year of Jubilee, it inspired people to campaign for debt relief for the poorest countries in the world, in the spirit of Leviticus 25.8-24.

Initially it was mainly churches and youth groups of older denominations who took part. A feature of the campaign was that local groups were active in letter-writing, advocacy and education on international debt issues across the whole of the UK. A key moment was in 1998 when between 50,000 and 70,000 people demonstrated at the G8 meeting in Birmingham England. Archbishop Justin Welby writing in 2017 described it as *"perhaps the churches finest hour in dethroning Mammon... Sustained support from Christians and others across the world led to the cancellation of more than $100 billion of debt owed by 35 of the poorest countries."*

Some Church Decisions

In 1968 Pope Paul VI promulgated 'Humanise Vitae' - 'Of Human Life': After a long period of consultation, he rejected all forms of artificial contraception including within marriage except for medical emergencies. Many Roman Catholic couples ignored it.

In 1985 a Church of England report 'Faith in the City' criticised Conservative policies on social welfare and determined to fund many social programmes in Urban Priority Areas.

In 1994 the General Synod of the Church of England voted in favour of the ordination of women as priests.

Islam

The first purpose-built mosque was built in Britain in Woking. Built in 1889 for the benefit of visiting dignitaries to Leitner's Oriental Institute it became a fully functioning mosque after 1912. Muslim presence in Britain, and in the West in general, then was tiny, although that did not stop the European powers drafting 3.5 million Muslims to fight in the two great wars. Hundreds of thousands of migrant workers were brought into Europe after 1945, from Pakistan and Bangladesh to Britain, from North Africa to France and from Turkey to Germany. They brought their families and mosques began to be a familiar part of the street scene.

Barriers to Belief

In 1988 Donald Soper, West London Methodist Mission, wrote: *"Whereas Wesley could count on an overall sense of guilt among his hearers, the preacher today can only, initially at least, count on a sense of doubt."* (From John Wesley - Contemporary Perspectives 1988, p.187)

Bill Wilson, writing in 'Alcoholics Anonymous' in 1939 said, *"The word God still aroused a certain antipathy. When the thought was expressed that there might be a God personal to me this feeling was intensified. "I didn't like the idea. I could go for such conceptions as Creative Intelligence, Universal Mind or Spirit of Nature, but I resisted the thought of a Czar of the Heavens, however loving His sway might be. I have since talked with scores of men who felt the same way."*

So what were the questions?

Maybe:
Why should I believe?
And if that can be answered,
Is a spiritual life possible?

YOUR OWN REFLECTIONS

What would you say to someone who says, 'You don't have to go to church to be a Christian'?

Is religion good for society? For me?

PART 2
THE 21ST CENTURY
THE FIRST TWENTY FIVE YEARS

Introduction — 102

War and Politics — 103
   Liberalism and International Cooperation — 103
   Democracy and Autocracy — 105
   Populism and Autocracy — 107
   Terrorism — 111
   The Axis of Terror — 112
   War — 114

Economics — 119
   Growth — 119
   Boom Years — 119
   The Crash — 120
   The Rich World — 120
   China expands — 121
   Digital Currencies — 122

Climate Change and Other Disasters — 125

Health — 129
   Public Health - Pandemics — 129
                - Other Issues — 133
   New Medical Science — 137
           Gene Therapy — 137
           Microrobots, nanorobots, AI — 138
           Synthetic Biology — 139
           The Magic CRISPR — 140

Science & Space — 143
- Graphene — 143
- Space telescopes — 144
- In the dark — 144
- Space — 145
- Archaeology — 146

Technology and Communication — 148
- Computers - the hardware — 148
- Computers - the software — 151
- Internet issues: Censorship — 154
  - Cybercrime — 154
  - Pornography — 155

AI — 157
- The history of AI — 157
- AI applications — 158
- Large Language Models — 159
- An AI future — 160

Cultural Shifts - Sex — 162
- Relationships — 162
- Sexual Practices — 164
- Surrogacy — 165
- Sexual Orientation — 165
- Some Definitions — 165
- Transgender Issues — 171
- Gender-fluidity — 173
- Safeguarding against abuse — 174
- Women Arising — 175
  - #MeToo — 175
  - Politics — 176
  - BBC — 176
  - Higher positions — 177
  - A Teen View — 177

Entertainment and Media — 178
Social Media — 178
Gen Z and Social Media — 183
Video Games — 185
The Best of the Rest — 188

Religion — 190
Statistics - UK — 190
More Statistics - USA — 191
Yet More Statistics - World — 192
Sexual abuse in the Church — 192
The Makin Review — 194
Reacting to the Sexual Revolution — 195
The New Atheism — 197
Mindfulness — 197
A Land of Faiths — 199
Islam — 202
Church Theology — 203
Church Worship — 204
Messy Church — 205
Food banks — 205
Pope Francis — 206
Pope Leo XIV — 207
New Age Religions — 207

What is the question? — 210

THE 21ST CENTURY
THE FIRST TWENTY FIVE YEARS

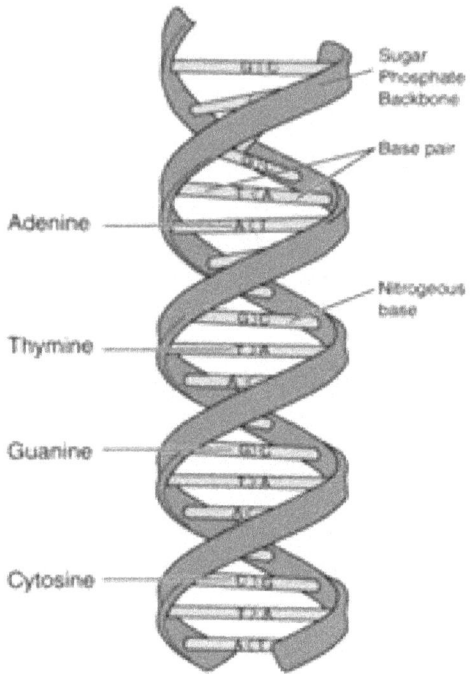

INTRODUCTION

The pace of change since 2000 has been bewildering. In so many areas, people are confronted with a completely new reality, with the promise/threat of even more fundamental change during the rest of the century. Only a proper though necessarily brief description of each of these changes needs to be made. So a brief description of the past twenty five years is going to occupy more pages than the last two thousand.

WAR AND POLITICS

The Prussian general von Clausewitz (1780-1831) famously wrote, "War is the continuation of policy with other means." (Beginning of his book 'On War')

The first two decades of the century have seen an amazing change in the outlook for the world. In 2000 democracy, liberalism and co-operation seemed firmly embedded in the international order. In 2025 the world seems to be succumbing to autocracy, populism and war. How did we get here?

Liberalism & International Co-operation

The century opened in a golden glow of international co-operation. The International Space station got its first crew in November 2000. The African Union replaced the Organisation of African Unity. In 2002 Russia became a partner of NATO and in 2004 seven East European countries joined. By 2015 nineteen member states had joined. And twelve EU member states adopted the euro as their currency. By 2008 all except Ireland had implemented the Schengen agreement, which provides open borders for citizens of 26 European states.

The International Criminal Court was founded in July 2002, and put Radovan Karadzic on trial for genocide in Bosnia during the civil war of 1992-1995. In 2016 he was sentenced to forty years in prison. In 2006 the UN founded the Human Rights Council.

These developments were bolstered by a series of high-profile centrist political leaders, notably Angela Merkel of Germany (2005-2020), Tony Blair, Gordon Brown and David Cameron in the UK (1997-2016) and Barack Obama in the USA (2009 -2017).

A potent example was the Good Friday Agreement in May 2007 which established a joint Executive for Northern Ireland between the Democratic Unionists and Sinn Fein. (The same month the SNP - Scottish Nationalists - came to power in Scotland). In 2016 Sadiq Khan became the first Muslim mayor of a major European city.

In 2010 Obama signed the Affordable Care Act into law, extending health insurance to 20 million Americans. In 2015 full diplomatic relations between the USA and Cuba were restored after 53 years.

In 2005 the Kyoto protocol to limit climate change came into force when Russia signed. In 2016 the Paris agreement was signed with the aim of keeping the rise of global temperature to well below 2% against pre-industrial levels. The Madrid talks in 2019 failed to come to an agreement due to opposition from United States, Russia, India, China, Brazil and Saudi Arabia.

The resources of liberalism were severely tested by the refugee crisis which erupted because of the Syrian civil war. This produced a staggering increase in refugees trying to move to Europe, arriving first in Greece and Italy. Numbers went from 309,040 in 2011 to 1,322,825 in 2015. These figures only account for 17% of those fleeing conflicts. The vast majority are accommodated in the least developed countries, in particular most Syrian refugees were in Turkey, Lebanon and Jordan.

In 2015 Germany granted protection to 140,915 out of a total asylum applications of 476,609. The largest refugee camp in Europe with about 8,000 people was the Calais Jungle established in January 2015 and demolished twenty one months later. In 2022 there were 29.4 million refugees and 57.3 million internally displaced people worldwide.

Democracy and Autocracy
EU, The European Union has been the most successful driver in encouraging democratic norms. Applicant countries have to guarantee democracy, the rule of law, human rights, respect and protection of minorities and a market economy. The application process typically takes nine years. This millennium the following countries have become full members: Estonia, Cyprus, Czech Republic, Hungary, Latvia, Lithuania, Malta, Poland, Slovakia, Slovenia (all on 1st May 2004), Bulgaria (2007) and Croatia (2013).

USA, In 2008 the USA convincingly elected Barack Obama as the first African-American President, a sign of hope to many around the world, and he was re-elected in 2012. However he was succeeded in 2016 by the business mogul Donald Trump. As Obama said the day after the 2016 election, *"We zig and zag, and sometimes we move in ways that some people think is forward and others think is moving back. And that's okay."*

The Arab Spring 2011
In the first months of 2011 a wave of popular protests swept the Arab world. It seemed as if democracy was abut to win a major victory. But their fortunes were mixed

Tunisia. *Success*: Ten days of popular demonstrations in Tunisia ended the 23 year rule of the President who fled the country on 14/1/11. This led to it becoming of a free democratic and prosperous country, with free trade with the EU.

Libya. *Failed success or successful failure?* Libya has two natural centres of power, Tripoli in the west and Benghazi and Tobruk in the east. A full-scale revolt against Gaddafi started on 17/2/11 leading to a civil war between Benghazi and Tripoli. After Gaddafi was overthrown in November 2011, there were elections in 2012, but the government quickly fragmented. In 2012 Islamic militants killed the American ambassador and three others inside the embassy. There was civil war from 2014 up to a ceasefire in 2020. At least nine different militias operate in different parts of the country, including Islamic terrorist groups. A ceasefire was agreed in 2020 together with an attempt to create a unity government without great success. In April 2024 the UN envoy resigned due to the "lack of political will and good faith" by politicians. The breakdown of law and order has made Libya a major route for refugees trying to get to Europe.

Egypt. *First success, then failure:* Egypt is the largest Arab country with over 95 million people. On 25/1/11 mass demonstrations in Egypt led to the resignation of President Mubarak. Social media was crucial in the success of the demonstrations.

In June 2012 the Muslim Brotherhood obtained a narrow election victory with Morsi as Prime Minister. Following mass demonstrations of 15 million in July 2013 the army seized power. General El-Sisi retired from the army and was elected President in May 2014, bringing about a highly repressive regime and making democratic elections a charade.

Bahrain *Failure:* In March 2011 there were mass protests by the Shia majority against the Sunni ruling class, but within a month a crackdown with thousands of arrests and systematic torture crushed it. Amnesty reports that since then systematic injustice and political repression have ruled.

Syria. *Failure:* In March 2011 there were demonstrations in Damascus and Aleppo demanding democratic reforms and release of political prisoners. These were violently suppressed. A loose coalition of anti-government forces came together to form the Syrian National Council in August 2011. Violence gradually intensified, with terrorist bomb attacks. Russia sided decisively on the side of Assad's regime. Syrian government forces took Aleppo from rebel forces in December 2016 after massive bombardment and finally after use of chemical weapons. Out of a population of 22 million, 6 million have been internally displaced and around 5 million Syrians have become refugees externally, principally in Turkey (3.5 million), Lebanon, Jordan, Turkey and Iraq. One million have applied for refugee status in Europe. In 2024 the civil war had reduced to an uncomfortable stalemate around Idlib in the north-east, with occasional interventions by Turkey. This was followed by the astonishing defeat of the Assad regime in just eleven days in December by a coalition of opposition groups from the north and the south.

Populism and Autocracy

UK The 2008 global financial crisis, created by excessive risk-taking by banks such as Lehman Brothers, led to massive bailouts of financial institutions to prevent the possible collapse of the world financial system. A severe recession followed. This led to a rise in populism - a mind-set based on nationalism and a distrust of elites and experts. Leaders of such movements often seek to disregard normal democratic safeguards such as the independence of the judiciary in favour of a narrative of national self-assertion and an increasingly authoritarian system of government. In Europe this trend is seen in Poland and Hungary, and among the right-wing parties in France and Germany. The Brexit referendum campaign in the UK, which voted 52% - 48% to leave the EU, created bitter divisions in the country, exacerbated by the capture of the Labour party by Left-wing militants with Jeremy Corbyn. During the campaign Jo Cox, a Labour MP, was murdered for her pro-Remain views. The Grenfell fire of 2017 in which 76 people died exposed deep fault lines between classes in Britain. In 2025, Nigel Farage's right wing Reform Party became a significant political force.

EU. There are strains within the EU when right-wing parties are elected when the fundamental principles of the Union are seen as at risk. In 2010 Victor Orban became prime minister of Hungary for the second time, promoting what he calls 'illiberal democracy'. The Polish elections of 2015 and 2020 were won by the Law and Justice Party (PiS), promoting right wing Catholic and eurosceptic views. However, in 2023 Donald Tusk led his Civic Coalition to election victory, to the relief of many EU Council members.

India. The same trend was seen in India with the landslide election wins for the Hindu nationalist BJP (Bharatiya Janata Party or Indian People's Party) in 2014 and 2019. However, in 1924 the BJP lost its majority in the Lok Sabha, Lower House of Parliament.

USA. In 2017 Donald Trump became President of the US, promising to clean up the 'Washington swamp' and make America great again, bringing in anti-immigration policies and withdrawing from the Trans-Pacific Partnership trade negotiations and the Paris Agreement on climate change. He willed the end of the judicial appeal structure of the WTO, World Trade Organisation, so that there is now no legal authority to settle disputes between countries. In May 2018 Trump unilaterally withdrew from the 2015 nuclear deal with Iran (the Joint Comprehensive Plan of Action), with both countries now apparently drifting towards war. The most serious action of Trump was to refuse to acknowledge his defeat in the 2020 election and to instigate a mass attack on the Capitol building on 6th January 2021. His insistence that the election was stolen has been adopted widely by the Republican Party, seriously threatening the normal checks and balances of the democratic process.

Trump won a decisive election victory in November 2024. His new presidency has been marked by an anti-liberal foreign policy, an attack on US government institutions and universities, and a chaotic trade war with the world, specially China.

Turkey. Turkey has a population of 80 million. It was a secular democracy up to 2016, when, after an attempted coup, Recep Tayyip Erdoğan, the President, effectively carried out his own coup, incarcerating tens of thousands of individuals, including teachers, journalists and police officers. In 2017 the constitution was changed, replacing the parliamentary republic with an executive presidential system. It was actively involved in the civil war in Syria.

Myanmar. A military dictatorship ruled Myanmar (formerly Burma) from 1962. In 2010 the army, 'the Tatmadaw', allowed elections which were boycotted by opposition parties. Free elections were held in 2015 in which the National League for Democracy (NLD) won convincingly. Its leader, Aung San Suu Kyi, had been under house arrest for fifteen of the years 1989 to 2010. She was then appointed State Counsellor, similar to Prime Minister. In the 2020 election the army-backed Union Solidarity and Development Party (USDP) suffered a humiliating defeat, taking only 33 of the 496 elected seats. On 1st February, the day of the opening of the parliament, the army arrested leaders of the NLD and declared martial law. This was met by huge demonstrations, which the army put down with extreme violence. Up to 2024 at least 2,900 protesters have been killed and 17,000 imprisoned. The Internet and social media have been blocked. A multidimensional civil war is now being waged.

Russia. Vladimir Putin became Prime Minister of Russia in 1999 and President from 2000 to 2008 and again from 2012 to 2018. He was ruthless in prosecuting the war in Chechnya and in disabling political opponents and basic freedoms. In 2014 he invaded Crimea occupied Crimea, part of Ukraine, and started a prolonged proxy war in the Donbas, eastern Ukraine. In 2022 he invaded Ukraine with massive force and made Russia into a totalitarian state with no freedom of speech. Ukrainian resistance forced him to withdraw from Kiev and central Ukraine. In western Ukraine the war is becoming a destructive stalemate.

China. Xi Jinping became President in 2012 and swiftly centralised power to himself, increasing censorship and mass surveillance and creating a country-wide cult of personality.

In 2018 he effectively made himself president, or paramount leader, for life.

Following pro-democracy protests in Hong Kong, China's National People's Congress passed the National Security Law of Hong Kong severely curtailing freedom. No longer 'one country two systems'.

Political dissent is quashed by a loose but blanket surveillance system incorporating facial recognition cameras, mobile phone tracking devices, various powerful units within the police and party and millions of informants.

Disinformation. A key issue is the ability for politicians to use social media to spread disinformation. Hugo Rifkind in The Times wrote, *"online disinformation is less about liars than it is about believers. When somebody has gone wrong, I learnt, it is no use to tell them the truth. For they don't want the truth. They want the belief. And they will find a way to keep it."*

Terrorism

9/11 The iconic moment was 9/11, i.e. 11th September 2001, when the Islamic terror group al Qaeda flew two planes into the Twin Towers of the World Trade Centre, New York, demolishing both buildings. 2,996 people died. Less than a week later George Bush declared a 'War on Terror', citing North Korea, Iran and Iraq as the 'Axis of Terror'.

Terrorist incidents, both by Islamic militants and right-wing groups, made news. In 2004 190 were killed in Madrid. The first major incident in the UK was the bus and tube bombings in London on 7/7/05 with 56 killed including the four terrorists. Four days later 259 people were killed in terrorist bombings in Mumbai. 129 were killed in 2015 in Paris and 12 by a lorry in a Berlin market in 2016. This is just a selection.

The Axis of Terror

Afgahnistan. US forces invaded Afghanistan in October 2001 to overthrow the Taliban; UN forces took over in 2003. The democratic Islamic Republic of Afghanistan was established in 2004, but had to face a protracted Taliban insurgency. 100,000 US troops returned between 2011and 2014. In February 2020 a conditional peace deal was signed between the US and the Taliban. On 1st May 2021 Joe Biden unilaterally withdrew all 2,500 remaining US forces. The Taliban started the Summer Offensive and captured Kabul in August, establishing the second Islamic Emirate. Their strict interpretation of the place of women has had devastating consequences for half the population.

Iran. Iran is the largest state in the Middle East after Egypt with 82 million people. After the 1979 Revolution which overthrew the Shah, it became a theocratic democracy, with ultimate authority wielded by the Supreme Leader, assisted by a Guardian Council of twelve jurists who supervise the elected President and Parliament. It supported the predominantly Shia government in Iraq after the 2003 Gulf War as well as the Alawite government of Syria and the Houthis in Yemen.

Its ambition to create nuclear missiles was put on hold after the Joint Comprehensive Plan of Action agreed in April 2015. The USA withdrew from the agreement in May 2018. Relations between Iran and the USA have deteriorated into low grade hostility, and Iranian pursuit of the capacity to produce nuclear weapons continues. It carries out low-level wars through proxies such as Hezbollah, Houthis and Hamas.

North Korea. On 4th July 2017 North Korea tested its first hydrogen bomb and its first ICBM - InterContinental Ballistic Missile. It continues to conduct test missiles, ratcheting up tension in the whole region. It also possesses various types of chemical weapons, including nerve, blister, blood and vomiting agents, as well as some biological weapons, including anthrax, smallpox and cholera.

Iraq. An outstanding failure in the fight to combat terrorism was the invasion of Iraq in March 2003 the by US and Great Britain; the allies invaded Iraq in the Second Gulf War, based on the false assumption of Saddam Hussein having a stockpile of chemical weapons. Hussein was overthrown in a month, but the inept handling of the resulting vacuum led to a many-sided insurgency using surface-to-air missiles, suicide bombers and IEDs - Improvised Explosive Devices. In 2008 it was estimated that 4.7 million Iraqis had been displaced, 16% of the population. Between August and December 2009 at least 383 Iraqis were killed and 1,734 injured in bombings in Baghdad. A year later all US troops were withdrawn. They returned in 2011. Armed conflict between Sunni and Shia, massive corruption and intervention by Iran continued, with Sunnis protesting against the Shia monopoly of power.

In 2014 the extreme Islamist group Islamic State took over large swathes of the country including Mosul and Fallujah, carrying out gruesome massacres and executions. In June 2014 their leader Abu Bakr al-Bhagdadi proclaimed himself caliph of the new Islamic State, calling on Muslims to unite and capture Rome. Thereafter government and allied forces stemmed IS's advances. War continued until 2017 when the Iraqi army with the help of US troops recaptured Mosul and all IS's strongholds. In October 2017 the IS capital of Raqqa in Syria was finally captured by Syrian anti-government forces. But Iraq's basic problems remain.

War

Israel In September 2000 Ariel Sharon sparked off the second Palestinian Intifada by his provocative visit to the Haram-al-Sharif/Temple Mount in Jerusalem. He became Prime Minister the following year, occupying Gaza and West Bank towns. Over the next five years 1,000 Israelis and 4,700 Palestinians were killed. In 2006 he withdrew Israeli forces from Gaza and West Bank towns and began building the Separation Wall. In 2007 Hamas won the election in Gaza and took control. Straightaway Israel instituted an economic blockade of Gaza by land, sea and air. Three wars followed, killing 3,500 Palestinians and 84 Israelis and destroying 17,200 homes. Israeli policy towards the West Bank continues to support Jewish settlers and oppress Palestinians.

On 7th October 2023 Hamas launched a series of attacks on southern Israel, when 1,139 people were killed and 252 taken hostage. Israel launched one of the most destructive bombing campaigns in recent history and invaded Gaza on 27th October.

Because of the elaborate system of underground tunnels, Hamas was weakened but not destroyed, while at least 54,000 Palestinians have been killed, 100,000 injured with the added threat of mass starvation and disease. In May 2024 the prosecutor of the International Criminal Court sought arrest warrants against three Hamas leaders: Yahya Sinwar, Ismail Haniyeh, and Mohammed Deif, and against Israel's Prime Minister and Defence Minister, Benjamin Netanyahu and Yoav

Gallant, over alleged war crimes. Israel then made war on Hezbollah in Lebanon and bombed Iran.

As at April 2025 Israel has continued to bomb and attack Palestinians in Gaza and to support settler attacks in the West Bank.

West Africa. In Nigeria the jihadist group Boko Haram started an armed rebellion in 2009, with 10,000 deaths in 2014, the capture of several towns, and massacre of 2,000 people in Baga. In June 2014 10 generals and 5 officers in the Nigerian army were court-martialled for supplying arms and information to Boko Haram. The warfare continues to disrupt all the West African countries bordering the Sahel, the semi-arid zone between the Sahara desert and the savannah plains. The increasing desertification has brought traditional cattle herders and farming pastoralists into bloody conflict.

Congo. The Second Congo War lasted from 1998-2003 in the Democratic Republic of the Congo, but violence still persists in the eastern part of the country. This war has caused the death of 5.4 million, principally through disease and starvation, with perhaps 860,000 deaths directly attributed to the war and 400,000 women suffering rape. The election in December 2018 was marked by huge fraud.

Sri Lanka. In 2009 the 26-year- civil war in Sri Lanka came to a conclusive and bloody end with many civilian casualties. 100,000 may have died during the course of the war and a further 100,000 at its conclusion, with war crimes perpetrated by both the Sri Lankan military and the Tamil Tigers. Reconciliation is a long way off.

Yemen. Yemen was created as a unified state in 1990 after thirty years of intermittent hostilities between North Yemen and South Yemen. The population is 27 million. Instability continued which allowed Al Quaeda and later Islamic State to establish their bases there. An attempted revolution in 2011 was met with police gunfire. In 2015 Shia Houthis from North Yemen were fighting against Al Quaeda, Islamic State and Saudi Arabia. It is basically a proxy war between Saudi Arabia and Iran. More than 50,000 children have died of starvation and over a million Yemenis have been affected by cholera.

South Sudan. A civil war between 2014 and 2020 caused the deaths of 400,000 with more than 4 million people displaced.

Ukraine. When the Soviet Union collapsed in 1991, Ukraine became an independent neutral state. The economic crisis which followed up to 1999 resulted in it losing 60% of its GDP. Democratic elections thereafter were marked by corruption and fraud, with constant swings between pro-Russian and pro-EU candidates, including the attempted poisoning by Russia of a leading opposition candidate. In 2013 and 2014 there were large street protests, which resulted in 10,000 injured protesters on 18th and 20th February 2014. Members of Parliament dismissed the pro-Russian president and new elections were held in May. Putin responded by taking over the Crimea on 20th February and starting a long undeclared war attempting to annex the Russian-speaking provinces of Ukraine. There was continual warfare between Ukrainian forces and up to 42,000 Russian 'volunteers' for the next six years.

On 24th February 2022 Russia carried out a full-scale invasion of Ukraine, aiming to take Kyiv and seize the whole country. Determined Ukrainian resistance forced the withdrawal of Russian forces from central Ukraine in April who then concentrated on conquering the eastern province of Donbas with heavy bombardment of cities. Despite two major Ukrainian advances It is turning into a long, grinding war. In the first three months 10,000 Ukrainian soldiers died.

Ukraine has been supported with additional weapons by Western countries, with a dramatic expansion of NATO. The economic consequences have been felt worldwide, from German anxiety about how to survive without Russian gas and oil, to countries in the Middle East and Africa at risk of severe hunger because of the interruption of grain imports from Ukraine and Russia.

It is also a new kind of war, a net-worked war. The internet and electronic communications are vital to the Ukrainian war effort and for the continued functioning of civil society. Russian cyber warfare and physical attacks were countered by the use of Elon Musk's 'Starlink' satellite communication system. And the use of drones has changed the battlefield. In one week in 2023 Ukrainian drones destroyed 75 tanks and 101 big guns. Russian drones have carried bombing raids on Ukrainian towns and cities and have enabled small advances not the battlefield.

The novelty of battle drones is their cheap microchips which let intelligence sit inside millions of low-level munitions.

We may soon see them being used by militias, terrorists and criminals.

YOUR OWN REFLECTION

Psalm 7.11 says, "God is a righteous judge, and a God who has indignation every day." Do you find this verse comforting or frustrating? Are there any events in which you can see God at work in a hidden way?

ECONOMICS

The four big stories of the economics of the 21st century so far are extraordinary growth, extraordinary debacles, the growing gap between the rich and the poor and the growth of China.

Growth
In 2000 the population of India was over 1 billion, only possible because a new variety of rice, !R8, produced in 1966, saved much of Asia from starvation. By 2018 electricity had reached every Indian village. World population in 2019 stands at 7.8 billion, up from 1 billion in 1804 and up from 6 billion in 2000. It is expected to reach 10 billion by 2050.

Boom Years
The century began with the bursting of the dot-com bubble. In the late 1990s there was a rush to buy internet related stocks and shares, by both financial institutions and by individuals. Many of these had yet to show any profits, or in some cases any trading. The bubble duly burst and the NASDAQ, the stock market index of information technology companies, lost 78% of its value between March 2000 and October 2002.

This was followed by a spectacular recovery. The World Bank data shows that between 2004 and 2009 world GDP (Gross Domestic Product) averaged $4,252 billion, up from $1,950 billion in 2001. The average house price in the UK, adjusted for inflation, doubled from £137,613 in 2000 to £282,000 in 2024.

China's GDP grew by at least 10% per year from 1991, becoming the second largest economy in the world in 1999. In 2001 China joined the World Trade Organisation.

The Crash
The financial crash of 2007 - 2010 originated in the subprime mortgage crisis, fostered by lower lending standards, higher-risk mortgage products and fevered housing speculation. This led to the indebtedness of American households as a percentage of personal disposable income rising from 77% in 1990 to 127% in 2007. When the bubble burst in 2007, house prices fell by 30% and the stock market by 50%. 9 million people in the US became unemployed. In September 2008 the investment bank Lehman Brothers became the largest bankruptcy case in US history, owing over $600 billion.

The effects were worldwide. There were massive bailouts of financial institutions. In October 2008 the UK government announced a bailout of three major banks totalling £500 billion. A global recession was the result. The Eurozone went into recession in 2009 and there was a global decline in GDP of $1,678 billion. In 2012 Eurozone unemployment hit 12%.

The Rich World
By 2010 global GDP was back to $4,229 billion. In 2018 the value of shares in Apple and Amazon briefly spiked at over a trillion dollars. The gap between the rich and the poor continued to escalate. According to Forbes magazine, in 2019 the two richest men in the world were Jeff Bezos (Amazon), net worth $113 billion, and Bill Gates (Microsoft) with $98 billion. In 2025, the richest person in the world was Elon Musk with a net worth of $432 billion. According to an Oxfam report in 2017, the top eight billionaires own greater wealth than half of the world's population, i.e. over 3,700,000,000 people.

One example of the rich world is a parking space in Hong Kong which was sold in 2017 for £664,000. In 2010 Dubai opened the tallest building in the world, Burj Khalifa, 828m. 2,717ft. Saudi Arabia is now building the Jeddah Tower which will be 1,008 metres.

In 2018 electricity finally reached every village in India. This was also the year when twelve camels were disqualified from King Abdulaziz's Camel Beauty Festival in Saudi Arabia because their lips had been injected with botox. (That's just 0.046% of the 26,000 camels taking part).

In 2014 the US pledged $14 million investment in Africa over ten years. At the same time China pledged to invest $175 million.

The election of Donald Trump as the 47th President of the United States ushered in a new era of protectionism instability and lower economic growth.

China expands
In 2013 China launched the 'Belt and Road' initiative. ('Belt' refers to road and rail links; 'Road' refers to sea lanes). China is spending roughly $150 billion per year in 68 countries underwriting infrastructure development aiming to create a unified trading area in the Eurasia land mass and becoming a major player in Africa. It has a target completion date of 2049.

There is the fear that the countries with infrastructure projects may become permanently indebted to China and therefore will fall under Chinese control.

From July 2018 the US, under Donald Trump, started a trade war with China (and most of the rest of the world). It imposed a series of punitive tariffs on Chinese goods, claiming unfair trading practices and intellectual property theft. In 2018 the US imposed tariffs worth $250 billion. China retaliated in kind with tariffs worth $110 billion. The trade war with China intensified in Trump's second presidency.

The US tried to have a global ban on the Chinese technology firm Huawei being allowed to take part in the roll out of the 5G network, (fifth generation technology standard for cellular networks). The Chinese response has been to try and make itself independent in information technology. It is already a world leader in facial recognition, with records of 1.4 billion of its citizens.

In 2019 the six largest economies by GDP were:

US	$21,439 billion
China	$14,140 billion
Japan	$5,144 billion
Germany	$3,863 billion
India	$2,936 billion
UK	$2,743 billion

Followed by France, Italy, Brazil, Canada, South Korea, and Spain. By leaving the EU, the UK decided to leave the only trading bloc other than the US that can compete with China.

Digital Currencies

On 31st October 2008 Bitcoins, the first digital currency, came on the market. Bitcoin is a virtual currency, not based on the value of gold or of a country's economic prospects. Instead its value comes through 'mining' algorithms on the internet, which limits the amount of virtual currency that can be created and then used as a medium of exchange. Value is created by the extreme difficulty of solving complex mathematical sums, which are made progressively harder so as to maintain the value of the Bitcoin. This defines it as a 'cryptocurrency'. Exchanges are made purely electronically, but a record of each transaction is kept in a 'blockchain'. The value of each Bitcoin has fluctuated around £5,000, depending on the stock market.

Whether this will be the future or not is open to debate. There have been three Bitcoin bubbles and collapses, 2011, 2013, 2017, in which the stock value of the company lurched from $20,000 down to $4,000, as did the share prices of other crypto-currencies.

In December 2017 the Venezuelan government announced the creation of a cryptocurrency backed by the county's gold and oil reserves, to cope with Venezuela's hyper-inflation. It was a spectacular failure and died in January 2024.

Governments and banks are exploring the possibility of issuing digital currencies linked to the normal currency to facilitate transactions. The Chief Scientific Adviser to the UK government has advised that a blockchain-based digital currency should be considered.

Facebook (now Meta) tried to launch its own crypto-currency, the Libra, later called Diem. This was a permissioned blockchain digital currency, backed by a basket of currencies and US Treasury securities. It collapsed in 2022 through concerns over monetary sovereignty, financial stability, privacy, and antitrust issues.

Crypto-currencies will probably emerge as means of trading rather than storing value, but the Bank of England is opening its doors to all payment providers, not just traditional banks, to enable them to store funds overnight in interest-bearing accounts.

Non-fungible tokens (NFTs) are digital assets that represent art, collectibles, gaming, etc. Like cryptocurrencies, their data is stored on the blockchain. NFTs are bought and traded using cryptocurrency. They are seen by creative artists as a way to increase their copyright income, and are becoming increasingly popular.

Digital currencies could be the future, but quite a long way in the future. One danger is that the more anonymous cryptocurrencies are, the more they are attractive to criminals. But the world, even the world of banking, is changing.

YOUR OWN REFLECTION
Jesus said, "It is easier for a camel (or possibly a ship's hawser) to go through the eye of a needle than for a rich man to enter the kingdom of God". (Mark 10.25).
Jesus clearly thought that money was dangerous. How should we deal with this as individuals and as a global society?

CLIMATE CHANGE AND OTHER DISASTERS

In March 2001 the world's largest oil and gas field – an estimated 50 billion barrels of oil and 300 trillion cubic feet of gas, was discovered in the Caspian Sea, but it took till 2018 for Russia, Iran, Azerbaijan, Kazakhstan and Turkmenistan to agree how to share it out. This of course feeds into global warming. Currently at least 30 countries supply 20% of their energy needs through renewable energy – wind, solar energy, biomass etc. and this is increasing.

In December 2015 195 countries signed the Paris Agreement to keep the increase in temperature to under 2%. In June 2017 Donald Trump announced the US's withdrawal from the Paris Agreement; withdrawal was due to take effect the day after the presidential election in 2020. The head of a large insurance company said that a world which had a temperature rise of 4ºC would be 'uninsurable'.

In June 2013 flooding in North India killed up to 10,000 people. In May 2015 a heatwave in India caused 1,800 deaths in one week. The hottest year on record is 2024.

Hurricane Patricia (2015) was the most powerful on record with winds of 215 m.p.h.

In 2023 the cost of natural disasters in the USA was $93 billion. In October 2024 a year's worth of rain fell in one day in Valencia, Spain and over two hundred people died.

"There is medium confidence that approximately 20-30% of species assessed so far are likely to be at increased risk of extinction if increases in global average warming exceed 1.5-2.5 °C (relative to 1980-1999). As global average temperature increase exceeds about 3.5°C, model projections suggest significant extinctions (40-70% of species assessed) around the globe." 2007 IPCC Fourth Assessment Report (UN Intergovernmental Panel on Climate Change).

Note: In the Cretaceous extermination, in which the dinosaurs perished, about 75% of species became extinct. In 1991 it was accepted that this was caused by a massive meteor crashing into the Gulf of Mexico. In June 2002 a large asteroid missed the earth by just 75,000 miles, a third of the distance of the moon from the earth.

Even 'ordinary' disasters can have great impact. On 15th April 2010 the Icelandic volcano Eyjafjallajöull exploded, grounding 107,000 flights over most of Europe for nine days and intermittently for another three weeks affecting 10 million passengers. Between 11th and 15th March 2011 an earthquake and tsunami caused the meltdown of the Fukushima Daichi nuclear reactor in Japan. As a direct result, two months later the German government announced that it would close down all its nuclear reactors by 2022. By September 2013 Japan had itself closed down all its nuclear reactors.

The increase in global warming may now be unstoppable. In 2018 the ice in Antarctica melted at a rate of 200 billion tonnes a year and this rate is accelerating, and the sea is itself warming and thus expanding, with consequent changes in sea levels, ocean currents and weather systems, i.e. more drought. Massive engineering projects, like the one protecting

Rotterdam, Netherlands, are being considered around the world. *"(The ocean) will rise slowly, like a tide, its encroachment as imperceptible from moment to moment as it is inexorable."* (The Economist 17/8/19)

Counter measures

Scientists all over the world are working on ways to decarbonise the economy. It will take time. Alternative internal combustion engines are being developed, including hydrogen-diluted natural gas and ammonia and electric vehicles. A key task for technology is how to increase hydrogen production massively while using low-cost zero-carbon electricity, and how to create heavy duty electrical battery storage. In 2017 the Hydrogen Council was formed, a coalition of global chemical, car and oil companies looking at ways to a carbon-neutral future. The timescale could be:

- 2025-2035: battery and hydrogen-fuelled long distance lorries and home heating;
- 2030's synthetic hydrocarbons for ships and planes;
- 2040's hydrogen and CCS (Carbon Capture and Storage) for industry, especially cement;
- 2050's full-scale carbon removal from the atmosphere.

It's a massive task but do-able. But is it already too late? In 2024 the average global temperature was already 1.5ºC above pre-industrial levels.

Solar energy is a hopeful factor. In 2024 solar energy provided 6% of the world's electricity. Its use is increasing exponentially with a ten-fold increase in each decade. By 2035 it could be the world's biggest producer of electricity. Much of the equatorial belt such as Africa will start to feel energy-rich. It won't solve the climate crisis, but it could ameliorate it. New possibilities are tidal power and solar power from space.

Around the world cities and governments are trying to mitigate the effects of extreme heat events, e.g. three days or more of temperatures above 90ºF / 32.2ºC. The World Health Organisation estimates that each year there are 489,000 deaths globally (176,000 in Europe) due to extreme heat – often linked to extreme humidity.

The City of London has adopted a seven year strategy aiming at net zero for direct emissions by 2027, with net zero for the full supply chain being achieved by 2040. The aim is to build in resilience to cope with increasingly extreme weather. For example, heavy rain is leading to localised flooding, and in the summer of 2022 temperatures in the City reached 43ºC. (London is typically 7ºC warmer than Essex). There is an increasing need to provide cool spaces in the summer, and churches are ideally placed to offer this. But resilience is not cheap. The City has budgeted £68 million to bring about net zero by 2027.

A possible emergency solution is geo-engineering. This is when reflective particles are sent into the upper atmosphere, with an effect similar to large volcanic explosions. These reflect back some of a the sun's rays so cooling the earth below. But by how much? You could try to get international agreement (probably impossible), or one large country might take unilateral action, leading possibly to some form of ecological warfare. It doesn't bear thinking about.

YOUR OWN REFLECTION

Genesis 6-9 tells the story of the great flood which wiped out all living beings, apart from Noah, his family and pairs of animals. Might climate change be a punishment for human greed and self-centredness? Why do poor people bear the brunt? Will sustainable energy be beyond their reach?

HEALTH

Public Health - Pandemics

Pandemics are not new. The earliest evidence we have of them is from about 3,000 BCE which wiped out entire villages in north-east China. They have had some major impacts on human history. Here are some of them:

541-542 CE Plague of Justinian.
10% of the world's population may have died and may have fatally weakened the attempted revival of the Roman Empire.

1346-1353 The Black Death.
50% of the population of Europe may have died. The result was the dismantling of the feudal system.

16th century
Diseases brought to the Americas by Europeans, e.g. smallpox and measles, wiped out up to 90% of native Americans. African slaves replaced the original population.

17th/18th century
Great Plagues such as London in 1665, Marseilles in 1720-23, Moscow 1770-1772 killed about 100,000 people each time.

18th century
An estimated 400,000 people in Europe died of smallpox each year. The first vaccination discovered was for smallpox in 1796.

1918-1919
Spanish Flu infected 500 million people, a third of the world's population and killed 20-50 million, possibly even 100 million.

Unusually, it was particularly deadly for young adults. (It was only called Spanish because Spain, being neutral, did not have war censorship and so reported the facts).

1981-present
HIV/AIDS has killed 25-35 million worldwide, and has effectively wiped out an entire generation in Africa, so that children are typically brought up not by their parents but by their grandparents. In 2007 it was estimated that there were 12 million AIDS orphans. Currently there are 40 million sufferers worldwide, 64% in sub-Saharan Africa.

Pandemics since 2000
Influenza The WHO estimate that between 250,000 and 500,000 people die of seasonal flu annually.

2002 SARS
Severe Acute Respiratory Syndrome. A coronavirus disease, with the main outbreak in China, spreading to Hong Kong, Taiwan, Canada and Singapore. Total deaths worldwide: 774

2009 Swine Flu
The same virus that caused the Spanish flu pandemic.
A reassortment of bird, swine and human viruses probably coming from Mexico. Between 700 million and 1.4 billion were infected. About 284,000 people died in Africa and South East Asia.

2012-2019 MERS
Middle East Respiratory Syndrome, known as camel flu.
A coronavirus that infects bats, camels and humans. A rare but severe disease.

Out of 2,519 cases, 866 died. In South Korea, the municipal governments instituted quarantine for those in contact with infected persons. 6,729 were quarantined and only 38 (2% of cases) died.

2014 Ebola
A viral haemorrhagic fever, originating in the Congo in 1976, and spread by direct contact with blood and body fluids. The average death rate is 50%. In West Africa 2013-2016 there had been 28,454 cases and 11,297 deaths. The WHO stated *"the Ebola outbreak has decimated families, health systems, economies, and social structures".* Vaccines have now been developed.

2013-16 Zika
Zika fever is a virus spread by daytime mosquitoes, coming from the Ziika forest in Uganda in 1947. In 2013-2014 it spread from Africa to the Americas. It affected the whole of America, North and South, and spread to Southeast Asia in 2016. In pregnant women it can spread to the unborn child and cause reduced brain and head development. Six Latin American countries advised women to delay pregnancy. The main response is to release genetically modified mosquitoes which do not grow to maturity.

2020 Covid-19
Coronavirus Disease 2019 was first identified in Wuhan, China in December 2019 and has since spread to every corner of the world. It is marked by the lengthy time that someone can be infected and infectious, but be without symptoms, normally for 5 days, but it can be for 2 to 14 days.

The most common symptoms are fever, breathing difficulties and loss of sense of taste and smell. Most people recover quickly, but some go on to develop acute respiratory distress and multi-organ failure. In the UK it was declared a pandemic on 11th March 2020. The result was a shutdown of most normal travel and social and economic activities around the world. By 2022 worldwide about 5 million people have died from the virus.

Partly due to previous research into SARS and MERS development of vaccines was rapid. The genetic sequence of the virus was shared openly on 10th January 2020. As of April 2022 over 11 billion doses of Covid 19 vaccines had been administered worldwide, about half by high-income countries comprising 14% of the world's population. It is now being treated by most countries as an endemic disease, with health services only dealing with serious or life-threatening cases.

YOUR OWN REFLECTIONS
In the Bible God frequently produced plagues, e.g. Genesis 12.17, Exodus 12.29, Exodus 32.33, Numbers 14.12, 2 Samuel 24.13. Should we blame God for the recent plagues?

PUBLIC HEALTH - OTHER ISSUES

Smoking

In 2004 Ireland became the first country in the world to ban smoking in workplaces and public places. That year the British Medical Journal published a study of almost 35,000 British male doctors who died 1951-2001, showing that half to two thirds of all persistent smokers would eventually be killed by their habit. In 2007 all parts of the UK banned smoking in workplaces and indoor public places. This was 45 years after the first Royal College of Physicians report, 'Smoking and Health'. Most of the rest of the world has enacted various levels of smoking bans in public places, partly dependent on whether the government is federal or centralised. About half of the states of the US have bans on smoking in workplaces and public places, with ten states having no statewide ban. A 2016 survey of 77 research studies from 23 countries showed a dramatic decline of hospital admissions for heart disease and strokes, particularly among non-smokers. We now take smoke free trains, buses, pubs and restaurants for granted.

Air pollution

Different factors are at work between ambient (outdoor) air pollution, caused principally by traffic and manufacturing, and indoor air pollution. Health risks outside are caused by microscopic particles (particulate matter) which get into the lungs and bloodstream. Indoors, damaging health effects are produced by tobacco smoke, solvents and air fresheners, and in the developing world burning wood or dung for cooking.

In 2016 the Royal College of Physicians stated that air pollution was linked to 40,000 early deaths.

In 2020 the WHO reported that an estimated 4.2 million premature deaths globally were linked to ambient air pollution, mainly from heart disease, stroke, chronic obstructive pulmonary disease, lung cancer, and acute respiratory infections in children.

Cities are major air polluters. I remember visiting the Great Pyramid in Egypt in 1995, and seeing the thick brown smog hanging over Cairo, then a city of 17 million inhabitants. Climate change will only make the situation worse. Governments are slowly addressing the issue. The UK will ban the sale of fossil fuel cars by 2040. London charges owners of cars older than 2005 within the central 'Ultra Low Emissions Zone', applying a standard set out by the EU.

Following the 'great smog' in central, eastern and northern China, China has taken active measures such as Beijing restricting the number of new vehicles to 100,000 a year and closing all its big coal-fired power stations, despite allowing the provinces to build big new ones. From 2018 to 2022 the number of 'blue-sky' days (good air quality) increased from 176 to 226 days per year.

The other side of the coin is India. In 2018 nine of the ten most polluted cities in the world were in India. In 2016 the annual mean concentration of particulate matter smaller than 2.5 micrometers (just one of the four major air pollutants) was 143 in Delhi, 73 in Beijing and 27 in Milan.

A virile (not viral) mystery

In 2017 an international research project (Israel, Denmark, US, Brazil and Spain) found that human sperm count had been decreasing steadily, in terms of both quality and quantity, for almost 40 years, 1973-2011, with a total decline for both of 28.5%.

For unselected Western men the decline was 52.4% in quality (concentration) and 59.3% for quantity. There is no sign of these declines coming to an end.

Why is this happening? What does it mean? No one knows. Apart from the Daily Mail whose banner headline read, *"Huge drop in sperm count could lead to human extinction: Study reveals 60% drop in fertility since 1970 – driven by the unhealthy Western lifestyle."* (25 July 2017)

Addictions

According to the charity Action on Addiction, 1 in 3 people are addicted to something.

Addiction is defined as not having control over doing, taking or using something to the point where it could be harmful to you. The substance addictions are well known and include alcohol, illegal drugs, solvents, tobacco as well as legal drugs like anti-depressants.. Behavioural addictions can be equally harmful: gambling, sex, internet pornography, work, even shopping. "Shopping becomes an addiction when you buy things you don't need or want to achieve a buzz; this is quickly followed by feelings of guilt, shame or despair." (NHS online page, April 2015)

In 2005 the UK government passed the Gambling Act, with the aim of gradually creating a network of 'super-casinos' to rival Las Vegas. Two years later Gordon Brown pulled the plug on a super-casino in Manchester. According to the NHS long term Plan 2019 there are 400,000 problem gamblers in England with a further 2 million at risk. That's a lot of family heartache!

In 2018 Canada legalised the sale of cannabis, joining the legal drugs of alcohol and coffee. In the same year the WHO classified gaming addiction (video gaming) as an addiction.

Euthanasia

In 2001 the Netherlands legalised euthanasia, including physician-assisted suicide. As of 2018 active voluntary euthanasia is legal in Belgium, Luxembourg, Colombia and Canada. Physician-assisted suicide is legal in Switzerland, Germany, the state of Victoria in Australia and in ten states of the United States, including California and Washington D.C. In the UK, France and Germany, Australia, India and Argentina passive euthanasia is legal, i.e. the agreed withholding of treatment. It is an issue that is hotly debated in many countries of the world. At the time of writing it is being debated in the UK Parliament.

YOUR OWN REFLECTIONS

There seems to be an indirect relationship, but a relationship nonetheless, between human self-centredness and a lot of human suffering.

Does the idea of original sin have any wisdom to offer?

NEW MEDICAL SCIENCE

Precision/personalised medicine - gene therapy

Knowledge of the human genome has enabled radical new ways to treat disease by analysing people at the genetic and even molecular level. We are now able to specify what sections of a population are susceptible to particular diseases and so target preventative treatment, and what side effects can be expected.

A classic case is the coronavirus pandemic. The Covid-19 Genomics UK consortium (Cog-UK) analysed the genetic code of viral samples taken from more than 20,000 people infected with coronavirus in the UK. Then, like a gigantic version of a paternity test, the geneticists attempted to piece together the virus's massive family tree. This, combined with data on international travel, showed that the virus was brought in from abroad at least 1,356 times, 80% between 28 February and 29 March, 76.5% of cases coming in from Spain, France and Italy (BBC, 10 June 2020).

Personalised medicine or gene therapy uses genomic information at an individual level to correct a single defective gene which causes a genetic disease. One example is the rare genetic disease of spinal muscular atrophy, caused by a loss of motor neurones. It can now be cured with a single injection - costing $2 million. Perhaps not excessive in the case of a child of 2 who otherwise would not have lived beyond age 5. But still phenomenally expensive.

My brother Martin, a former Professor of Health Services Research at Cambridge, said, *"The ability of science and medicine to provide effective treatments will outstrip the abilities of most countries to pay for them."*

Microrobots, nanobots & AI

Some definitions:

AI is the ability of computer algorithms to approximate conclusions without direct human input.

A minirobot is less than 10 cm, a millirobot less than 1 cm, a microrobot less than a millimetre, and a nanobot less than a micrometre or one thousandth of a millimetre.

Artificial Intelligence uses complex algorithms and machine learning to analyse and interpret complex data for improved diagnosis, treatment decisions and patient monitoring. It is successful in reading breast scans, where the aim is to have as few false negative readings as possible; in that respect AI is superior to the readings of two radiologists. The NHS, the Mayo Clinic and others have developed algorithms for use in a variety of departments. As we take an internet world for granted, AI in health care will become completely normal. Its use will become standard in radiology & pathology.

In 2000 the first robots were used to assist surgeons in surgery for prostate cancer. The surgeon sits at a control panel and operates with the aid of four microrobots, one of which holds the camera. It allows the surgeon to make very tiny, accurate movements. The most widely used surgical platform is the da Vinci system. It is designed to perform complex minimally invasive surgical procedures with precision and accuracy, and is used in abdominal, kidney, throat and eye operations, though each type has its own particular challenges. Alongside the robot system are intelligent surgical instruments which can measure the microforces being applied and give aural feedback to the surgeon.

Of course, robotic surgery is much more expensive than the traditional way, and there are risks, particularly possible burning of tissue, but it does seem to be the future.

Nanobots are about the size of a red blood cell. In February 2018 researchers in America and China successfully used nanobots to enter the blood stream of a mouse with cancer and to inject blood clotting drugs to cut off the blood supply to cancerous cells. Bio-engineered bots made from DNA will shortly be able to deliver drugs with great precision, eliminating most side effects.

The global nanomedicine market was estimated to be worth $138.8bn in 2016, according to market research company Grand View Research. But is it a sensible use of resources, when the major health issues of the world are infection, diabetes, obesity and starvation?

Synthetic biology
Synthetic biology is the application of engineering principles to the fundamental components of biology to generate off-the-shelf biological parts with predictable characteristics. This involves taking genetic information that conveys useful functions in one organism and using it to design biological pathways to create desired products or devices in a desired organism. We can also change genes by inserting synthetic elements.

The scary bit is when we tinker with the human genome, e.g. by changing the gene which gives rise to Down's syndrome or the sex of a foetus, or upper body strength or intelligence etc. However, most synthetic biology is used to solve more specific problems, e.g. creating vanilla essence without the increasingly rare vanilla pods; or making a meat-free burger that tastes like meat. The advance in synthetic biology is led by private industry. From 2010 to 2018 the number of investment deals rose from 32 to 140 per year. It might be a way to manufacture biofuels and so wean us away from a carbon economy.

Governments could also, and here is the really scary bit, manufacture diseases, such as the 1867 influenza epidemic, or the Great Plague. Humanity has a poor record in not weaponising the latest scientific advances.

The Magic CRISPR

In 2003 the mapping of the entire human genome was completed. It took scientists working in twenty universities all over the world thirteen years. In May 2013 human stem cells were successfully cloned.

The really big story has the natty acronym of CRISPR, or rather less natty 'Clustered Regularly Interspaced Short Palindromic Repeats'. These are short sequences within an organism's DNA, first identified in 1987. It was not until 2007 that it was found that it served as a bacterium's immune system, and in 2012 that an artificial RNA, RiboNucleic Acid, one of the four main components of all forms of life, could trigger a surgical operation by the enzyme Cas9 on the CRISPR. This enabled scientists to edit DNA precisely and make detailed changes, for example to mosquitoes so they don't carry malaria, to crops making them more nutritious, and to the creation of hornless dairy cows. In the past, it might have cost thousands of dollars and weeks or months of fiddling to alter a gene. Now it might cost just $75 and only take a few hours. (Vox December 2018).

CRISPR/Cas9 can also be used to alter the human genome, first by doing away with genetic diseases such as Huntingdon's disease, but also to produce designer babies. In 2018 a Chinese scientist Juinkui ignored the worldwide moratorium against altering the human genome by making twin girls genetically resistant to the HIV virus. There was worldwide condemnation in the scientific community and China put him in prison.

In October 2017 President Putin of Russia spoke to a group of young people at the World Festival of Youth in Sochi: *"Genetic advances will open up incredible opportunities in pharmacolgy, new medicine, altering the human genome if a person has a genetic disease. But there is another part of this process. It means we can already imagine it, to create a person with the desired features. This may be a mathematical genius. This may be an outstanding musician. But this can also be a soldier, an individual who can fight without fear or pain... You are aware that humankind will probably enter a very complicated period of its development, and what I have just said may be more terrifying than a nuclear bomb."*

Or maybe not. Stephen Hsu, co-founder of Genomic Prediction, which provides advanced genetic testing for IVF, has welcomed the developments: *"Sex is for recreation. Science is for procreation."*
(Last two quotes from BBC2 Storyville - the Gene Revolution 27/1/20)

YOUR OWN REFLECTIONS

All religions affirm in some sense that the universe does not explain itself, but that there is a Creative Spirit beyond and within all things bringing creation to birth. Have we now replaced God? If humans can make fundamental changes to our DNA, are we still 'made in the image of God?' Whose image are we made in?

SCIENCE & SPACE

Scientists continue to push the boundaries of human knowledge.

Graphene

After more than fifty years of scientific examination of graphite sheets of single-layer atoms, in 2004 two researchers at Manchester University isolated and were able to pull a graphene layer from graphite with the aid of Scotch Tape. They won the Nobel Prize for Physics "for groundbreaking experiments regarding the two-dimensional material graphene." Graphene is a monolayer of carbon atoms bonded in a repeating hexagonal pattern. It is the thinnest known material, 200 times stronger than steel, flexible and an excellent conductor of heat and electricity. Theoretically you could make a television out of graphene, then fold it up and put it in your pocket. In fact like the discovery of coherent light or lasers in the 1960's, it is a solution looking for a problem.

Some may have been found. 8% of CO_2 released each year comes from making concrete. If just 0.01% of graphene is added to concrete, it makes it 30% stronger, and less is needed, a significant factor in the struggle against global warming. It is used to improve surgical gloves and can be used to create high-altitude (30km) balloons capable of launching satellites into space.

Space telescopes

In 2008 the Large Hadron Collider started up. It lies in a 17-mile tunnel 574 feet underground, with over 10,000 scientists taking part in experiments into the nature of subatomic particles. In July 2015 it demonstrated the existence of a pentaquark. (It is a very very, very small bit/wave of an atom.)

The Hubble Space Telescope was launched in 1990 on an orbit 340 miles above the above the earth and designed to be serviced in space. It has an estimated lifespan of 30 - 40 years. In May 2011 The Alpha magnetic Spectrometer went into operation to search for dark matter, which is estimated to comprise 94% of the universe. In 2012 light from the earliest stars in the universe was found, 500 million years after the Big Bang. In March 2013 the European Space Agency calculated that the universe was 13.82 billion years old.

In 2021 the James Webb space telescope was launched in an orbit 930,000 miles above the earth. It is expected to provide data on the formation of the first galaxies. The total cost of creating it was $10 billion.

In the Dark

It was only in 1998 that scientists discovered evidence for dark energy. It is only possible to study it indirectly through its effects, for instance in the unexplained increase in the speed at which supernovae move away. Dark matter consists of 27% of the universe while everything else visible is just 5%. But there is even less we know, namely why the density of dark energy kept increasing for five billion years and then started to decrease. Why?

Space

In 2002 Elon Musk founded Space Exploration Technologies Corp, known as SpaceX, with the aim of bringing down the cost of space transportation. Ten years later came the first commercial docking of SpaceX Dragon at the International Space Station. Private investment in space exploration now (2019) comes in at $2 billion a year, 15% of the total, and due to rise.

Half of that is contributed by Jeff Bezos, the founder of Amazon and described by Forbes in September 2018 as "by far the richest person on the planet." He funds Blue Origin, with the aim of making the human race multi-planetary. Planned projects include a permanent manned outpost on the moon near the poles (which have substantial frozen water) at a suggested cost of $7 billion. The US plans to send Americans back to the moon, using a partially completed replacement of the International Space Station 'Gateway'. China sent its first crewed space mission in 2003 and plans to send people to the moon by 2035. India is becoming the fourth big player in space alongside Russia. Meanwhile, Elon Musk's SpaceX company sent two astronauts to the International Space Station in May 2020, followed by the latest of eight missions launching 60 satellites at a time, totalling 482 satellites. By 2023 SpaceX had created a constellation of 4,300 satellites called Starlink, and plans to send out 40,000 more, bringing broadband to everyone. Crucially Starlink was provided to Ukraine within days of the Russian invasion and played a vital support for Ukraine's forces and society. China, Russia and the EU are joining the constellation dance.

The likeliest uses of space in the foreseeable future are communication satellites, tourism for the rich, and mineral exploitation. Annual revenues of space could increase to $800 billion by 2030 according to UBS. But there are risks. There are already 2,000 satellites in orbit and over 500,000 bits of debris hurtling round at over 27,000 km an hour. This debris is made up of items over 10cm in diameter. At 27,000 km an hour, even a flake of paint can cause damage. When China conducted an anti-satellite missile test in 2007, it increased the amount of debris in space by 25%. And now China and India, as well as Mexico, the EU and others, have joined the space game.

All this is likely to put strains on international co-operation, which is governed by the 1967 Outer Space Treaty. It says that no nation state can claim sovereignty in space. Things could get complicated as private firms became major players, especially as the military get involved. Trump planned to set up a 'Space Force', as does France. China and India are also increasing their destructive capabilities, such as blinding military satellites with lasers, jamming their signals to earth or even blowing them up.

Meanwhile Elon Musk and Jeff Bezos of Amazon are on the brink of normalising space travel.

Archaeology
In April 2015 stone tools were found in Kenya, dated to 3.3 million years ago. Three years later the world's oldest brewery was found in Haifa, Israel, supplying its customers with beer in 11,000 BCE.

FOR YOUR REFLECTION

'When I look at your heavens, the work of your fingers,
the moon and the stars which you have established,
what are human beings that you are mindful of them,
mortals that you care for them? (Psalm 8.3,4)

Has the advance of science decreased or increased our sense of wonder at the universe?

TECHNOLOGY AND COMMUNICATION

COMPUTERS - THE HARDWARE
In 1943 Thomas Watson, head of IBM, is alleged to have said, *"I think there is a world market for maybe five computers."* Of course, at that time a computer would fill an entire room.

The first successful mass-market home computer with a mouse and graphical user interface was the Macintosh in 1984, followed by Microsoft's Windows PC the following year. Today there are probably 3.8 billion computers in the world (AI estimate), quite apart from multitudes of computer-like devices: from washing machines, to car engine management and aircraft navigation systems. There is more computing power in an ordinary smartphone than was available to the NASA astronauts in 1969.

Mobile phones
In 1991 the first 2G digital mobile phones were produced (2G = 2nd generation) replacing the old analogue phones. In 2001 3G phones came with higher data capacity and 4G in 2008 enabling access to the World Wide Web, gaming services, mobile TV, 3D TV, mobile conferencing etc. 5G technology can handle the exponential increase in data transfer.

In 2007 Apple released a new generation of thin smartphones, the i-Phone. By the mid-2010s, almost all smartphones were touchscreen-only, and Android and iPhone dominated the market, with Android being more popular in developing countries, and the iPhone being more popular in developed countries. In 2013 there were shipments of over 1 billion i-Phones. By 2014 90% of the developed world and 20% of the developing world had an i-Phone or smartphone.

Tablets

Android released the first tablet (or tablet computer) in 2009. In 2010 Apple released their equivalent, the i-Pad. By 2017 360 million had been sold. By 2018 out of 4.4 billion devices, Android accounted for 2 billion, Apple 1 billion and remainder were PC's in various forms.

Social impact of computers

In the developing world mobile phones have brought enormous benefits, because you do not have to set up a physical infrastructure. In 2015 90% of Nigerians had a mobile phone, with almost 30% being smartphones. 90% of earth's 7.2 billion people have mobile connections with 3.7 billion unique subscribers. It is providing accessible banking, marketing for subsistence farmers, educational resources, political information, health monitoring and more. There are now more mobile phones in the world than people.

The impact of the new technology was seen when Western Union sent its last telegram at the start of 2006 and the fact that now in Luanda, capital of Angola, Africa, you can use the internet to order live goats for parties to have them killed and cooked on the premises.

Quantum computing

Today quantum computing is being actively researched. It uses the physical properties of sub-atomic physics. Whereas the classical computer is binary, i.e. calculations are made with 'bits' which are binary, with signals being either on or off, quantum computing works on the basis of qubits when can be in both states simultaneously. In 2019, Google AI and NASA announced that they had achieved quantum supremacy with a 54-qubit machine, performing a computation that was impossible for any classical computer. Investment is pouring in, but use of quantum computing is still largely experimental and hypothetical. In the future the use of encryption to safeguard private data may be a thing of the past.

Metaverse/virtual reality

Does the metaverse exist? Facebook thought so. In October 2021 it rebranded itself as 'Meta', staking a claim on the new digital future. Matthew Ball, author of 'The Metaverse: and how it will revolutionise everything' (2022), defined it as 'an interoperable network of 3D virtual worlds that can be accessed simultaneously by millions of users, who can exert property rights over virtual items'.

At the moment virtual reality worlds are accessed through headsets which act like a digital blindfold. Augmented reality (AR) sets use the technology to paint information on to the real world.

Billions already use virtual worlds in video games, many of which involve trading virtual items. If it becomes possible to trade items not only within virtual worlds but between them, that would create an extraordinary virtual economy. A major problem, though, could be the intellectual property rights held by the creators of video games.

Meanwhile through the Metaverse Standards Forum (MSF) the major players (other than Apple) have committed themselves to open, interoperable technical standards so that an avatar designed for use in one company's virtual world should work without trouble in another's. Billions are being spent on developing these technologies. But no one is sure yet if this is really the future of computing.

COMPUTERS - THE SOFTWARE

The Internet

In 1990 Tim Berners-Lee developed all the basic tools needed for the World Wide Web. By 1995 it had started to take off, with users growing at between 20% and 50% per year. In 2005 16% of the world's population used the internet, 50% of the developed world. In 2017 the figures were 48% worldwide and 81% in the developed world.

The internet has changed human communication more than anything since the dawn of humanity. It took the telephone 75 years to reach 50 million users. It took television 13 years. It took the internet 4 years. It took the game of Pokemon Go 19 days.

Here are some of the key players:

Netflix

Netflix started in 1997 as a mail-order company sending out rental DVDs on demand. In 2007 it introduced streaming videos on demand over the internet. By 2018 it had 139.26 million viewers-on-demand, its revenue was $15,794,000 and a debt of over $22 billion. In 2019 it had about half its library as self-produced content, including the six-part series 'The Crown' 2016-2023. In 2021 it won more Academy Award nominations than any film studio.

i-Tunes

At the start of 2001 Apple released i-Tunes as the "World's Best and Easiest To Use Jukebox Software". In 2003 it was made compatible with Windows. Over the years it has expanded, or got bloated, by accessing videos, podcasts, e-books and university lectures.

Its success in promoting individual songs led to the disappearance of music albums. In 2019 Apple split it between Apple Music, Apple TV and ApplePodcasts.

Wikipedia

Wikipedia was launched in 2001 as a free internet encyclopaedia. By 2006 it had 1 million entries, receiving 18.3 million unique visitors. Currently (2024) there are 6.8 billion entries in the English Wikipedia and visitor numbers are stable at 4.3 billion.

Social media

The first social network service website was Sixdegrees, which lasted from 1997 to 2000. The Chinese company TenCent launched its social media website QQ in 1999 and has over 800 million users. In 2004 Mark Zuckerberg launched TheFacebook from his dorm room for his university, Harvard. Twitter was created in 2006, Instagram in 2010 and Snapchat in 2012. In 2016 the Chinese company Bytedance launched Douyin, a platform hosting user-generated videos. They expanded it internationally in 2017 as Tik Tok. It is especially popular with Gen Z, but western governments fear its links to the Chinese state. In 2022 the billionaire businessman Elon Musk bought Twitter and rebranded it as 'X' with fewer constraints on disinformation and hate speech.

Currently (May 2024) 62.6% of the world's population or 5.07 billion people, use social media, with a daily average use of 2 hours 20 minutes. Its use and impact is considered in more detail on pp. 176-182.

Google

On 1st April 2004 Google was launched as a search engine. Its mission statement is "to organise the world's information and make it universally accessible and useful". It has added a comprehensive range of services, G-mail, the world's most popular email server, as well as Google Chrome, Maps, Translate, Docs, Calendar, YouTube etc. By 2011 there were more than a billion unique visitors per month, generating $50 billion in revenue in 2012. In 2023 it generated $305.63 billion.

Podcasts

Podcasts, starting around 2004, are a form of downloadable radio which can be created by anyone from ex-convicts to duchesses. The name is an amalgam of i-Pod and broadcast, and its winning feature is its transparency. Instead of formal interviews, you get sprawling conversations. Anyone can converse and be heard through people's earbuds on the train or tube. 43% of American internet users and 30% of Britons listen to a podcast at least once a month. Tech companies are starting to use video to increase their audience.

Zoom

Zoom was founded in 2011 in California as a videoconferencing app. By 2013 it had a million users. Then Covid 19 struck. In April 2020 it had 300 million users (including the author). Microsoft launched its competitor 'Windows Teams'. The technology has transformed places of work enabling homeworking, social interaction and church programmes.

Tech profits

"America tech giants make ungodly amounts of money." (Economist 30/4/22). In April 2022 Alphabet (the company owning Google) announced revenues of $68 billion and $16.4 billion net profit. Microsoft took in $49.4 billion with net profits of $16.7 billion. Meta (Facebook etc.) had sales of $27.9 billion and net profits of $7.5 billion, i.e. $7,500,000,000.

Internet Issues: Censorship

But not everyone agrees with a free internet. Internet censorship varies between countries. In 2004 North Korea banned mobile phones; it only allows access to the web to privileged citizens via its own intranet. Iran blocked Google in 2012. China operates detailed censorship and blocks Facebook and Twitter. In 2018 it banned 'Pepper Pig' as subversive. In October 2006 Julian Assange founded Wikileaks and in February 2012 disclosed 5 million confidential US government emails. In January 2012 the US tried to pass the 'Stop Online Piracy Act' to deal with copyright infringement in 2012 but failed due to massive protests organised by Google and others. Egypt took down the internet during the Arab Spring of 2011. Web service operators operate a basic policy of 'deplatforming' some extremist sites, but often after political pressure has been brought to bear. In May 2018 Uganda started taxing social media sites 'to stop gossip'. But government control of the internet is hard to maintain, because it is largely privately owned.

Internet Issues: Cybercrime

The internet has spawned whole new dimensions of crime. Here are some of the crimes available: financial theft – stealing money electronically; stealing people's identities; child pornography and child grooming; national or commercial espionage; ransomware (threatening to take down a site unless money is paid); malicious viruses, malware and denial-of-service threats to organisations and individuals; copyright infringement (which was the grounds of the FBI shutting down Megaupload in 2012, re-launched as Mega a year later); planning terrorist outrages and building of weapons; trolling or cyberbullying, especially against women; sextortion (blackmailing the victim for sexual favours with images downloaded from the internet). Finally there is governmental cyberwarfare such as the Russian use of denial-of-service attacks, hacking, and political disinformation. In 2014 the damage of cybercrime was estimated at $445 billion. It is estimated that by 2025 cybercrime will cost the world $6 trillion.

Internet Issues: Pornography

There has been an explosion of pornography in popular culture through the internet. Statistics in this area are a minefield. Here are some from a digital technology consultant, Bas van den Belt in 2011: 24.6 billion websites and 25% of all search enquiries are porn related; the most popular viewing day is Sunday; the average porn site visit lasts 6.5 minutes (10 minutes in 2018 according to the Guardian). The porn industry is bigger than Hollywood or Netflix. A key player is MindGeek which is a holding company for most of the big names in porn, including Pornhub, which reported 33.5 billion visits in 2018. MindGeek's website announces that it has *"Industry-leading exclusive technologies driving unparalleled performance"*, with over 115 million daily visitors, 15 terabytes of content uploaded on a daily basis, over 1,000 employees and offices in Luxembourg, London, Los Angeles, Bucharest, Nicosia and Montreal. About a third of visitors to porn sites are women who prefer to use smartphones, as do teenagers. Use of chat rooms and sexting is common – 1 in 4 teens receive unwanted sexts (psycom.net).

Typically boys start looking at porn at 11.
So, is it a problem? In 2011 the Guardian published an article with the heading: "The government is playing to the crowd with its opt-in plan for online porn, ignoring the positive role it can play". In 2017 Martin Daubeney, writing in the Daily Telegraph quoted a report reviewing 50 previous studies. It concluded that *"porn consumption has no negative effect on women's sexual satisfaction"* but that there was "an overall negative effect of pornography on men's sexual and relational satisfaction". He continued, *"Last year, sexual psychotherapists at Nottingham University Hospital told us there are now as many British men in their teens and twenties with erectile dysfunction as men in their fifties and sixties. The cause is almost always early-life and unchecked access to unlimited porn."*
In 2018 it was revealed that 24,000 attempts were made to access pornographic websites from devices in the Palace of Westminster in six months. (Evening Standard 28/4/22) That is 400 attempts to access porn every working day in Parliament. Perhaps not the ideal way of governing a country.

YOUR OWN REFLECTIONS
The Christian faith spread partly because Greek was spoken throughout the Roman Empire. The Reformation was created by the new technology of printing. The internet could be the next advance in Christian evangelisation. But are there too many competing voices?
What are the differences between an online discussion group and a person-to-person one?

Does the internet increase or decrease the total sum of human happiness?

AI

The History of AI

Artificial Intelligence is the use of micro-electronics to mimc the neural patterns of the human brain. The phrase as a branch of computer science was first coined in the Dartmouth Conference in 1956. There was little advance for forty years, but there was an explosive development when an exponential increase in computing power and storage ability took place in the 1990s. AI is designed to outperform human beings at specialised tasks in very specific environments. In 1997 the chess-playing computer Deep Blue defeated Garry Kasparov, the world chess champion, (though Kasparov said the rules had been bent). In 2016 Google's Alpha Go beat the world champion of Go, Lee Sodel. Go is more complicated than chess by a factor of many thousands). In 2018 Google developed AlphaGoZero which was able to become a world-beater at chess or Go simply by being told the rules of the game. The computer then learned by itself how to win. More technically, it recognises useful patterns in disorganised data sets without human supervision. AI then makes connections and draws usable conclusions. Problems can arise around who develops the algorithms, what the developers look for or don't think about.

In the 2000s Amazon, Google and Baidu used AI to their huge commercial advantage, especially in collecting masses of data about their customer base, targeting advertisements and offering to people information about their personal preferences. In 2011 Apple introduced Siri, the first integrated virtual assistant; this was overtaken in 2014 by Amazon's Alexa.

They are activated by a command word and can then respond to a wide range of questions as well as activating electronic systems around the home, such as the washing machine or the heating system. Facial recognition systems are able to 'read' a person's feeling from their face and respond appropriately.

AI applications

Currently in development are autonomous, or driverless, cars. AI machines will transport us around cities, grow our food, deliver packages to our doorstep and even save lives. By the end of 2020 AI drones were clearing landmines. AI is transforming medicine, providing more reliable diagnoses than human doctors, performing surgical procedures by tiny robots (nanobots) within the body, and targeting and destroying cancer cells. Fully autonomous AI robots will eventually be used for space exploration.

Face recognition, voice recognition and language learning are all part of today's AI. China is pioneering many aspects. Baidu has developed an algorithm that can mimic someone's speech from a 30 minute speech audio. (What a gift for 'fake news'!) With a population of 1.4 billion, Chinese AI will have face recognition of almost the whole population, 1.3 billion, be able to predict their social, political and economic behaviour, and control city lighting and traffic systems. The advanced AI available to the Chinese government enabled them to control the spread of coronavirus more rapidly than other countries.

In Wuhan, China, there are hundreds of driverless taxis; by 2030 it was expected that 50% of traffic in Chinese cities will be autonomous vehicles. US companies are developing them, but occasional accidents have caused the companies to pause the roll-out of robotaxis.

The defeat of the 'go' grand master by the computer programme AlphaGo in 2016, led to a workshop on the implications at China's Academy of Military Science one month later. In 2024 the Royal Navy commissioned Microsoft and Amazon to create a command-and-control software dubbed Stormcloud. It was the world's most advanced kill-chain. Even two years ago it was miles ahead, in terms of speed and reliability, of human officers in an conventional headquarters. (Quoted in the Economist 20/6/24). It is feasible that we could get into a version of the First World War in which attacking and defending forces grind rapidly to a stalemate. Then what?

Large language models

AI charged on to the human scene on 30th November 2022. The American research company Open AI developed a chatbot and virtual assistant called Chat Generative Pre-Trained Transformer or Chat GPT for short. A chatbot simulates human conversation either spoken or by text. It is based on large language models (LLMs), by which vast amounts of data are fed into the LLMs during a computationally intensive self-supervised and semi-supervised training process. This enables the user to ask very specific questions and get back suggestions in a second. For instance, in February 2023 I asked Chat GPT how best to market my latest book 'Daily Prayers from the World's Faiths'; I instantly received a very helpful response. In less than a month, Chat GPT had racked up over 100 million users. It is not always accurate; but it is like having one's own junior research assistant. It is now a 'freemium' site, so the basic level is free but additional benefits are charged.

Researchers are now experimenting with teams of LLMs, known as multi-agent systems, which can handle more complex tasks, and can plan and collaborate on joint tasks without explicit instructions.

An AI future

In 2023 the boss of IMB said that they would replace about 7,800 jobs with AI over the next five years. An average of top AI researchers believe that there is a 50% likelihood that machines will outperform humans in all tasks in 45 years. What will be the impact on society and on individual well-being? Might we end up with a small minority of the super-rich and the vast majority (say over 7 billion) imprisoned in workless poverty? How long would that last?

The really scary bit is when we assume that at some point machines will be able to increase their own intelligence and continually rebuild themselves. Would they be able to write their own programmes? To write their own rules? For instance, if AI were told to produce as many paper clips as possible, it might not rest until the earth is full of paper clip factories and the human race is extinct. Perhaps humans are just too slow to control the AI we have created.

In October 2023 Rishi Sunak the Prime Minister, while not wanting to be alarmist, said, *"Get this wrong and it could make it easier to build chemical and biological weapons. "Terrorist groups could use AI to spread fear and disruption on an even greater scale. Criminals could exploit AI for cyber attacks, disinformation, fraud and even child sexual abuse. And in the most unlikely but extreme cases, there is even the risk humanity could lose control of AI completely through the kind of AI referred to as super-intelligence."*

As Eliezer Yudkowsky, founder of the Machine Intelligence Research Institute, said, *"The AI does not hate you, nor does it love you, but you are made up of atoms which it can use for something else."*

A Google engineer made this worrying remark to Tom Chambers as he researched a book on AI: *"I don't expect your children to die of old age."*

YOUR OWN REFLECTIONS
A prayer in the Anglican Church talks of men and women as 'the crown of all creation'. Are we about to be replaced?

CULTURAL SHIFTS

SEX

RELATIONSHIPS

In June 2019 BP (British Petroleum) and Nutmeg (an online investment company) published a joint advertisement extolling the virtues of 'going steady', thus proving that oil and money are several decades behind the times. In the 1950s, the notion of 'going steady' was really popular. At its centre was a desire for security and commitment. 'Playing the field' and 'playboy' became negative terms. The '60's brought the notional paradise of 'free love', made possible by the wide use of contraception.

In the 21st century 'going steady' and 'free love' are no longer on the scene. Here are a some current (I hope) words:

Benching: Casually dating a partner without commitment - keeping them on a string;

Catfishing: Stealing someone else's information and photos to create a false identity;

Cuffing: Entering into a comfortable live-in relationship for the winter;

Curve: In a relationship but deflecting (curving away) or not committing;

Cushioning: Being in a relationship but keeping your options open;

Dry dating: Abstaining from alcohol during dates;

Freckling: Entering into a comfortable live-in relationship for the summer;

Ghosting: Stopping active engagement on social media with one's former partner without telling him/her you want to move on;

Groundhogging: Going into relationships with similar people, expecting different results;

Love bombing: Unhealthy/manipulative showering of gifts or flattery;

Pocketing: Refusing to introduce a partner to family or friends or on social media;

Situationship: An undefined relationship;

Slow fade: Ending a relationship by slowly withdrawing, not having honest communication;

Soul tie: A deep emotional or spiritual bond;

Skinny love: Being in a relationship for one's own needs without engaging seriously with the other person: a relationship with no weight;

Stashing: Keeping the social media relationship minimal but still active while exploring other possibilities;

Vibing: Feeling connected with someone; sharing energies, whether emotionally, intellectually or sexually; a positive word.

Mind you, the enormous popularity of 'Love Island' on ITV demonstrates how popular good old-fashioned romance still is. Series 5 in 2019, started with 3.9 million viewers and ended with over 6 million, more than half in the age group 16-34. It follows a similar formula to the gladiatorial games in Ancient Rome, though playing with emotions instead of swords, nets and tridents. The hopes it raises are summed up in the poem which one of the winners, Greg, wrote in July 2019:

> *"I'm going to keep this short and sweet,*
> *just like when we first came to meet.*
> *Up in the Hideaway sheltered from the trouble,*
> *we instantly connected and formed our own bubble."*

SEXUAL PRACTICES

The pornography industry has led to a 'pornification' of society, in which thoughts previously unexpressed are now seen as part of the spectrum of normality. For instance, in one high street games shop there is a card conversation starter entitled 'Who should I be with?' One of the cards for a couple to discuss has the binary statements: "Threesomes can help a couple stay together/Threesomes are always a disaster". That would have been inconceivable a few years ago. In 2016 Channel 4 showed a series, continuing to this day, in which men and women choose a date based on seeing their potential dates in full frontal nakedness. Channel 4 went further in 2022 with a reality series 'Open House: the Great Sex Experiment'. This shows real-life couples exploring sex with other people. *"They hope that sex with other people will help future-proof their romance, but roping in newcomers soon stirs up all manner of unexpected emotions."* (Radio Times 29/4/22).

Eight European countries have similar TV programmes. Whereas bisexuality used to be seen as a perversion, it is now marketed as just one option alongside heterosexuality and homosexuality (male and female).

The Covid 19 pandemic increased the sales of sex toys by a third, so that now at least 30% of adults in the US and UK are the proud possessors of sex toys.

Alongside has come some sort of acceptance of prostitution as an at least temporary career choice as a sex worker. At the same time the criminal and horrifying practice of human trafficking and sex trafficking blights the lives of women throughout the world.

SURROGACY

The first legal, compensated surrogacy cases started in America in the 1980s. That is where a woman is paid to carry a foetus and bring it to birth on behalf of someone else. It used to be rare, but in the San Francisco Bay area of California it is becoming a recognised option, either because a woman is not able to conceive or bring the baby to term, or because a homosexual couple (about a third of cases) want to bring up a child. It is so accepted now that there are 'fertility concierges' who help with finding and matching a surrogate, and both Google and Facebook, (as well as Uber, Lyft and Pinterest) offer $20,000 to employees to help with surrogacy fees which can typically reach $150,000. Today California, tomorrow the world?

SEXUAL ORIENTATION

Since the decriminalisation of homosexual acts between consenting adults in the UK in 1967, there is a wide-spread acceptance of same-sex relationships, based on the liberal consensus that private relationships of whatever sort should not just be accepted but celebrated. The term LGBT (Lesbian, Gay, Bisexual, Transgender) started being used in the US in 1988, and was adopted by Stonewall, a leading British gay rights group, in 2015. LGBTQ is the most popular self-description today (Q = queer).

World-wide atitudes of homosexuality are patchy. The Netherlands was the first country to legalise same-sex marriage in 2000, followed by one US state in 2001 and all 50 states in 2015. In the UK same sex couples could enter into civil partnerships in 2005 and be married in 2013. Same-sex marriages are celebrated in Europe, North America, most of South America, Australasia and South Africa. At the end of 2018 there were over 60,000 married same-sex couples in the UK. Nasdaq is a digital stock exchange based in New York City with 5,000 companies listed with a major focus on technology. In 2021 it required many companies to have within five years two 'diverse directors' on their boards, one a woman, the other to be gay, lesbian, bisexual, trans or of another 'underrepresented minority'.

On the other hand, same-sex intercourse was illegal in Russia up to 1993, and there is no move to stop discrimination against gay people there. Indeed, in 2011 the head of the Russian Orthodox Church, Patriarch Kirill, said that the idea of same-sex marriage was *"a very dangerous sign of the Apocalypse."* The attitude of China is summed up by the three 'no's': no approval, no disapproval, no promotion. It was removed from the list of mental illnesses in 2001. In 2017 the Indian Supreme Court struck down a law inherited from the British Penal Code making homosexuality illegal. Homosexual relationships are not recognised in Vietnam and Indonesia, and are punishable by life imprisonment in Pakistan, Myanmar and much of East Africa and by death in Saudi Arabia, Sudan, and Iran.

In 2006 the Equality Act (UK), created a public duty to promote equality on the ground of gender. The Act was updated in 2010, mirroring the four EU equality directives.

The Act protects people from being discriminated against in employment and provision of public and private services for these nine categories: age, disability, gender reassignment, marriage and civil partnership, pregnancy and maternity, race, religion or belief, sex, and sexual orientation

In 2021 a 27-country survey was carried by IPSOS, an international market research and consulting firm. The global country average for sexual attraction was:

- only attracted to the opposite sex: 70%

- mostly attracted to the opposite sex: 13%

- only attracted to the same sex: 5%

- mostly attracted to the same sex: 4%

In Great Britain 9% said they were only attracted to the same sex.

SOME DEFINITIONS

Chromosomes: The DNA of humans and animals consist of 24 pairings, 23 of which are identical between male and female. Only one has a difference between men and women: XX chromosome results in developing as female and XY in developing as male. The Y part can only be handed down from the male. Most people have a clear binary physical sexual development. In an online UK survey in 2007 90.9% of respondents identified as heterosexual. In 2017 a BBC survey found that here was a significant difference between generations. Those who identified themselves as exclusively heterosexual or straight were:

Baby Boomers (b. 1946 - 1964)   88%
Generation X (b. 1965 - 1980)   85%
Millennial (b. 1981 - 1995)   71%
Generation Z (b. 1995 - 2015)   66%

Within Generation Z this figure varied between the sexes: men 73%, women 59%.

Homosexual (male)
A male who has romantic or erotic attraction to the same sex. Male homosexuality has been promoted ever since Plato's dialogue 'The Symposium' (360 BCE), and lesbianism from the time of the Greek female prophet Sappho (as reported c 200 BCE). Around 6% of the UK population are homosexual (arrived at by the Government when assessing the financial implications of the Civil Partnership Act in 2005). There is a higher proportion among people under 30.

Homosexual (female), lesbian
A female who has romantic or erotic attraction to the same sex.

Bisexual
A person who has romantic or erotic attraction to both sexes. The concept of bisexuality was inherent in the 6-point Kinsey scale in his 1948 report on male sexuality, though Kinsey

himself disliked the term. It varies enormously between cultures, ranging from non-existent to universal as in some Melanesian cultures.

Pansexual or omnisexual
A person whose romantic or erotic attraction is not affected by someone's sex or gender identity. The term seems to have surfaced in the 1990's, its true meaning being hotly debated within the bisexual community.

Asexual
A person who does not feel sexual attraction. The term asexual was first used in public in 2001 with the foundation of the Asexuality Visibility and Education Network.

Demisexual
A person who only feels sexually attracted to someone they have an emotional bond with. It can refer to being halfway between sexual and asexual.

Transgender
A person who does not identify with his/her physical identity and experiences distress in living as such. The term was coined in 1969. A trans man is someone who was born female but whose gender identity is male; a trans woman is someone who was born male but whose gender identity is female, whether or not they have undergone medical reassignment. At most, a third of transgender people have surgery.

Transsexual
A person who does not identify with his/her physical identity and experiences distress in living as such to the extent that they

undergo hormone and surgical treatment to reverse their birth identity. 'Transsexualismus' was coined in Germany in 1923 where the first operations took place. The term was introduced in England in 1949. In 1952 the 'Ex-GI blonde beauty' riveted America, after he had surgery and hormone treatment in Denmark and became Christine Jorgensen. Another notable person undergoing a sex change was the author James/Jan Morris who had her sex re-assignment in 1972 and wrote about it in 'Conundrum'.

Cisgender
A person who is not transgender, from the Latin pronoun 'cis' meaning 'on this side of', or the opposite to 'trans'; In other words heterosexual. It was one of the gender options provided by Facebook in 2014.

Intersexual
A person who has disorders of sex development (DSD) and may self-identify as male or female or intersex. It used to be called hermaphroditism. The term intersex was coined in 1917; the term 'disorders of sexual development' (DSD) has been used in clinical settings since 2006. About 1.7% of babies are born in this condition. The practice of 'normalising interventions' has been strongly criticised. *"As an experience of being born with sex characteristics that do not fit social norms, intersex can be distinguished from transgender, while some intersex people are both intersex and transgender."* (Wikipedia)

Metrosexual
A term invented in an article in 'The Independent' in 2002: "The typical metrosexual is a young man with money to spend, living in or within easy reach of a metropolis – because that's

where all the best shops, clubs, gyms and hairdressers are. He might be officially gay, straight or bisexual, but this is utterly immaterial because he has clearly taken himself as his own love object and pleasure as his sexual preference."

TRANSGENDER ISSUES

In 1990 Judith Butler, Professor at Berkley, the University of California, published 'Gender Trouble', an academic book that argued that gender was 'performative' and unrelated to biological sex, and that terms like 'man' and 'woman' should be reimagined.

It has become part of the post-modern social science canon.
In 2004 the UK passed the Gender Recognition Act. In it people can present themselves as they wish, but cannot change the sex on their birth certificate without a psychological evaluation and two years in one's preferred gender role.

In 2014 the Indian Supreme Court ruled that "it is the right of every human being to choose their gender." The number of children in the UK asking for gender reassignment has mushroomed, from 40 in 2009-10 to 1,806 in 2017-18. In the US clinics have supported social transition for children as young as 3, and there is advocacy for mastectomies for girls as young as 13. Earlier there was general belief that children growing up would normally go through a variety of identities, such as schoolgirl 'crushes'. Indeed there have been cases where people have had their re-assigned gender reversed with unhappy consequences. And if children cannot think about their gender by first looking at their bodies, then they rely on teaching manuals and websites using 'typical' male and female stereotypes like pictures of Barbie and G.I. Joe - just what we thought we were getting away from!

The right to gender self-ID became a political cause in the UK after the 'Marriage (Same Sex Couples) Act 2013'. It has spread particularly through social media and has become a political litmus test of acceptablity. When Kathleen Stock, a philosopher at Sussex University, wrote a post about the lack of discussion about gender self-ID within academic philosophy, there was a flood of posts from transactivists demanding she be sacked.

The number of referrals to the UK Gender Identity Development Service (GIDS) has grown thirty fold in 10 years. (This has now been replaced by regional service centres). In 2018-19 they reached 2,590. In January 2020 a 23-year-old woman, Keira Bell, joined a legal challenge against the over-prescription of puberty blockers and cross-sex hormones to over 1,000 teenagers and children, some as young as 11. In her short life, Ms Bell has transitioned, had a double mastectomy and detransitioned (The Economist 1/2/20).

Also in 2020 NHS England commissioned the Independent Review of Gender Identity Services for Children and Young People, commonly called the Cass Review, after its chair Hilary Cass, a retired consultant paediatrician. The final report was published in 2024; It found some evidence that hormone treatment improves psychological outcomes after 12 months, but found insufficient/inconsistent evidence regarding physical risks and benefits. The report stated that insufficient evidence was available to assess whether social transition in childhood has positive or negative effects on mental health, and that there was weak evidence for efficacy in adolescence. The review advised that there should be a 'clear clinical rationale' for the prescription of hormone therapy under 18 years of age. These guidelines have now been extended to adults.

In the week after the release of the final report, Cass described receiving abusive emails and was given security advice to avoid public transport. She also said that 'disinformation' had frequently been spread online about the report. Cass stated *"if you deliberately try to undermine a report that has looked at the evidence of children's healthcare, then that's unforgivable."*
There are two main issues: gender-fluidity and transgender rights

Gender-fluidity
The term gender-fluid started in the 1980's, but only became popular around 2010. It is an aspect of being transgender, of personal gender identity. It specifically refers to people who feel they are different genders at different times. By 2011, 'gender-fluid' had 37,000 hits on Google. In 2018, this had increased to a staggering 2.3 million. Businesses are being encouraged to take account of these various gender identities in their employment practices and commercial plans. In a Dutch study quoted in Psychology Today in 2018, 5% of those born male and 3% of females had an ambivalent sexual identity, i.e. genderqueer.

In a May 2016 Guardian article, a young woman Payton Quinn explained, *"My friends started using male pronouns and one day someone referred to me as male, but I felt uncomfortable. It got me thinking – am I sure about this?"* It was then that Quinn found out about gender fluidity. *"I would say I am gender fluid but also non-binary and trans. My gender is an evolving thing, like my sexuality, the more I explore it the more it changes. The only reason why I feel I should put a label on it is just to make it easier for other people."*

Transgender rights

Transactivists actively promote the right of transpeople to be allowed to use the public space of their chosen gender. This has run head on into fears of women feeling at risk from people who are still biologically male, though living as women. The problem is not trivial. In 2018 Karen White, a trans woman with a record of sexual offences against women was put in a women's prison and assaulted several other prisoners.

In San Francisco a number of women have been sued for not doing 'Brazilian' waxing treatment on genital areas for trans women, because they feel uncomfortable doing such intimate action around the penis. In 2016 Obama directed that trans students in school and college had the right to use public bathrooms of their chosen gender; the directive was blocked by the courts within three months and in 2017 Trump overturned it. In May 2019 the City of London ruled that under their new gender identity rules trans women should have right of access to the women's-only pond which has been a single sex haven since 1926. An overwhelming majority of the 21,000 consultation responses said there should be no discrimination against trans women. But as one woman, a law professor, said, *"It's a place where women feel safe, and now it won't be the same."* However, it is likely that women will feel safer following the UK Supreme Court's ruling on 16th April 2025 that 'woman' means 'biological woman', and that if a space or service is designated as women-only, a person who was born male but identifies as a woman does not have a right to use that space or service.

SAFEGUARDING AGAINST ABUSE

On 4th August 2002 two 10-year old girls, Holly Wells and Jessica Chapman, were murdered by Ian Huntley, the school caretaker. Then it was found that he had been investigated about sexual assaults but never tried, and that the school had not taken up references. The outcry over this led the government to institute the Independent Safeguarding Authority in 2006, to protect children and vulnerable adults. It merged with the CRB (Criminal Records Bureau) to create the Disclosure and Barring Service in 2012. The aim was to make sure that no one slipped under the radar again, though it did not provide any review of family members, by whom the majority of rapes are committed. The effect was to make public institutions safer, but also to create a general atmosphere of suspicion and make the world more bureaucratic.

The context is important. In England in 2016-17 there were 43,522 recorded sexual offences against children under 16 years old, and a further 11,324 offences against young people aged over 16 and under 18.
Police recorded 6,009 rapes of children aged under 13 years, and 6,299 rapes of children under 16 years.

In 2012 Jimmy Savile was identified as a serial sexual predator for the 60 years. 90% of sexual abuse is carried out by those known to the child. A third of abused children do not tell anyone about it. The internet has brought a whole new dimension to the abuse and grooming of children. The issue is huge.

WOMEN ARISING
#MeToo: On 9th October 2017, after months of allegations, Harvey Weinstein, the powerful Hollywood film producer, was sacked from his own company and three years later imprisoned for rape. Around noon on 15th October 2017 the actress Alyssa Milano tweeted the phrase #MeToo to draw attention to sexual harassment and assault. (She credited the phrase to Tarana Burke who used it in 2006 to highlight the plight of young black women). The phrase was tweeted 500,000 times

in two days, and 4.7 million people posted 12 million posts on Facebook within 24 hours. It has been a game changer, creating discussion about sexual harassment in the music industry, sciences, academia and politics. The New York Times reported in October 2018 that in one year 2021 powerful men had been ousted, such as Kevin Spacey (actor), James Levine (Conductor at the Metropolitan Opera) and Bill Hybels (lead pastor of Willow Creek Church).

Politics: For centuries women have been able to hold power, but crucially only because of the family they were born into or the man whom they had married: Pharaoh Hatshepsut (d. 1458 BCE), Empress Matilda (1102-1167), Mary I, Elizabeth I, Catherine de Medici, Queen Anne, Catherine of Russia, Maria Theresa of Austria, Victoria, Elizabeth II. In the 20th century women became political leaders through the ballot box, such as Sirimavo Bandaranaike (Sri Lanka), Indira Gandhi (India), Benazir Bhutto (Pakistan), Aung San Suu Kyi (Myanmar), Margaret Thatcher and Angela Merkel. Now it is taken for granted that the commanding positions in any aspect of society, business or politics can be held by women. Examples are Nancy Pelosi, Speaker of the House of Representatives, Christine Lagarde, Chairman of the International Monetary Fund, Janet Yellen, head of Federal Reserve, Katherine Jefferts Schori, Presiding Bishop American Episcopal Church 2006-2015, and, from 2018 to 2022, Jodie Whittaker as Dr Who.

BBC: In July 2017, as part of the renewal of the Royal Charter, the BBC released figures of salaries over £150,000. 62 men and 34 women were over the threshold. As a result some leading male presenters took a pay cut. It's all part of a new and equal world.

Higher positions: At least half the researchers in life science worldwide are women, rising to over two thirds in the Ukraine, Kazakhstan and El Salvador among others. The proportion is less in engineering and computer studies. And the glass ceiling still applies. For instance in 2011 in the University of the West Indies, women represented 51% of lecturers but only 32% of senior lecturers and 26% of full professors in 2011. In Germany, the coalition agreement signed in 2013 introduced a 30% quota for women on company boards of directors.

Elsewhere: In Saudi Arabia women were finally allowed to drive in 2018, the same year as the Irish Republic held a referendum which voted 66.4% to legalise abortion.

A Teen Viewpoint: A British teenager Ty (age 16, 2019) said, *"I believe that women aren't of equal status to men. They're actually above men at the moment. They act above, I mean. To get a girlfriend you have to try a lot harder than 10 or 15 years ago."*

FOR REFLECTION

At the start of the Bible, Genesis 1.27 states: 'So God created man in his image, in the image of God he created him, male and female he created them.'

(Some translations use the word 'humankind' for 'man'). 'God', of course, despite being usually referred to as 'he' has obviously no gender.

Did S/He create humans as binary creatures in his/her image? What are the physical issues? The psychological issues? The spiritual issues?

ENTERTAINMENT AND MEDIA

SOCIAL MEDIA

The first proper social media site was Six Degrees in 1997. It offered profiles, friends' lists and affiliations. It was followed in 1999 by QQ, a Chinese site. Facebook was created in 2004. The essential ingredients of social media sites are that they are internet-based, use user-generated content, enable users to create profiles and facilitate online social networks. Here are the number of users for the biggest social media sites in April 2024; ('users' refer to monthly active users):

Facebook:

Over three billion users. Created 2004. In 2006 it opened up to anyone over the age of 13 and became a public company in 2012 at a valuation of $104 billion. It has over 2 billion monthly active users, i.e. almost a third of the human race, at least half of whom connect via mobile devices. It acquired social media rivals Instagram (2012 - $1 billion) and What'sApp (2014 - $19 billion). It has been criticised for privacy violations, negligence in allowing fake news, hate posts and tax avoidance.

People create a customised profile with information about themselves – accurate or not. They can post text, photos and multimedia to share with anyone who has agreed to be their 'friend', and use embedded apps, join groups, and get notifications of their friends' activities. It has brought a whole new meaning to the word 'friend'. A friend is now someone who likes your posts. Businesses can use 'Pages' to increase their market visibility. Over 70% of American internet users have an account on Facebook.

YouTube:

Almost five billion users. YouTube is a video-sharing website created in 2005 and bought by Google in 2006. Users can upload, view, rate and share user-generated and corporate videos. The advent of the smartphone has made video-sharing a key social media activity for millions. It raises most of its revenue from advertisement placed on free videos, but there are also subscription and premium channels. About five billion videos are being watched every day. TED curator Chris Anderson asserted that "what Gutenberg did for writing, online video can now do for face-to-face communication". (TED is an annual conference of short talks on Technology, Entertainment and Design; TED started in 1984 and has been free to view since 2006). An activist during the Arab Spring said they used "Facebook to schedule the protests, Twitter to coordinate, and YouTube to tell the world."

Instagram:

2 billion users. The name is a conflation of 'instant camera' and 'telegram'. and is a photo and video-sharing social networking service. It is hugely popular in the 18-24 age group. It was developed in 2010 and bought by Facebook in 2012. In 2016 it moved from a chronological listing of feeds to one based on algorithms. They responded to the outcry by saying, "You may be surprised to learn that people miss on average 70 percent of their feeds. As Instagram has grown, it's become harder to keep up with all the photos and videos people share. This means you often don't see the posts you might care about the most. To improve your experience, your feed will soon be ordered to show the moments we believe you will care about the most."

The stories feature is used by over 500 million users daily.

WhatsApp:
2 billion. Started 2009, bought by Facebook 2014. It is a messaging app that lets users text, voice message, chat, share videos. It has privacy issues over access to phone numbers. It is particularly popular in Africa, where it is often the only social media that people access. A major problem is how it has been used to spread fake news to influence elections.

TikTok:
1,582 million users, the international branch of the Chinese site Douyin. Launched internationally in 2017, it hosts short videos of 15 seconds to 10 minutes. It had phenomenal growth and now has 1,582 million users. There have been concerns about its addictive quality, and its censorship of social and political content.

WeChat:
1,343 million users. A Chinese messaging, social media and payments app started in 2011. Known in China as 'the app for everything'.

Facebook Messenger:
1 billion users - was developed by Facebook in 2008 to provide live chat. It moved to a standalone app in 2011.

Telegram:
900,000 users, originally Telegram Messenger. It started in 2013 as an instant encrypted messaging site with its headquarters in Dubai, allowing users to exchange messages, post stories and hold private and group video calls. It is particularly popular in Asia and Africa. The app has been criticised due to violent organisations like ISIS, Proud Boys and the Myanmar junta

using the app to communicate, both privately between members and publicly through channel posts.

Snapchat:
800,000 users. Launched in 2012, Snapchat is a multimedia messaging app whose content, using messages, audio and video, is usually only accessible for a short time, so it is conversational in nature. It is popular with millennials. "The primary use for Snapchat was found to be for comedic content such as 'stupid faces' with 59.8% of respondents reporting this as the most common use". (Wikipedia ed.)

Douyin:
755,000 users. The parent company in China of TikTok.

Kouaishou:
700,000 users. A Chinese short video sharing platform.

Twitter:
611 million. Created 2006; in 2012 100 million tweets being sent and it adopted the famous blue bird logo. Originally limited to 140 characters per tweet, in November 2017 this increased to 280 (but not for Chinese, Japanese or Korean). After 2015 growth slowed. There have been a number of security issues over the years and issues of hate crime and fake news. In the year September 2015 to August 2016 it suspended 360,000 accounts. It is used at all levels of politics, Famously it was used by Donald Trump voraciously to boost his 2016 campaign to run for President, particularly as they were quoted by mainstream media. On the day of the election over 40 million tweets were sent. It has been criticised for providing a channel of support for Islamic terrorism. In 2015/2016 it banned 360,000

accounts for promoting extremism. Twitter is banned in China, Iran and North Korea, and intermittently by other countries. But in 2010 many Chinese tried to evade the censors when the Japanese porn actress Sor Aoi joined Twitter.

Its real-time character has made it valuable in responding to emergencies. It has been used to organise protests in Moldova, Austria, Iran, Gaza, Germany, Egypt, Greece and Italy. In 2008 the Wall Street Journal said, "Fans say they are a good way to keep in touch with busy friends. But some users are starting to feel too connected, as they grapple with check-in messages at odd hours, higher cellphone bills and the need to tell acquaintances to stop announcing what they're having for dinner."

In April 2022 Elon Musk, owner of Tesla and SpaceX, bought Twitter outright with $44 billion of his own money. *"This is my strong, intuitive sense that having a public platform that is maximally trusted and broadly inclusive is extremely important for the future of civilisation."* (TED talk April 2022). He then sacked 6,000 of the 7,800 staff. There has been an increase in the amount of hate speech on the platform.

The six people with most followers in 2024 were Elon Musk, Barack Obama, Cristiano Ronaldo, Justin Bieber, Rihanna and Katy Perry.

Twitterbots or Xbots:
There are a type of software that controls a Twitter/X account. They autonomously perform actions such as tweeting, retweeting, liking, following, unfollowing, or direct messaging other accounts. *"Benign twitterbots may generate creative content and relevant product updates whereas malicious bots*

can make unpopular people seem popular, push irrelevant products on users and spread misinformation, spam and/or slander. These can amass significant influence and have been noted to sway elections," (Wikipedia)

Spotify:
602 million active users, 236 million subscribers in April 2019. It is a Swedish platform launched in 2008 which audio-streams music and pays royalties. It's what Gen Z listen to on their headphones.

Weibo:
598 million users. A Chinese microblogging website available only in China, launched in 2009.

QQ:
554 million users. Released in China in 1999, it was one of the earliest social media sites. It is a Chinese instant messaging service, with social games, music, shopping, group and voice chat.

GEN Z & SOCIAL MEDIA
Gen Z people will typically use multiple social media sites for different purposes. In 2019 the Economist reported on a 24-year old American woman living in London:

"Instagram is her natural home. She's also on Linked-In for work and status anxiety, Tumblr for private expression, Twitter for news, song lyrics, stream of consciousness, retweeting memes and political outrage. But Instagram is queen. It is the engine of her life, the medium of her job, the thing she is on at three in the morning telling herself 'five more minutes, five more minutes'". (The Mind of a Millennial, Economist Feature)

"As well as feelings of crippling loneliness and the concern that everyone hates me, Instagram often leaves me feeling utterly inferior.... One of my best friends says, 'It feels like self-sabotage. I sink hours into unproductive scrolling and then feel shit about myself.'" - Emily Clarkson, Evening Standard 29/1/19

According to research quoted in a TED talk, 10% of women are on their smartphones during sex and 35% immediately afterwards.

Another voice on what it means to live in a social media world comes from Samuel, a 16-year old from Derby, England: *"This nagging, heightened habit of 'emulating and exaggerating, emulating and exaggerating'. My generation depends on popularity. The pressure they put on themselves for more popularity is higher than any older generation's experience."* (Guardian Weekend 9/3/19)

The whole social media thing can be summed up by an advertisement that an insurance company placed on London Underground in 2020:
> *Imagine your phone is stolen, lost, or broken.*
> *Life without Facebook, Tinder or Google.*
> *You'd have no mates, love or answers!*
> *Love it - Cover it Phone insurance,*
> *so you'll always exist.*

FOR REFLECTION
Christians and Jews try to follow the basic commandment "Love your neighbour as yourself". Since the advent of social media, who is my neighbour?

VIDEO GAMES

Video games were first successfully marketed in the 1970s, but it was Nintendo who revitalised it in the 1980s partly by bundling its Famicom console more commonly known as the Nintendo Entertainment System (NES) with the Super Mario Bros game. Since the 1990s many games can be played directly via a web browser, using Java or Flash, or though cross-platforming. The development of broadband, smartphones and social media this century has created even greater popularity. Over 2 billion people now play video games worldwide – a quarter of the human race.

Games can be for one player, using a third-person viewing perspective such as in the horror games 'Bloodborne' and 'The Last of Us', which have very detailed graphics.

There are team games, of various genres, in which you join a global team of 4 or 6 players such as the Nintendo game of 'Splatoon', 'Riot Games' or 'League of Legends'. The last has 100 million unique users and holds huge tournaments of esports.

Also worth mentioning are 'first-person' shooters such as 'Call of Duty' and 'Battlefield', a really popular genre of gaming and a big trailblazer in multiplayer experiences and the rise of 'loot boxes'.

There are physical (fitness) games like 'Wii Fit', and 'Ring Fit Adventure' for the Nintendo Switch, often played in DIY arcade club-nights.

Massively multiplayer online role-playing games (MMORPG)

These games, such as 'World of Warcraft' created by Blizzard Entertainment in 2004, build particularly strong social networks. In 2016 they launched 'Overwatch', a 6vs6 multiplayer first-person shooter team game. After three years it had more than 50 million players.

'Minecraft' (2009/2010) can be played by single players. Fans connect over the internet and become co-creators of the fantasy world of Westeros, a complicated process. You share in creating a new world on your own – you don't need other players. You can take a four week training program to become a better 'builder'. At the time of writing the continent of Westeros is 1,300 square kilometres and the city of Kings Landing has 4,788 houses, all of which can be entered. Minecraft has sold (to date) over 100 million games.

When the Museum of London wanted to celebrate 350 years of the Great Fire of London, they commissioned Minecraft builders to re-create London before, during and after the fire.

But there is a downside. Although free to play, some games, such as Fortnite, cleverly encourage players to spend real money to level up, gain status and XP boosts, outfits, virtual weapons and different player/weapon skins. 'Loot boxes' or 'loot crates' offer rewards for success in games, but because those rewards are randomly selected, it can facilitate video game addiction, similar to gambling, even when real-world money is not involved (which it has been).

In 2018 the WHO named 'gaming disorder', along with gambling, as one of the 'Disorders Due to Addictive Behaviours', associated with anxiety, depression, obesity, sleeping disorders, and stress.

The Evening Standard columnist Emily Sheffield headlined in April 2019, *"I smashed the headset, stamped on the console... but I can't pull my sons away from Fortnite's addictive grip."*

In July 2019 a 15-year old Essex teenager, Jaden, and his 21-year old Dutch team-mate got second place in the Inaugural Fortnite World Cup and won £1.8 million. His mother said, *"He will have a lifetime supply of Uber eats, and I think that will do him, to be fair. Just sitting there playing video games and eating take-aways, Jaden would be in his element."*

Are video games perhaps being twisted away from the engaging, artful and communal form of media that they should be? Games such as Red Dead Redemption 2 are as engrossing and poignant as any Western novel/film; Breath of the Wild is artistically stunning as any water colour; Mario Galaxy as stimulating as any puzzle book; Bioshock as philosophical as any work of political fiction.

In 2019 the Victoria and Albert Museum put on a large exhibition on video game design. The opening display was a quote from Frank Lantz in 'Hearts and Minds':

"Making games combines everything that's hard about building a bridge and everything that's hard about composing an opera. Games are operas made out of bridges."

THE BEST OF THE REST

Media and the internet

The internet has been an earthquake for traditional entertainment organisations. The BBC music programme 'Top of the Pops' ended its 42 year history in 2006, and Encyclopaedia Britannica stopped printing in 2012, though it still operates digitally.

Despite this, there has been an explosion of books, not just printed books, but e-books and particularly audio books. Between 500,000 and 1 million books are published annually by traditional publishers. About 4,000,000 are self-published each year.

TV and films

A key difference between types of entertainment is where they take place. The TV is a domestic, home-based medium, and the eight most popular programmes reflect this. In 2023 the most watched terrestrial TV programmes (excluding sport) were: The Coronation of Charles III, Happy Valley (crime drama), Eurovision, I'm a Celebrity - Get Me Out of Here, Strictly Come Dancing, Death in Paradise, The Great British Bake-off and Planet Earth.

The film industry has gone for big spectacle, in which the size of the screen creates an immersive experience not available at home or on a laptop. The producers of 'The Matrix - Reloaded' (2003) created virtual cinematography in which characters, locations, and events can all be created digitally and viewed through virtual cameras, eliminating the restrictions of real cameras; this is called CGI (Computer Generated Imagery). It is the foundation of modern video games.

The four highest grossing films worldwide in 2023 were Barbie, the Super Mario Bros Movie, Oppenheimer and the Guardians of the Galaxy vol 3. In each case foreign takings were greater than domestic ones.

FOR REFLECTION

There are so many opportunities for recreation, from video games to hang-gliding. What works best to help us re-create ourselves?

RELIGION

Some Statistics - UK

In the 2001 census 71.6% saw themselves as Christian. In 2011 that had dropped to 59.5. In 2021 for the first time it was less than half the population, 46.2%. Equally significant was the movement of those calling themselves not religious. In 2001 that covered 15.9% of the population; in 2011 it was 26.1%; in 2021 the figure was 37.2%.

In 2001 2.7% said they were Muslim; in 2011 that increased to 4.5% and in 2021 the figure was 6.5%. In 2021 1.7% described themselves as Hindu, 0.9% as Sikh; 0.5% as Jewish, and 0.5% as Buddhists.

In 2008 over Europe as a whole 52.8% selected 'no religion' to describe themselves. (European Social Survey). Church-going in Northern Ireland dropped from 44% to 30% between 1998 and 2017. In New Zealand's 2018 census 49% described themselves as having 'no faith'; and only 37% identified themselves as Christian.

And yet - isn't Britain a basically Christian country? Back in 1989 I took part in a friendly discussion on Salman Rushdie's 'Satanic verses' with Zaki Badawi, Chief Imam of London Central Mosque. He was challenged when he made the comment that Britain was not a Christian country. He thought for a moment, then said, *"It's Christian by prejudice, not by belief."* That puts it well. But is it still true?

The British Social Attitudes Survey makes sobering reading for Christian folk. Between 1998 and 2019 those who felt sure of

God's existence dropped from 21% to 19%, while those who were certain there was no God rose from 10% to 21%.

"The number of 'confident atheists' in Britain has more than doubled in the past two decades." (The Times). This is significant, because 20% is the threshold at which attitudes can become key determinants of society.

In the UK, 33% of those over 75 identified themselves as Church of England; in the age group 18-24 only 1% did so. The average age of the population is 40; that of Christians is 51. The same decline is present in the general voluntary sector.

The Covid Effect

Clearly the Covid pandemic had a massive effect on church attendance, especially when all churches were closed from March to July 2020 and again in November. The Church of England had 1.1 million in their worshipping community before the pandemic. In 2021 this dropped to 966,000 but rose again in 2022 to 984,000. In 2023 it rose again by about 5% - but still below pre-Covid levels.

More Statistics - USA

The United States is a special case. It is the only major industrial country which is also very religious. A Gallup poll in 2024 found that 68% identified themselves as Christian: 33% as Protestants, 22% as Catholics and 13% as other Christian. Protestants were split equally between evangelical and mainline denominations. Other faiths accounted for 4%.

1,750 mega churches are thriving, i.e. Protestant churches with over 2,000 on Sundays. Although they account for just 0.5% of all churches, they have 7% of churchgoers. It is easy for people to choose their level of engagement and for large churches to have very specific groups; Life Church hosts a club for Dungeons and Dragons gamers.

However, even across the Pond, the tide is still going out. Those who said that religion was very important to them dropped from 59% to 45% between 2000 and 2024. Those with no religious affiliation increased from 14.1% in 2001 to 26.8% in 2024.

Yet more Statistics - the world

Current estimates (mid-point 2024) for the world are:

Christians: 2.63 billion Christians or 31.2% of
        which 1.2 billion were Roman Catholics,
        40% being in Latin America, with the fastest
        growth being in Africa.
        There are 656 million Pentecostals.
Muslims: 2 billion, or 24.9% of the world's population.
Hindus: 1.2 billion, or 15.2%.   "   "
Buddhists: 507 million, or 6.6% "   "
Secular/Agnostic/Atheist: 1.19 billion, or 15.6%   "

SEXUAL ABUSE IN THE CHURCH

The most newsworthy events in the worldwide church has unfortunately been the scandal of historic sexual abuse, not merely the abuse itself but the way that those in authority covered it up.

USA

In the USA, following the Boston Globe's investigations into the criminal prosecution of five Catholic priests in 2002, there was a flood of allegations, resulting in numerous claims for compensation.

Also in 2002 the Catholic Bishops commissioned the 'John Jay Report' which found that since 1950 there had been 11,000 allegations of sexual abuse against 4,392 priest, just over half being single allegations. Of the victims, 81% were male and 19% female, 73% being under 14. The perpetrators were about 4% of the total number of priests.

In 2018 The Pennsylvania Grand Jury found there were over 1,000 identifiable child victims of 301 priests, and that there were likely to be thousands more. State Attorney General Josh Shapiro, said in a news conference: "They protected their institution at all costs. As the grand jury found, the church showed a complete disdain for victims."

By 2012 the amount paid out by US Catholic dioceses came to $3 billion. Eight dioceses were bankrupted and five dioceses got bankruptcy protection.

Ireland

In Ireland the Sexual Abuse Commission 2009 found that "church institutions failed to prevent an extensive level of sexual, physical and emotional abuse and neglect." By 2018 over 1,300 clergy had been accused of sexual abuse and 82 were convicted. The result has been a widespread secularisation of Irish society, leading to two referendums approving same-sex marriage (2015) and abortion rights (2018).

Germany

In Germany a leaked report said that 3,677 boys, mostly under 13, had been abused since the Second World War; this probably is under-reported.

Poland

In 2019, after intense pressure, the Catholic Bishops' Conference in Poland said that over 30 years 382 priests had abused 625 children.

UK

In the UK the Church of England set up an Independent Inquiry into Child Sexual Abuse (IICSA) in 2016 and had its first public hearing in 2018; the Church of England faced 3,300 sexual abuse claims. In 2017 300 clergy were involved in abuse issues out of 20,000 active clergy. But there were also claims of abuse by churchwardens, and others with church connections.

The Makin Review

In November 2019 Keith Makin, a former chair of Southampton's Local Safeguarding Children's Board, together with a colleague Sarah Lawrence, undertook a review of *'the Church of England's handling of allegations of abuse by the late John Smyth QC. The review was commissioned by the Church's National Safeguarding Team acting on behalf of the Archbishops' Council. The objective of the review was to bring to light what the Church knew, or should have known, about allegations made against Smyth, evaluate its responses, and identify steps to help prevent similar abuses in the future.'* (John Smyth Review). It was originally planned to finish in May 2020 but was actually published in November 2024. (This was almost three years after Winchester College had published their own review).

The Review, usually called the Makin Review, found that Smyth had abused between 115 and 130 boys and young men from the mid-70s to his death in 2018. They included his own sons. *"His victims were subjected to traumatic physical, sexual, psychological and spiritual attacks."* Church officers and others were made aware of the abuse in a key report in 1982, but the recipients participated in an active cover-up. These were *'a small group',* all members of the Iwerne Trust. The Review stated that it had become an open secret within the Conservative Evangelical network. A diocesan safeguarding office reported it to her local police in 2013 but no action had been taken.

Five days after the publication of the Makin Review, Justin Welby, Archbishop of Canterbury, resigned, accepting that he needed to take *"personal and institutional responsibility"* for the failures identified by the Review. Subsequently the National Safeguarding Team identified ten clergy, including two bishops, who could be subject to the Clergy Discipline Measure. The Bishop of Newcastle refused to accept the authority of the Archbishop of York. It is an earthquake in the life the Church of England.

Reacting to the sexual revolution

One major shift in the landscape of society in the West has been the explosion of sexual choices. What was unthinkable twenty or thirty years ago is now taken for granted. I overheard a woman saying casually to her friend as they walked along: *"Oh, I'm definitely non-binary."* Gender-neutral public toilets are becoming the new norm. The Equality Act 2010 makes it unlawful to discriminate directly or indirectly against persons on the grounds of sexual orientation, whether homosexual, heterosexual or bisexual. This includes treating requests for maternity/paternity leave differently for same-sex couples. Harassment includes verbal 'jokes' to threats of violence. There are some exemptions in law for religions who have a specific theological conviction.

In 2019 an 8 year old boy at a C of E school wanted to transition to being a girl. Rev John Parker, the local vicar and school governor, resigned in protest at a training session given to teachers. He said: *"Many parents may well hold the view that sex and gender are fixed at birth and may wish to educate their children in line with those beliefs. Instead trans ideology was forced on their children as fact and without their knowledge."* The diocesan director of education said:
"Church of England schools are inclusive environments and nurture pupils to respect diversity of all kinds Our schools must comply with the legal requirements of the Equalities Act 2010."

The Roman Catholic Church holds firmly to the primacy of the family unit in teaching sexual mores. The Catholic Truth Society wrote a major review of the question of gender theory in education. Unfortunately it is almost completely unreadable, e.g.:
"In the light of a fully human and integrated ecology, women and men will understand the real meaning of sexuality and genitality in terms of the intrinsically relational and communicative intentionality that both informs their bodily nature and moves each one towards the other mutually."
(Male and Female He Created Them p. 19)
With friends like that, who needs enemies?

In 2004 the UK Parliament created civil partnerships for same-sex couples. This was extended to opposite sex couples in May 2019 and the first couples celebrated it at the end of December 2019. This led to a rapid pastoral letter from the Church of England repeating the previous line that such unions should be celibate. The Church Times printed an editorial under the headline **'Sex (again)'**

"There is no need to point out the exasperation that will be felt by readers of all opinions that, once again, the issue of sexuality has flared up, cementing the Church's reputation as a judgmental, sex-obsessed, and yet loveless body (and that's just the view of some of the bishops)."

The New Atheism

In 2006/7 three books were published contending that religion was not just wrong but false, harmful and authoritarian. The most popular was Dawkins' 'The God Delusion', followed by Christopher Hitchens' 'God is Not Great' and Daniel Dennett's 'Breaking the Spell'. Sam Harris had written 'The End of Faith' in 2004 in response to the 9/11 attack. The books struck a nerve in popular culture.

'The God Delusion' in particular sold over 3 million copies and has been translated into over 30 languages.

As Dawkins wrote in his book, chapter 2: *"I am not attacking any particular version of God or gods. I am attacking God, all gods, anything and everything supernatural, wherever and whenever they have been or will be invented."*

In December 2011 Hitchens died of oesophageal cancer, maintaining his anti-theism to the end, decrying death-bed conversions as *'bad taste'.*

Mindfulness

Mindfulness is a technique for stress-reduction, originating in Buddhist meditation, but developed by psychologists and neuroscientists. In the 1970s Professor Jon Kabat-Zinn found that an eight-week course was remarkably successful in helping people live with chronic pain. In 1979 he founded the Mindfulness-Based Stress Reduction (MBSR) programme at the University of Massachusetts to treat the chronically ill. Later three psychologists, Williams, Teasdale and Segal from England and Canada linked the programme to Cognitive Behaviour Therapy (CBT) to treat depression, 'Mindfulness-Based Cognitive Therapy'. In 2011 Williams (a professor and ordained priest) and Penman wrote 'Mindfulness - a Practical Guide to Finding Peace in a Frantic World'. This ushered mindfulness into general society. It is now used by businesses, schools and even some churches to help people manage stress. Transport for London introduced a stress-management programme in 2010 which included 'mindfulness' days; the result was that days off sick due to stress, depression and anxiety fell by 70%.

Children today are under enormous stress. Claire Kelly who works with the charity Mindfulness in Schools Project said: *"the average levels of anxiety for a teenager today is equivalent to the level of those being hospitalised in the 1950s."* It is no surprise that schools up and down the country are using mindfulness practices to help pupils cope with stress. One school in Harlow, Essex, installed a meditation pod. It is certainly popular. Recent books include *'Meditation for Relaxation', 'Mindfulness Activity Book for Kids', and 'The 5-Minute Mindfu*lness Journal'. However, a MYRIAD study in 2023 found that mindfulness did not improve the mental health of children age 11-16.

Kabat-Zinn describes mindfulness on his website as *"paying attention... on purpose, in the present moment, and non-judgementally."* It is best undertaken as part of an 8-week course in which one learns various meditation practices to cultivate inner attentiveness. There are three dimensions. Learning to pay attention to one's body, starting with one's breath; then to one's mind, non-judgementally; then to one's overall being, in which one internalises three blessings: *"May I be safe ad protected. May I find peace. May I live with ease and kindness."* (From Meditation and Prayer by Tim Stead)

Is there anything left over for religion to contribute? Or is there a fundamental problem with it as a panacea? Ronald Purser in his book 'McMindfulness: How Mindfulness became the new Capitalist Spirituality' (2019) says it acts as a *"reinforcement of Western individualism; it seems more like an entitled self-centred and myopic guide to happiness."*

A personal note: In February 2020 I took part in a free 8 week mindfulness course for the over-50s in Chelsea Library. I found it a bit helpful, but found the implicit approach of Centring Prayer, based on traditional Christian contemplation, more useful.

A Land of faiths

As you enter the Victoria and Albert Museum, South Kensington, you can either turn down the right hand corridor and discover the art and culture of China, Japan and Korea; or turn left and absorb that of mediaeval Islam, India and south Asia, all overseen by a multiplicity of gods, demons, monks and boddhisatvas. Nowhere is the multi-faith nature of our human world more clearly demonstrated. The new entrance on Exhibition Road now takes you directly to a small gallery on Buddhism. Or turn immediately to the right of the main entrance to see the wonderful collection of mediaeval Christian art.

This is not new. What is new is how in this century the multi-faith idea has captured the public space. In 1994 Prince Charles said that as monarch he saw his future role as *'Defender of Faith'* rather than 'the Faith'. In 2015 he clarified this by saying, *"while at the same time being Defender of the Faith you can also be protector of faiths".*

The Millennium Dome is a case in point. It celebrated 2,000 years since the officially recognised birth of Christ - quite an opportunity to wave the Christian flag. Instead, Tony Blair's government decided to celebrate the religious dimension with a 'Faith Zone', incorporating the history of Christianity, Key Life Experiences, How Shall I Live?, a contemplation area, and a Faiths Festival Calendar. Today it is hard to dredge up any element of surprise at this.

The 1996 Education Act set up SACREs (Standing Advisory Councils for Religious Education) to advise each local authority on the provision of Religious Education, in the absence of national guidelines. The composition of each Council is a relic of bygone days. There are four representative groups: the Church of England; teachers, local authorities, and just one group representing Roman Catholics, other Protestant and Pentecostal churches and all the world's faiths. It is frankly embarrassing.

As an example, the syllabus for primary schools in Sutton, Surrey, where I was a member of the SACRE, was:

Key Stage 1, ages 5-6
    Hinduism   a story of Krishna
    Islam   names of Allah
    Christianity   many messages

The Journey of Life Key Stage 2, ages 7-11

Hinduism	the blind men and the elephant
Hinduism	Puja ceremony
Islam	the Five Pillars
Islam	the Pilgrimage of Hajj
Judaism	the Shema
Sikhism	the Mool Mantar

Unless one came from a family who practised a religion, this is the default framework for thinking about religion for anyone born after 1990. The Hindu/Buddhist story of the blind men and the elephant sums it up. Four blind men were introduced to an elephant. One felt its leg and said "It's like a tree"; one felt its side and said "It's like a wall"; one felt its trunk and said, "It's like a snake"; one felt its ear and said, "It's like a fan"; one felt its tail and said "It's like a rope". And they came to blows over their disagreements. All were right, none were wrong, the actual elephant was a different entity altogether. This is a different understanding from that of more dogmatic faith communities like Christianity and Islam which together make up 75% of religious adherents worldwide.

Governments now encourage different faith communities to set up their own faith-based schools, mostly in the state sector. They have to teach the national curriculum but can choose what they teach in religious studies. The number of children at non-Christian religious schools has gone up from 64,000 in 2011 to 94,000 in 2018.

Now 60% of Jewish children attend Jewish schools and 5% of Muslim children attend Muslim schools; these numbers are rising fast. Parent with strong religious affiliation tend to send their children to private faith-based schools. Is this likely to create a more integrated society?

Christian schools have a long history of serving society as a whole. Some years ago a vicar was told by a Muslim mother how much she appreciated her local Cafe school, because it removed her anxiety about infiltration by Muslim fundamentalists. And a Muslim reporter on the Sun newspaper commented how she had enjoyed the annual nativity plays and how jealous she was when her brother landed the part of Joseph. There is often a natural sympathy as well as competition between religions which the secular mindset doesn't get.

Then there is the secular counter-movement to remove all traces of religion from the public sphere, most obviously so in France and the United States. In March 2017 the European Court of Justice ruled that firms could ban staff from wearing religious symbols including head scarves.

Islam

Muslims make up 6.0% of the population in Britain, 10% in France, about 6.5% in Germany and 1.1% in the USA.

9/11 brought Islam into the forefront of public consciousness, but not in a good way. The rapid rise of Daesh/Isis with their brutal military campaign in Syria and Iraq and their success in attracting young Western Muslims into their ranks (5,800 from Europe, 8,300 from the former USSR) and the 676 people in the West killed in jihadist terror attacks has increased the fear factor, while at the same time Islam has become openly accepted as part of the mix of society. (The outburst of a Muslim bystander to a terrorist attack in Leytonstone in December 2015 got front page headlines, *"You're no Muslim, Bruv."*) Between 2014 and 2016 a million came to Europe from the civil war in Syria, half of them accepted by Germany.

A key question has been the training of imams. It has become unacceptable to governments as well as third-generation Muslims that imams, often Urdu-speakers from south Asia, have no understanding of their host societies, indeed often not speaking the language of the host country. British mosques now routinely bring in a second English-speaking Imam to keep the younger generation. A quarter of Britain's 1,700 mosques do not have facilities for women to worship.

But Islam is changing. The Muslim Council of Britain runs a six month course to train women to take up positions of leadership. Western Islam now includes the whole spectrum from the most conservative to the most liberal. A training centre for gay imams has opened in France. A former Catholic nun in Germany founded the Islamic Liberal Bund in 2008, modelled on Liberal Judaism. Islam is changing. An American Salafist preacher (the most rigorous stream of Islam) said *"While old-school Salafists are arguing over the minutiae of Islamic law, their children are debating whether or not God even exists."* Islam is learning for the first time how to live as a minority within non-Muslim society. Often imams are happy to engage in interfaith dialogue as they see the church as an ally in their struggle against secularism and lament its decline.

Church theology
The Church has made no response to the modern world in terms of theology. Despite maverick voices like Richard Harries and David Tomlinson, no new thinking has been done, or at

least has not filtered through to the person in the pew. The most prophetic voices today remain John Robinson's 'Honest to God' (1963) and even Charles Gore's 'God and Us' (1922).

Church worship

New thinking about worship has been limited to three movements. One was Pope Benedict XVI's 2007 permission for Roman Catholic priests to use the 400 year old Tridentine mass in Latin. Another is the Evangelical Anglicans' embrace of soft-rock as the main vehicle for worship, aimed at creating an atmosphere of spiritual intimacy and emotional openness. A third is 'Messy Church' (see below).

Pentecostal Christianity has at least 500 million adherents worldwide, to which must be added those denominational churches which have adopted the pentecostal-charismatic use of emotive soft-rock as the principal way or worship, in which the general adoration of God led by a worship band forms the first main phase of the church service.

"People who are interested in Christianity or your church have already checked you out long before they visited you. And if you have an online service, they've been with you for at least a week, and sometimes months or beyond. Trust me: if they have spiritual questions, they've googled their way to spiritual answers long before they set foot in your door.

All of which means...the foyer moved. When people come to your church these days, fewer are looking for information about God; they're looking for an experience with God." (Carey Niewhof's blog)

Messy Church

In 2004 Lucy Moore was part of the team at the Bible Reading Fellowship which started the Messy Church movement. It was created to reach out to children and parents with whom the Church had no contact, and 60% of attendees come under this heading. It is all-age and is made up of a long, messy time of creativity, a celebration with story, prayer and song, and a sit-down meal together. Discipleship is understood as 'following Jesus'. Most meet once a month, not on Sunday, and are female-led. About half have communion and baptism. There are currently 2,800 Messy Churches registered in England, predominantly Anglican, and 3,885 worldwide. Median size of congregations is 43, a third more than many normal congregations. It is welcoming, non-dogmatic and involves adults and children together.

Food banks

In 1997 Paddy and Carol Henderson used a legacy to help street children in Bulgaria. In 2000 they opened their first food bank in their home town of Salisbury. This has now mushroomed to over 12,000 food bank centres up and down the UK. In 2018-2019 the Trust distributed 1.6 million food parcels. In 2023-2024 the number rose to 3.1 million. Because it is typically done through churches, there is no need for the bureaucracy that would be inevitable if it was funded by local government. The most remarkable feature is that every person coming is offered a supportive talk with a volunteer. Two thirds of food banks are run by Christian bodies, compared with 4% by avowedly secular bodies.

Pope Francis - dangerous radical or godly reformer?

On 13th March 2013 the Argentinian cardinal Jorge Bergoglio was elected Pope at the age of 76 and took the name of Francis, the first Jesuit pope. (Jesuits have been at the forefront of catholic evangelism for 400 years, and are therefore sensitive to the needs of their local communities). On the Saturday after his election he said: *"How I would like a poor Church, and for the poor."* Although conservative in his theology, he is radical in his overturning of ancient traditions to make his papacy serve the poor and marginalised, such as washing the feet of prisoners on Maundy Thursday. His clear wish to support those who have failed, such the divorced or homosexuals, has divided the Roman Catholic Church, but has enabled the rest of the world to hope for a newly relevant and listening church. On 24th September 2015 he was the first Pope to address both houses of the US Congress. Speaking to reporters on a flight back from Brazil, he said: *"If a person is gay and seeks God and has good will, who am I to judge him?"* (Umm - well, you're the Pope...?) Pope Francis, the first Franciscan pope, has abandoned the traditional luxury of the papal role and lives in a small flat in the Vatican guest house. But he has embraced modern means of communication. In 2014 he had 9.06 million Twitter followers.

A story of Cardinal Vincent Nichols' visit to Pope Francis illustrates the tension. On leaving, the Cardinal said:
"I will pray for you, Father."
"What did you say?"
The Pope replied:
"I said I will pray for you."
"Oh please do. So many are praying against me."

Pope Leo XIV

On 21st April 2025 Pope Francis died. His successor, elected seventeen days later, was Robert Prevost, the first American citizen to become Pope, being then 69. He had spent many years as a missionary bishop in Peru and holds joint American and Peruvian nationality. He is committed to following the path laid out by the Second Vatican Council. He took the name of Leo XIV, referencing Pope Leo XIII (1878-1903) who established modern Catholic social teaching during the late industrial revolution. A similar challenge faces the Church in the age of Artificial Intelligence.

New Age Religions

Statisitics
The 2021/2 UK censuses reported the following figures for the six largest movements:

> Pagan 93,686,
> Wicca 13,056,
> Shamanism 7,904,
> Heathenry 4,791,
> Druidy 2,527,
> Pantheism 2,380,
> Witchcraft 1,044.

Witchcraft
According to the 2021/22 censuses there are 1,044 witches in the UK.
Inbaal Honigman came to witchcraft through the 'gateway drug' of tarot. She says: *"Witchcraft is a nebulous concept and*

can include anything from working with crystals, affirmation or astrology, to casting spells with candles or performing rituals with herbs."
Its rise has gone hand in hand with feminism and environmental issues.

Robert Poole, a professor of history, said: *"What is called 'witchcraft' today is a modern, New Age religion which celebrates nature, spirituality, and female empowerment."*

Tarot cards, healing crystals and books of spells are all readily available from Amazon and on the High Street.

Neo-Paganism

The Pagan Federation started in 1981 as a support group linking paganism to people seeking a nature-based spiritual path, and as a spokesperson to the wider society, e.g. the Home Office, police, hospitals and prisons. This includes Shamanism, Witchcraft and Wicca, Druidry and Heathenry. The last focuses on the traditional Norse Gods (as seen in the English days of the week). The bewildering complexity of this sub-culture is shown in this letter from the editor of 'The Troth' to the author of 'Secret Religions'.

"Do we count Norse Wiccans? Do we count dual-tradition folks, or AFD (Irish) Druids with a Norse cultural focus, or assorted other eclectic types? Do we want to include the Wotanist white supremacists? Who gets counted as Heathen could be contentious."

Astrology and Tarot

We only have to open a newspaper or woman's magazine to see how widespread the use of astrology and tarot cards has become. Princess Di had a six year relationship with her personal astrologer Penny Thornton. Another astrologer, Stina Garbis, said: *"There are multiple benefits to getting a tarot reading. You can get insight into your situation and determine the best actions to move forward regarding your love life, career or whatever question that you may have. You can find out the motivations of others."*

As G K Chesterton wrote, *"When men choose not to believe in God, they do not thereafter believe in nothing, they then become capable of believing in anything."*

Author's note: The general Christian view, from the time of Jesus onwards, is that there are spiritual forces around that can be inimical to or parasitic on people and places. It is wise not to meddle, but equally not to be extravagantly fearful.

SO WHAT IS THE QUESTION?

In November 2018 there was an advert on the Underground for Etihad United Arab Emirates Airways. It had the simple statement:
'We are our choices'

It enshrines the current mindset precisely. We are not composed of our commitments, beliefs, duties, or relationships. We are individuals with the absolute right to make whatever choices we want. The more choices the better. Attitudes to gender are a perfect example. But how do we make choices? What guidance is there other than immediate sensation? Ultimately, we say of ourselves what people in the past used to say of God:
"Is there anyone there?"

The best question I have come across to encapsulate the current mindset was put to me by a young man, Elian Odunlami, block manager for our local estate agent.
"I keep chasing tomorrow. How can I live in the now?"
   T S Eliot reflected in 'The Rock' (1934):

"Where is the Life we have lost in living?
Where is the wisdom we have lost in knowledge?
Where is the knowledge we have lost in information?
The cycles of Heaven in twenty centuries
Bring us farther from God and nearer to the Dust."

YOUR OWN REFLECTION
Does it matter what happens to the institutional Church provided individual Christians are happy?

THE CHURCH HAS A PAST HAS IT GOT A FUTURE? PART 3

BEING CREDIBLE IN THE POST-MODERN WORLD

1	Introduction: Who's listening?	213
2	Good, bad or both? The Natural History of Religion	217
3	Danger! Stories!	222
4	Is 'God' past its sell-by date?	229
5	God in 3D	234
6	The Bible is not the word of God; it is more interesting than that.	241
7	Jesus - the Facts	248
8	Why did Jesus die - according to Jesus?	254
9	Whose Son?	256
10	The Only Way?	266
11	What's the Problem? - The Problem of Sin	275

12 What's the Problem? - The Puzzle of Good and Evil   283

13 Sex and Society   291

14 A History of Hell   303

15 Death etc. - The Psychic Realm   313

16 Death etc. - The Realm of Light   317

17 Transformations   327

18 Conclusion: Crisis? What Crisis?   337

Bibliography   347

INTRODUCTION

WHO'S LISTENING?

Today's word on the street

In September 2024 Lauren Windle, author, journalist and presenter, wrote an article for the Christian online magazine 'Seen/Unseen'. The headline was 'Christianity's Big PR Problem'; it commented primarily on the way Christianity is portrayed in the media.

A friend of mine just completed her master's in counselling from Oxford University. On the first day, the group of elite academics sat around and debated the most pressing challenges facing modern society. A huge majority agreed that Christianity was a big concern. They described Christians as 'deeply problematic'...

A recent Netflix chart-topping film 'Wicked Little Letters' showed a gracious and timid Christian woman, who constantly quoted scripture, receiving vile poison pen letters... As the story progressed she was shown as suppressing darkness and completely unhinged. This kind of depiction of Christians – as suppressed and dangerous – is pretty standard...

Every documentary maker is now on the lookout for extremists, abusers and cult-leaders performing horrific acts 'in the name of Jesus'. And they're finding them... For example, 'Shiny Happy People' (Prime 2023) 'was a damning portrait of a Christian organisation that created a power structure leaving so many of its followers open to abuse, and a profile of exactly how that played out in one family.'

The agony for a practising Christian is that, in all their detailed research and shocking-details, at no point do any of the documentary makers explain that these horrific actions and principles are not reflected in the Bible but are in fact (sometimes deliberate, sometimes ignorant) user error.

General attitudes

As a small experiment, I surveyed twenty people in 2023, ten women and ten men, chosen at random in the Victoria and Albert Museum, Picturehouse Central and Caffe Nero. They were born between 1987 and 2004. I asked them for their instant responses to five words: religion, Jesus, Islam, Buddha, and Mindfulness. Mindfulness was the clear winner. Then came Islam, Buddha and last Jesus.

What seems to be taking the place of Christianity as the social 'glue' of our society are individual human rights especially around sexuality. In the 2024 election the Lib Dem candidate for Sutton was deselected from standing because of his religious views on abortion, gay marriage and legal sex change. Rowan Williams, former Archbishop of Canterbury, said, that it could set a *"worrying precedent... If it is indeed impossible to hold dissenting views, this ought to make it impossible for Orthodox Jews and most Muslims as well as Catholics and other Christians to represent the party... The precedent is a worrying one."* (Church Times 20/9/24).

While society and the powers-that-be value some of the social actions which faith groups engage in, (food banks, yes, supporting refugees, not so much), any idea that Christianity may have wisdom and iconic stories to offer is at best disregarded if not dismissed. We see this in the debate on assisted dying.

The general point of view on religion in Britain today is benign indifference. And for younger people, *"benign indifference can tip over into outright hostility on LGBTQ+ issues."* (Stephen Hance - 'Seeing ourselves as others see us – perceptions of the Church of England' – Grove Books)

And now

In 2019 Douglas Murray, a British journalist and topical commentator, said on the Triggernometry YouTube channel: *"Going from belief in God to non-belief in God as a society is one of the biggest changes that can happen. I'm a non-believer myself , but I think it's very unwise for non-believers to pretend that it's all business as usual. Very unwise."*

Is there a way back to being a Church which can even be heard by the wider society? That is the question this part of the book poses. Is it possible for the Church (in whatever form) to have a future in the public square?

A view from the shore

As I was growing up, the schools I went to assumed that Christianity, the Church of England version, was the norm. I willingly took part in prayer and church worship and have done so all my life. But relatively few in our society think like me. So in the next part, Being Credible in the Post-Modern Age, I try to take the standpoint of the interested but sceptical outsider and see what sense can be made of 'Christian-speak' outside the charmed circle of the Church.

Cyprian of Carthage (210-258) wrote that the Church is like an ark, or ship, outside of which there is no salvation: *'extra Ecclesiam nulla salus'.* Quite deliberately I am standing on the shore, watching the ship making heavy weather. The questions I ask as an outsider are: 'Does this make any kind of sense? Is it anything I can even hear in order to disagree with? How does it fit with the scientific description of the world? What's the evidence?'

However, there are also major questions which the secular mindset ignores. The most certain thing we can say about ourselves is that we will all die. Our society refuses to consider whether or not there might be human experience beyond death, whereas there is significant evidence that there is. I relate some examples in the chapters on 'Death etc.' The chapter on 'Transformations' gives many examples of spiritual enlightenment. Society disregards these. The only exception in our society are the twelve step groups like Alcoholics Anonymous with their recognition of a 'Higher Power'. Outside of these, stories of such personal transformations are regarded as either embarrassing or simply weird. Perhaps we should be more open.

Enjoy the ride.

RELIGION GOOD, BAD OR BOTH?

THE NATURAL HISTORY OF RELIGION

Good, bad or both?

In his preface to 'The Screwtape Letters' C S Lewis wrote: *"There are two equal and opposite errors into which our race can fall about the devils. One is to disbelieve in their existence. The other is to believe, and to feel an excessive and unhealthy interest in them."* Exactly the same can be said about attitudes to religion.

One attitude to religion is to dismiss it completely. Richard Dawkins wrote: *"I am attacking God, all gods, anything and everything supernatural, wherever and whenever they have been or will be invented."* (The God Delusion, ch 2)

I once tried to read Bertrand Russell's book 'Why I am not a Christian'. I gave up when I read the sentence "If Christianity were true, it would have produced something better in two thousand years than the crusades and the Inquisition." (Well, it did. How about hospitals and the abolition of slavery for a start?) The problem with this attitude is that it wilfully only sees one side of the picture.

The other attitude of total acceptance is fuelled partly from ignorance and partly from a fear of being discriminatory. The result is that religions are taken at face value, their rituals and rules treated as privileged.

Examples are some attitudes to Jewish laws and Muslim sharia (in contrast to France where secularisation is in a privileged position). And secular misunderstanding of religion feeds into the abandonment of traditional religious bases of festivals like Christmas and Easter. I remember in 1987 Lambeth Council decided to stop placing a large Christmas crib on Streatham Common. There were loud complaints from the churches, and from the local mosque.

Making sense of religion

So how can we understand religion? The way for me is an historical and developmental approach, 'the Natural History of Religion'. Religion always goes through three stages. These three stages apply to all religions everywhere. Religions are of course not static entities; they grow and change over time and are constantly re-inventing themselves. So the same three stages will make a series of re-appearances within a religion's life cycle.

STAGE 1

Revelation or faith

This is when someone has a direct encounter with the divine. It could be Moses at the burning bush, or Peter saying to Jesus, *"Lord, to whom shall we go? You have the words of eternal life."* It could be Siddhartha Gautama's 'awakening' as a Buddha or enlightened one; or the revelation to Mohammed in a cave outside Mecca in 610 CE.

A classic example is John Wesley's spiritual transformation at a Moravian meeting in London on 24th May 1738. *"In the evening*

I went very unwillingly to a society in Aldersgate Street, where one was reading Luther's Preface to the Epistle to the Romans. About a quarter before nine, while he was describing the change which God works in the heart through faith in Christ, I felt my heart strangely warmed. I felt I did trust in Christ, Christ alone for salvation, and an assurance was given me that he had taken away my sins, even mine, and saved me from the law of sin and death."

I believe that such an experience, an in-breaking of the divine into our ordinary consciousness, is always life-giving. It moves the person to being God-centred and other-centred rather than self-centred and ego-driven. At last one feels truly free. What's not to like? But until one has this experience, it sounds like a foreign language.

STAGE 2

Religion

The second stage is when the revelation moves from being simply private to being shared. The revelation is put into words, e.g. the Buddha's Eight Noble Truths, the Bible, the Qu'ran etc. It is heard, remembered and recorded by others and eventually written down as a formal account. The stories and teaching of Jesus seems to have been handed down by word of mouth for twenty or thirty years before being committed to writing, as were many of the revelations to the prophet Muhammad. Then people are designated to explain the teachings, buildings are built to do the teaching in, and a hierarchy of learning is appointed to make sure the original revelation is properly interpreted. In other words, a religion is created. Indeed, the Muslim calendar is dated from the movement of Islam from stage 1 to stage 2, the emigration (Hijra) from Mecca to Medina where Mohammed was able to create a Muslim society.

This is inevitable because men and women are social beings. But it is a two-edged sword. It is meant to be a signpost, but it can all too easily become a tentpole. As a signpost it points men and women back to the original source of revelation, so that they too may have a direct encounter with the divine; or at least be on a life-path with such an encounter as the end-point. But all too easily it becomes a tentpole, a centre of domesticity, fencing off the original revolution [revelation?] with a set of expectations, aesthetic decorations and house rules so that it becomes our ego-identity. "This is me, and I will fight anyone who tries to take it away".

The former leads to a radical de-selfing, in which we become open to God, the world and our fellow beings. The latter enshrines our egoism, which we sanctify in the name of a higher purpose. Our ego is happy that it has a club of like-minded humans around it and so confirms our hope that we are OK. Clubs, by definition, have borders, entry rules and normative activities. People in other clubs can then be viewed as the enemy, or if not the enemy, as at least peculiar. The history of all religions amply reflects this pattern. (So also does nationalism, politics and football. It is a basic human trait.)

STAGE 3

Power

When religions attain power, they can become seriously toxic. It is easy to make a list: the Crusades, the Inquisition, Islamic terrorism, Hindu nationalism. More subtle is the 'soft power' used to dominate a group. Group loyalty is proclaimed as an overarching good.

Freedom to have one's own thoughts or relationships are heavily policed and wrong ways punished by exclusion from the group. Examples are the patriarchal subjugation of women, the manufacture of guilt feelings, the persecution of those who wish to follow a different way. Those who want to open themselves to the original inspired revelation may well find it outside their inherited faith community.

I am a member of the Church of England, which I recommend because it is relatively powerless. But when it did have power, in the reign of Charles II (1660-1685), it was a persecuting church. John Bunyan, the author of 'Pilgrims Progress', was imprisoned for twelve years. The quarterly 'Meetings for Sufferings' of the Society of Friends (Quakers) tried to help Quakers being persecuted, and remembered those who had recently died in prison. Traditionally the Shiite branch of Islam did not seek political power. Just look at what it has turned into since the Iranian revolution of 1979!

So – is religion good, bad or both? The answer is, Yes.

DANGER! STORIES!

Sapiens

In his magisterial book 'Sapiens' (2011) the Israeli historian Harari sets out to cover the whole of human history. The crucial period was the Cognitive Revolution of 70,000 to 30,000 BCE. Suddenly, (in a geological sense), 100,000 years ago, Homo Sapiens seems to have been able to co-operate in combinations much larger than the small face-to-face groups our hunter-gatherer ancestors had managed hitherto. Suddenly whole tribes, towns and ultimately cities became possible. How did we do this? Through inventing stories.

Peugeot

Harari's classic example is the French car company Peugeot SA. In 1896 Armand Peugeot took steps in accordance with the French legal system to create the company Peugeot SA as a new legal entity. No one doubts the existence of the Peugeot company, but it would still survive if all the factories, offices and employees were lost in some catastrophe. It could still survive and start trading again. *'If somehow we convince millions of people to believe particular stories about gods, or nations, or limited liability companies, (then) it enables millions of strangers to co-operate and work towards common goals... An imagined reality (such as money) is something that everyone believes in, and as long as the communal belief persists, the imagined reality exerts force in the world'.* It would only disappear if we all stopped believing in limited liability companies.

Understanding ourselves

Stories are crucial because it is how we understand ourselves and our lives. My father wrote an account of his life. He grew up in Germany, came to England in 1933 because of Hitler and studied medicine. He married Mum in the war. Later in 1960 he worked for two years in Uganda and I went out there for the longer holidays. In 1963 we went on holiday to Munich at the invitation of the City Council – a very healing experience. Lots of stories which help to make me the person I am.

The same holds true for societies. It is not surprising that the teaching of history in schools should become a political battleground. Conservatives champion the telling of great moments in our nation history such as the defeat of the Spanish Armada in 1588. Left-wing parties maintain we should use history to include the various cultures which make their home here and to appreciate that we live in an inter-connected world. History should be about justice and compassion, so the trans-Atlantic slave trade is key.

Not so harmless

Normally stories are relatively harmless. But they can be weaponised. The book 'The Protocols of the Elders of Zion' described a Jewish plan for global domination. It was published in Russia in 1903 and became a worldwide phenomenon in the 1920s, despite proof that they were forgeries. Hitler promoted it and it led directly to the Holocaust and the murder of some 6 million Jews. Right now we see how Putin is proclaiming that his military intervention in Ukraine is to rescue the poor subjugated Ukrainians from the evil Neo-Nazis, of whom the Jewish Zelensky is supposedly a prime example. Sadly stories do not have to be true to have a disastrous impact. It is enough

for them to create hatred between people and so spark off violence, as we saw in Rwanda, Zimbabwe, former Yugoslavia etc. It may be that Homo Sapiens acted just this way when they came across groups of Neanderthal and other humans.
Maybe genocide is in our genes, and it only needs a good dramatic story to set it off.

Of course, stories can also do good, they can encourage mutual help and understanding between different people groups, as in Jesus' parable of the Good Samaritan.

A good example of how stories work is seen in the statue of Edith Cavell just north of Trafalgar Square. She was an English nurse in Belgium when Germany invaded in 1914. She treated wounded from both sides, and then was involved in smuggling 200 British soldiers to neutral Holland. She was arrested and shot. In 1920 the Liberal-Conservative Coalition government put up the very large monument just off Trafalgar Square with the rather jingoistic inscription *'For King and Country'.* When Ramsay MacDonald formed the first Labour government in 1924 a further inscription was squeezed in with the actual words Edith Cavell wrote just before her death: *"Patriotism is not enough. I must have no hatred or bitterness to anyone."* Which to choose?

How stories work
The story of Edith Cavell illustrates perfectly how stories work. Here is a diagram:

What happened → The story → a meaning

The facts of what happened to Miss Cavell are clear and undisputed.

The story could be told to highlight Edith's heroism and Christian faith; or to denounce the brutality of the German occupation forces and the need for patriotic soldiering. You pays your money and you takes your choice.

The same goes for the story of the Spanish Armada in 1588. It was perhaps the largest military force the world had seen. And yet it failed, partly though bad decisions of the Spanish commander, partly though atrocious weather. What did the defeat of Spain's 'Great Enterprise' mean?

The English were clear. God intervened by sending just the wrong sort of weather for the Spanish fleet at the right time. God was on our side.

The Spanish were equally clear. The English seamen were better than the Spanish ones. Anything so as not to say that God was against them.

The facts were the same, the stories not dissimilar, the meanings quite different.

The birth of religions

Religions are large communities combining millions, sometimes billions, of adherents. It is stories which glue these communities together. It may be that only a small minority of adherents study them 'religiously'. For the majority it is likely that these stories are more like a passive background to their lives. Here are some of the founding stories:

Classical Greece
The two great poems of Homer, the Iliad and the Odyssey, were the backbone of how Greeks understood their place in the universe. They are essentially accounts of human actions, but with divine forces at work.

Hinduism
The Mahabharata tells of a civil war happening about 900 BCE. It was made into the longest poem in the world between 500 and 1,000 years later. It includes the devotional book of the Bhagavad Gita in which Krishna tells the prince Arjuna how to work and love and live.

Buddhism
The foundation story is of a young prince Gautama who left his palace to seek the answer to suffering. He discovered the principle of non-attachment, the basic Buddhist view of life and salvation.

Judaism
Judaism proclaims a God who is beyond the universe and yet is active in history, especially in the escape of the Hebrew slaves from Egypt, about 1200 BCE. The story is told and reflected on in the first part of the Bible, which Jesus called the Law and the Prophets.

Christianity
The Christian message is centred on Jesus, primarily on the impact which his death and resurrection had on people then, and still have today.

Islam
In 610 CE Mohammed received his first vision of God/Allah. There were subsequent revelations as set out in the Our'an.

Because God spoke to Mohammed in Arabic, the actual text of the Qur'an is in Arabic, they are the words of God. Adherents are commanded among other things to pray five time a day and to complete once in their lives the pilgrimage to Mecca.

Finding meaning

But the bare stories are not the whole of it. Recall the diagram:

What happened ↠ The story ↠ a meaning

The stories will have some relationship with actual events, in the Mahabharata's case, minimal, in the New Testament's case quite fundamental. But the stories are what we have and what people revere. Their significance goes far beyond the actual stories. They enshrine their own linguistic 'game', to use the Austrian philosopher Wittgenstein's word. A 'game' is the whole context, usage and grammar in which words are used, and you cannot use another 'game' without falling into nonsense. One example he gave was his experience as a soldier in the First World War. A consecrated 'host' or bread was brought to give communion to troops in the front line. It was protected by a bullet-proof steel case. Mysticism meets military hardware. Faith encased by fear.

St Paul

We have a prime example of stories providing meaning in a letter of St Paul. In 1 Corinthians 11 he says:

I received from the Lord what I also handed on to you, that the Lord Jesus on the night when he was betrayed took a loaf of bread, and when he had given thanks, he broke it and said, 'This is my body that is for you. Do this in remembrance of me.' In the same way he took the cup also, after supper, saying, 'This cup is the new covenant in my blood. Do this, as often as you drink it, in remembrance of me.'

Here is a story that explicitly goes back to actual events – in fact probably the earliest account we have of the Last Supper. What point is Paul making?

First, to assert that the death of the Messiah is the central paradox of the new Jesus community.

For as often as you eat this bread and drink the cup, you proclaim the Lord's death until he comes.

Second, wealthier members of the local fellowship should stop bringing their own private food to the common sacred meals. Everyone should be treated with respect, whether rich or poor:

When you come together, it is not really to eat the Lord's supper. For when the time comes to eat, each of you goes ahead with your own supper, and one goes hungry and another becomes drunk. What! Do you not have homes to eat and drink in? Or do you show contempt for the church of God and humiliate those who have nothing?

Third, discern the body, whatever that means!

Fifteen hundred years later the meaning had grown more elaborate. Thomas Cranmer, in his exhortation in the 1552 Book of Common Prayer said: *Then we spiritually eat the flesh of Christ and drink his blood; then we dwell in Christ, and Christ in us; we are one with Christ, and Christ with us.*

We have come quite a long way from a simple "Do this in remembrance of me." But that's stories for you.

IS 'GOD' PAST ITS SELL-BY DATE?

An unfortunate word

There is so much wrong with 'God'. It is supposed to refer to an overwhelming mystery, but 'God' is really inadequate. Hard 'g', hard 'd' and little 'o'. It may be no coincidence that it spells 'dog' backwards. There is nothing in the sound that suggests the ultimate mystery. It's even worse if you are orthodox Jewish, where the word appears as G_d.

The word 'God' sounds suspiciously like the word 'good'. Indeed, that is how St Thomas Aquinas (1225-1274) understood it (though writing in Latin) when he produced the most elegant argument for atheism I have encountered:

"It seems that God does not exist. For if of two opposites one were infinite, the other would be altogether absent. Now 'God' means infinite goodness." (Quoted in a footnote by John Hick in 'Evil and the God of Love').

However, the roots in Sanskrit have nothing to do with goodness or morality. They apparently come from Sanskrit words meaning either to pour (as a libation), or to invoke while offering sacrifice. In other words 'God' refers to the direction in which we place ourselves rather than an entity above and beyond us.

But nobody understands it that way today, although within the context of prayer and worship we use it to place ourselves in a spirit of prayer.

Many people today have a visceral reaction against the very word.

"The word God still aroused a certain antipathy. When the thought was expressed that there might be a God personal to me this feeling was intensified.

I didn't like the idea. I could go for such conceptions as Creative Intelligence, Universal Mind or Spirit of Nature, but I resisted the thought of a Czar of the Heavens, however loving His sway might be. I have since talked with scores of men who felt the same way." (Alcoholics Anonymous p.12, 1939)

And yet we do need some form of words to use that are appropriate.

Oh Lord!

One that is much used in Christianity is 'Lord'. There are three problems with this:

1. it is too male;
2. it is too patriarchal – implicitly demanding obedience;
3. It is a mistranslation.

The word 'Lord' in the Old Testament – or in translations of the Tanakh (the Jewish scriptures – Law, Prophets, Writings) – is actually written in capitals to show that is not what the text says. In hundreds of instances it should be properly rendered as 'Jehovah', or more likely 'Yahweh'.

The reason for the change was that later on the rabbis and teachers of the Law felt that the name of God was too sacred to use, (as they do still today) so they used the vowels usually attributed to the word (in Hebrew one does not write out vowel sounds), and then added random consonants which happened to spell the Hebrew word for 'Lord'. So for instance, in Psalm 86 'Lord' occurs eleven times, four being a mistranslation of 'Yahweh'. In Psalm 96 all ten occurrences of 'Lord' are mistranslations of 'Yahweh'.

The writer of St John's Gospel so disliked the word that he did not use it once to refer to God. Today Liberal Jewish synagogues replace it with the phrase 'the Eternal', perhaps because they want to move away from patriarchy. This isn't bad as it does link up with idea of 'to be', as in the original Hebrew.

'Yahweh' however can be useful in meditation. It can be used to relate to the sounds of one's breath, so it could accompany breath-focused meditation.

Father!

Jesus' favourite word was 'Father', as it was for the author of John's Gospel. Again, this is eminently usable as a form of prayer, depending on one's own experience of one's own father. It was constantly used by Jesus, who used the Aramaic word 'Abba' or 'Father'. It is worth noting that the chief of the Roman gods, Jupiter, has a name that comes from the head of the pantheon of gods in Sanskrit, 'Dyans-Pita'. These two words mean sky - father. In other words, 'Father in heaven'! In a convent I visit, the word 'mother' is equally used. But both are incomprehensible outside the community of faith.

Other voices

'Allah' isn't bad. It has an openness about it, and a pleasing flow in the sentence "La illaha illallah" – "There is no god but God."

It is used (in Maltese) by the Christian churches in Malta. And it is quite close to the Aramaic word for God which presumably Jesus used, 'Elaha'.

But it carries too many Muslim associations for the average non-Muslim.

Alcoholics Anonymous uses the phrase 'Higher Power', which is not bad. But both the word 'Higher' and 'Power' have problems, similar to calling God 'the Almighty'. Looking around the world we inhabit, with the challenges of populist politics and accelerating climate change, Almightiness does not seem much in evidence.

'Great Spirit' is a translation of the Native American tribe of the Sioux 'Wakan Tanga', which is probably better translated as 'Great Mystery'. 'Wakan' can also be translated as 'holy'. Not bad.

The Hindu sound 'Om' or 'Aum' has a suitable mysteriousness about it. It is Hinduism's most sacred mantra; it is described as a sound, which is the vibration of the Supreme and which allows you to feel the whole universe. It is a reality well beyond our world of sense perception and it is often chanted at the start and end of meditation. It is not a noun, or a verb, and cannot be used as part of any sentence.

Making sense of God

Before settling on a word or phrase, one needs some sort of understanding of what we are talking about. In Christian tradition there are two classic ways of referring to God, the Positive Way and the Negative Way (the Via Negativa). The positive way asserts that God is perfectly good, perfectly just, perfectly merciful, perfectly loving etc. The natural response is worship and prayer. The negative way is to take any such attribute and move beyond it for the Godhead (God beyond God) is so other than us that any human definitions are inevitably more wrong than right. The natural response is silence and contemplation.

For me, a useful definition of God comes from a phrase quoted by the 12th century 'Book of 23 Philosophers', the 16th century satirist Rabelais, and the 18th century sceptic Voltaire, which all go back to late pagan writings like Hermes Trismegistus: *'God is an infinite sphere, the centre of which is everywhere, the circumference nowhere.'*

A possibility

What we need is a word or phrase that can be used both in statements and in invocation. There is such a word in the Judaeo-Christian tradition. That word, specially but not uniquely, used by the prophet Isaiah, is *'the Holy One' or 'the Holy One of Israel'.* 'Holy' not only has a pleasant sound (in English), but there is the sense that the meaning is beyond our normal perceptual world, and even beyond moral categories. To say about someone that they are a holy person is significantly different from saying that s/he a good person, though it includes that.

For many Jews it is a synonym for the sacred Name of God itself. He is the One *"utterly transcending the realm of the finite, the fallen and the imperfect"*. (from Hebrew4Christians.com)

To call God the Holy One also refers to the essential unity of the Great Mystery, as is emphasised in the basic Jewish creed, "Hear, O Israel, Yahweh your God, Yahweh is One, (echad)." (This is sadly watered down in Christian liturgies by saying, "The Lord your God is one Lord.").

So: is 'the Holy One' or 'the Holy and Eternal One' a possibility?

GOD IN 3D

East and West

Here are some thoughts about what western Christians think is a great problem, and eastern Christians take as a fundamental truth.

There is a great little book called 'The Orthodox Way' by Kallistos Ware, explaining simply how Orthodox Christians (in Greece, Palestine, Egypt, Russia etc.) understand Christianity. The first chapter is 'God as Mystery'. God is in such a different category from us (Creator/created, Infinite/finite) that ultimately the best we can say about God is, 'I don't know'. Chapter 2 is about what instantly springs to mind when we start thinking about God. It is 'God as Trinity'. 'The Trinity is not a philosophical theory but the living God whom we worship." Surprising?

To Western Christians, yes. For example, in 'Christian Faith in Outline' (1830) by the celebrated 19th century German theologian Schleiermacher, the Trinity is relegated to the conclusion. *"The ecclesiastical dogma, however, that in the one and undivided nature there are three Persons of like nature and like power, has not in this form equal value with the other proper doctrines of the faith, but is simply a summary statement."* (p. 62)

Who is right?

Words, Words, Words

One major issue is the problem of language. Christian ministers talk about the Trinity being 'Three Persons in one God'. Some theologians talk about a heavenly dance with the three persons interweaving, rather like some celestial tea party. No wonder that Muslims think that Christians worship three gods (though traditionally they think that Christians worship God, Jesus and the Virgin Mary).

The difficulty comes with the word 'Person'. When the Church started, everyone in the Roman world spoke Greek. The New Testament was written in Greek and church services were in Greek. Greek was the 'lingua franca' of the Roman world, similar to English being the common language in British India. It was not until about 300 CE that Latin started to take over in the West.

The Greek theologians talked of God as having three 'prosōpa'. The word means 'face' or 'actor's mask' - the outward surface you show to the world. When Latin came to be used, 'prosōpon' was translated as 'persona'. This also means face or actor's mask, but increasingly it came to its modern meaning of the total person, inside thoughts and feelings and opinions as well as the physical outside. Anselm of Canterbury puts it precisely in the Prologue of the Monologion (1076): *"When I say that the supreme Trinity can be spoken of as three substances I follow the Greeks... For, with reference to God, the Greeks mean by substance what we mean by person."* Without clarity of thinking like this we quickly get to the stage of having three Gods with all sorts of difficult consequences (e.g. the God of the Old Testament is an angry God, Jesus is a loving God, the Spirit is little more than a ghostly presence).

If we stick to the original meaning, we can see that the idea of God as Trinity means to show us not three individuals, but three aspects or three dimensions of God.

Back to the Bible

The word 'Trinity', meaning three-in-one, was first coined by Tertullian (155-240 CE). But the idea goes back to the beginning of the New Testament. I find one particular passage illuminating: Paul's first letter to the Corinthians, c.56 CE, is one of the very earliest Christian writings we have. Paul is not trying to make a theological point here, he is simply trying to get these new Christians, both Jews and Gentiles, in the cosmopolitan port of Corinth, to stop squabbling with each other.

"Now there are varieties of gifts, but the same Spirit; and there are varieties of services, but the same Lord; and there are varieties of activities, but it is the same God who activates all of them in everyone." (1 Corinthians 12.4-6)

Paul says that it is the Spirit who gives us spiritual experiences, who works in us from the inside. The Lord is the title that Paul always gives to Jesus, referring to the Jewish name for God 'Adonai', and it is Jesus who inspires us to act as servants of others. For instance, in Mark 10.45 Jesus says: *"The Son of Man came not to be served but to serve, and to give his life as a ransom for many."* And when Paul talks about God 'working' in people, he uses the same word as is used for the creation of the world in Genesis 1.

In other words, we know God in three aspects or dimensions: Creator of the universe – clearly beyond us; the Son who teaches us to help others, shown to us in Jesus; the Spirit who lives in us and provides spiritual gifts.

To use the three dimensions of God – the One Beyond us; the One With us; the One In us – is helpful when considering other faiths.

Trinity and the world's faiths

Christianity, in all its forms, is the most widespread religion in the world. The next in order of adherents, though not of time, are Islam, then Hinduism, Buddhism, Sikhism and Judaism. (Other affiliations are secularism, including agnosticism and atheism, traditional religions, and spiritualism). How can Christians hold a world view which takes them seriously without falling into wholesale condemnation or a spineless tolerance? The answer is the Trinity. Here is how it can work out:

Islam

Islam holds a very transcendent view of God, so far beyond us that he cannot be questioned, yet he is 'nearer than the vein in your neck', both transcendent and immanent.

Hinduism

Hinduism holds a two-stage view of reality. The lower reality is everything we can touch and know, including divinities we experience, thousands of them. Some Christians think that three most popular gods, Shiva, Vishnu and Brahma, the 'trimurti', are like the Trinity. That is a mistake. The Trinity, God, the Godhead, is infinitely beyond the created order. The meditative teachings of the Upanishads talk of Brahma, the utterly transcendent One, and Atman, the utterly immanent One.

Buddhism

Buddhism is a devoutly agnostic faith, which spends no time in thinking about any kind of transcendent power, but where deep meditation practice can bring one eventually to transcendence or Nirvana.

Judaism

Judaism is rooted in the oneness of God: *"Hear, Israel, the LORD your God, the Lord is one."* I heard a rabbi expounding it as follows: God is not many – not lots of little gods; He is not three – as if Christians believe in three separate gods; He is not two – the principle of good on an equal footing as the principle of evil (Zoroastrianism); He is not none – atheism has got reality wrong. But within the Jewish Scriptures are hints that more is going on in creation, particularly though the Word and the Wisdom of God. The whole of Christian theology is an attempt to combine the unity of the Godhead with the three ways we encounter him through Christ.

I see the Trinity as an expression of God active within the whole range of human experience. Islam witnesses to the transcendence of God, God beyond us, the Father, Creator of everything. Hinduism and perhaps Buddhism witnesses to the inner work of God with in everything, including our hearts and minds.

What about the Son, the Word, the agent of God in revelation? This is only hinted in other faiths, though they all in some way witness to the reality. I find it fascinating that in the Hindu Upanishads there is just one description of the supreme spiritual reality, 'sat-cit-ananda' shortened to 'saccidananda'. 'Sat' means 'I am' – like the vision given to Moses at the burning bush. 'Cit' means something like intelligence, and is an exact parallel to the Logos or the Word at the start of the Gospel of John. 'Ananda' means joy or bliss - not a bad description of the Spirit.

It is my contention that all genuine movements of human spirituality can find a home within the framework of the Trinity.

Trinity and making sense

I once knew a vicar who had married a Russian woman, brought up in the Soviet Union. There was no hint of anything spiritual in her whole upbringing. But when she married an English vicar, she could relate to the idea of God. She had experienced that feeling of immensity and beyondness because she had lived by the sea. The Spirit she experienced in Christian worship. Jesus she found more difficult until she went to an Orthodox monastery in Essex, and Jesus came alive for her in the Jesus Prayer: *"Lord Jesus Christ, Son of God, have mercy on me, a sinner."* This is an example how people who are far from the Christian faith can be touched by each of the aspects of the Trinity.

My own experience is that when I talk with people for whom 'God' is a difficult if not a downright irrational concept, to describe 'God' as the one beyond us, and with us, and in us, the frequent response is *"That makes sense"*. The Trinity is a gift!

Trinity and prayer

The Trinity can also be a programme for growth in prayer.

Worship
If God the Father is the one beyond us and beyond all contingent beings, the source and fount of creation, then praise, worship and thanksgiving is the appropriate response.

Prayer for self and others
The prayer that Jesus taught his disciples, the Lord's Prayer ('Our Father', Matthew 6.9-13, Luke 11.2-4) both lifts our hearts to God beyond us, and brings our physical and spiritual needs before him. We are invited to bring to him our concerns, worries, or distresses.

Jesus also held to the command in the Old Testament/Tenakh, to *"love your neighbour as yourself"* (Leviticus 19.18). A simple way I use is to remember individuals and pray, *"God, bless x and give them what they need."*

Meditation/Contemplation
St Paul tells us that *"the Spirit helps us in our weakness; for we do not know how to pray as we ought, but that very Spirit intercedes with sighs too deep for words."* (Romans 8.26) It's when we run out of words and simply seek God in silence that we may well be closest to God and experience the Holy Spirit present in our hearts.

IN CONCLUSION
You can see that I am a big fan of the Trinity as a way of approaching God. To talk of God as the One beyond us and with us and in us makes sense to most people of any age. And of course it means that we will never have God 'sussed'. That's good!

THE BIBLE IS NOT THE WORD OF GOD

IT IS MORE INTERESTING THAN THAT

Introduction

In the 1990's a well-known Argentinian Pentecostal pastor, Juan Carlos Ortiz, caused offence at an Evangelical conference in England. He held a Bible high in the air and proclaimed: *"The Bible is not the word of God! Jesus is!"*

I hope to show that Juan Carlos is both right and a main-stream Christian, and how this approach makes the Bible much more exciting.

Revelation and reason

The Anglican position from the beginning is that we need to use revelation, tradition and reason. Richard Hooker (1554-1600) argued that we were entirely at liberty to use our reason about 'things indifferent', i.e. not central to a spiritually transforming faith. So forms of church government were 'things indifferent', even if there was a specific command in Scripture. We are free to think!

In the time of Jesus, Josephus tells us that 22 books of the Old Testament, or Tanakh (Law, Prophets, Writings) were authoritative, with the first five written by Moses. (Actually in our Bibles there are 28 books; Jewish tradition took the 12 minor prophets as one book).

So the first Christians did think that the Scriptures, 'the Law and the Prophets' were inspired. But that made them useful, not inerrant. *"All scripture is inspired by God and is useful for teaching, for reproof, for correction, and for training in righteousness."* (2 Timothy 3.16.) A prime example is in Acts 15 when James and the other apostles decided they could ignore the clear command of the Law: *'Any uncircumcised male who is not circumcised in the flesh of his foreskin shall be cut off from his people; he has broken my covenant.'* (Genesis 17.14) Many Christian men are rather glad they did decide to ignore it.

The New Testament explicitly refutes the idea that what we have are words directly transmitted by God. Here is how Luke opens his Gospel: *"I decided, after investigating everything carefully from the very first, to write an orderly account for you, most excellent Theophilus..."* In other words, Luke and Acts are the product, not of inspiration, but of investigation.

Paul in one place explicitly denies inspiration: *"To the rest I say — I and not the Lord... Now concerning virgins, I have no command of the Lord, but I give my opinion as one who by the Lord's mercy is trustworthy"* (1 Corinthians 7.12, 25). Not authority but opinion. The same goes, I think, when Paul writes about the place of women in the church.

Apostolic, not inerrant
The basis on which the Early Church Fathers chose what books should be included in the Bible was simple. Did they come from the original apostles, Peter, John, James, and, a late entrant, Paul? So the criterion was, do they come from good witnesses?

The Letter to the Hebrews was included because, although the eastern church did not think it was by Paul (and it certainly wasn't), the western church thought it was and they won. A similarly revered writing, 'the Shepherd of Hermas' did not make it in.

This means that we are at liberty to use our own brains. A friend once heard a church-warden read 1 Corinthians 11.2-16 as the second lesson during an evening service on Jersey, about how women should cover their heads during worship. She read it well, and ended with, *"I am not going to say this is the word of the Lord. It is just St Paul being silly."*

In the Church of England, men and women who are ordained priests are asked if they *'accept the Holy Scriptures as revealing all things necessary for eternal salvation through faith in Jesus Christ.'* In other words, all other matters are secondary, and if secondary not worth creating divisions over. Even back in 1562, when the English bishops drew up the 39 Articles of Religion, the Bible is instrumental: *'Holy Scripture containeth all things necessary to salvation: so that whatsoever is not read therein, nor may be proved thereby, is not to be required of any man, that it should be believed as an article of the Faith.... All the Books of the New Testament, as they are commonly received, we do receive, and account them Canonical.'* (Not necessarily inerrant)

I once had a conversation with a Muslim taxi driver who was puzzled on how Christians understood the Bible. I replied that we do not treat it like the Qur'an, as verbally infallible, but rather as the Hadith, (traditions of the oral teachings of the prophet Mohammed) as authoritative but not infallible. He said, *"That makes sense."*

Despite all this, I and millions of others still find the Bible amazing.

1 Amazing first person memoirs

Just imagine the Bible did not exist. Then in some ruins of Roman Thessaloniki some parchments were discovered which were a series of long letters sent by one of the first Christian leaders. It would be an amazing discovery, people would have to rewrite the whole history of the early church. Well, we have those letters: Romans, 1 & 2 Corinthians, Galatians. Even the most sceptical scholars agree that these were by St Paul, written between 55 and 57 CE. Paul himself even signed off one of them: *"See what large letters I make when I am writing in my own hand!"* (Galatians 6.11)

In the Old Testament we have the personal memoir of Nehemiah, Governor of Jerusalem c.440 BCE, a conscientious official, but not an easy person to get on with. Then in Isaiah, Jeremiah, and Ezekiel we have the actual words of Jewish prophets from 740 to 540 BCE. E.g.:
Now the word of the Lord came to me saying,
'Before I formed you in the womb I knew you,
and before you were born I consecrated you;
I appointed you a prophet to the nations.'
(Jeremiah 1.4-5, 627 BCE)

2 Amazing contemporary reportage

If we go to contemporary accounts, the evidence is equally mind-boggling. We have the clearly contemporary accounts of King David's adultery with Bathsheba and ensuing family dissensions and civil war, c.1000 BCE; and the grisly but gripping account of Jehu's bloody coup d'état in 841 BCE:

"When Jehu came to Jezreel, Jezebel heard of it; she painted her eyes, and adorned her head, and looked out of the window.

As Jehu entered the gate, she said, *'Is it peace, Zimri, murderer of your master?'* He looked up to the window and said, *'Who is on my side? Who?'* Two or three eunuchs looked out at him. He said, *'Throw her down.'* So they threw her down; some of her blood spattered on the wall and on the horses, which trampled on her. Then he went in and ate and drank; he said, *'See to that cursed woman and bury her; for she is a king's daughter.'* But when they went to bury her, they found no more of her than the skull and the feet and the palms of her hands." (2 Kings 9.30-35)

All this hundreds of years before the Greek writer Herodotus (484-425 BCE), 'the Father of History' wrote anything.

3 The gospel truth?
The Bible contains four accounts of the life of Jesus. It is my conviction that Mark is the earliest, written about 50CE by an early follower of Jesus who was present in Gethsemane when Jesus was arrested (Mark 14.51); Luke, I believe, was written about 60-62CE and is a reliable report; Matthew is a church product and tampers with the tradition, making Jesus more judgemental than the others do; and John is an enigma, though I now think it was written by a Jerusalem disciple who knew Jesus personally – but I could be wrong.

4 Problems, problems
In the 1930's Christopher Fry and some friends went on holiday to Cyprus, and to their surprise one of them was reading the Bible. When asked about it, he replied, *"Oh, it's a great read. God is such a shit!"*

Not the sort of reaction one hopes for. But if you read it without the filter of faith, it's a natural response. There is a lot of anger in the prophets (and in Jesus), random regulations like women being unclean for a week after giving birth to a son, and two weeks after giving birth to a daughter (Leviticus 12.2-5), chapter after chapter on architecture and animal sacrifice, as well as divine commands for genocide.

Thus says the Lord of hosts, *"I will punish the Amalekites for what they did in opposing the Israelites when they came up out of Egypt. Now go and attack Amalek, and utterly destroy all that they have; do not spare them, but kill both man and woman, child and infant, ox and sheep, camel and donkey."* (1 Samuel 15.2-3)

A big problem is when people take this literally. A rabbi taking part in a round table discussion on Israeli TV in 2011 on *"What should we do with the Palestinians,"* said: *"We will have to push them into Jordan, and if they won't go, we will have to exterminate them."*
During the current Gaza conflict, an Israeli minister explicitly referred to the Amalekites as a possible solution.

5 Nationalistic or universal?

It is clear that we need a moral criterion outside the Bible to determine what parts challenge us towards good behaviour and what parts can lead us to the worse, just as in the case of moderate Islam versus violent fundamentalist Islam. The distinction seems to me to be one of either a national perspective or a universal human perspective. Two examples of the latter in the Bible are:

> *Are you not like the Ethiopians to me,*
> *O people of Israel? says the Lord.*

*Did I not bring Israel up from the land of Egypt,
and the Philistines from Caphtor and the Arameans from
Kir?* (Amos 9.7)

And from Paul's speech in Athens: *'From one ancestor he made all nations to inhabit the whole earth, and he allotted the times of their existence and the boundaries of the places where they would live, so that they would search for God and perhaps grope for him and find him—though indeed he is not far from each one of us. For "In him we live and move and have our being"; as even some of your own poets have said, "For we too are his offspring."'* (Acts 17.26-28)

Chaim Weizmann, later first President of Israel, said to the World Zionist Congress in 1946: *"If you think of bringing the redemption nearer by un-Jewish methods, if you lose faith in hard work and better days, then you commit idolatry..."* If we use the Bible, or any religious text, in a way that brings division and barriers, we commit idolatry. And if we use the name of God to justify inhuman acts, we commit blasphemy. Maybe there should be a health warning on every Bible: *'Handle with care'.*

6 And yet
And yet, there is an undeniable spiritual power in the Bible. I recently met a Muslim who has started reading the Bible and finds it *"the most beautiful book."* In even the most unlikely places a verse may stand out to address us personally. Does the Holy Spirit, who was present with the writer of that particular part of the Bible, also create a response in us?

Let's continue to read the Bible, or to start reading it, but with intelligence as well as prayer.

JESUS – THE FACTS

What can we know about Jesus? We have four main sources. Here they are in my view of their order of reliability:

Mark. The first gospel to be written, I believe, with many indications it is a record of eyewitnesses. John Mark was probably the teenager in the Garden of Gethsemane who was almost caught by the soldiers, and was later assistant to both Paul and Peter.

Luke. He used large portions of Mark and recorded them accurately. An investigative historian and companion of Paul. Possibly researched and written 60-62 CE.

Matthew. A composite gospel written for the church later. It records what was written before but editorialises and sometimes invents stories to make a point. The least trustworthy.

John. The nearest we have to a classical biography with long passages of 'factional' dialogue. Written, I believe, by a Jerusalem disciple called John and a good witness to events in Jerusalem. (Apart from chapters 6 and 11 only 22 verses take place in Galilee).

Arguments for the above are made in blogs on the website bibleinbrief.org, namely 'Can we trust Mark? Luke? Matthew? John?'

So, what are the facts about Jesus?

Fact 1
He was Jewish and spoke Aramaic. His name was actually Yeshua, known as Yeshua Ish Natzeret or Yeshua bar Maryam or Yeshua bar Yusef. He was a practising Jew and was steeped in 'the Law and the Prophets', which Christians call 'the Old Testament' and what Jews today call 'the Tanakh', short for 'Law, Prophets, Writings'

Fact 2
He was brought up in Nazareth, an out-of-the-way village five miles from the developing city of Sepphoris in Galilee, northern Israel. When the ruler Herod Antipas heard about him, he said: *"John I beheaded; but who is this about whom I hear such things?"*. (Only Luke and Matthew tell us that he was born in Bethlehem).

Fact 3
He was baptised by John/Yechoanan in the river Jordan. Why?

At this time there were four main parties among Jews.
- Sadducees were the corrupt priestly elite who governed the temple in Jerusalem.
- Pharisees were an evangelical elite wanting all Israel to become a holy priesthood. Much respected, and the forerunners of today's rabbis.
- Essenes were a popular semi-monastic rigorist movement with communities in the desert, Jerusalem and Alexandria in Jerusalem. They would have nothing to do with the temple.
- Zealots were terrorists/freedom-fighters against Rome and its collaborators.

John the Baptist cut through all these distinctions. Baptism was something that was normally offered to Gentiles who wanted to convert to the Jewish way of life. John treated all of Israel as if they were Gentiles and had to make a completely fresh start. Clearly Jesus agreed with this.

Fact 4
After going under the water, Yeshua withdrew alone for a period in the wilderness. His practice later was to get up early to spend time in prayer. (Mark 1.35)

Fact 5
He preached around the villages of Galilee, saying: *"The time is fulfilled, and the kingdom of God has come near; repent, and believe in the good news."* The core of his message is in the Lord's Prayer, see Luke 11.2-4.

> *God is Father*
> *His kingly reign is coming.*
> *We are dependent on him for our needs.*
> *We need to forgive.*
> *A time of evil is coming.*

Fact 6
He told marvellous stories like the good Samaritan, the prodigal son, the Pharisee and the tax collector.

Fact 7
People around him got healed.
Prayer for healing was common in the ancient world, including among the disciples of the Pharisees. What was unusual about Jesus was that he did not pray. Indeed, he often didn't say anything. See Mark 5.29, Luke 7.10, John 5.50. What he

typically did say was, *"Your faith has healed you."* He seems to have carried healing around with him like an infection.

Fact 8
He commanded unclean spirits to leave the persons they were tormenting, whatever that means.

Fact 9
He drove the money-changers and animal dealers out of the Outer Court of the temple, and would not let people carry merchandise through the temple. (Mark 11.16)

Note: The temple had the only gateway on the east side of the city. Yeshua must have done this by having his supporters outnumber the temple police at the entrances. In other words, it was not a demonstration, it was an occupation.

Fact 10
Yeshua expected the climax of history to come soon, when people *"will see the Son of Man seated at the right hand of the Power and coming with the clouds of heaven."* This was Jesus' declaration in front of the Sanhedrin. It got him the death sentence. (Mark 14.62). It remained the vital Christian hope for decades and even centuries after.

Fact 11
'On the night when he was betrayed (Yeshua) took a loaf of bread, and when he had given thanks, he broke it and said, *"This is my body that is for you. Do this in remembrance of me."*

In the same way he took the cup also, after supper, saying, *"This cup is the new covenant in my blood."'*
(1 Corinthians 11.23-25)

Fact 12
The Jewish and Roman authorities colluded in sentencing Yeshua to the slow agonising death of crucifixion. At the end he cried out "*My God, my God, why have you forsaken me?*" (Psalm 22.1)

Fact 13
His body was laid to rest in a nearby rock-tomb.

Fact 14
He was first seen alive again by women. Paul, writing in 56 CE said,

'(The Messiah/Christ) appeared to Cephas (Peter/Rocky), then to the twelve. Then he appeared to more than five hundred brothers at one time, most of whom are still alive, though some have died. Then he appeared to James, then to all the apostles. Last of all, as to someone untimely born, he appeared also to me.' (1 Corinthians 15.5-8)

Fact 15
Jesus' resurrection unleashed God's Spirit into the world, either on the first Easter Day as in John or seven weeks later at Pentecost, as in Acts. Whenever he/she/it came, Holy Spirit became the unarguable experience of the first (and later) Christians. *'You have received a spirit of adoption. When we cry, 'Abba! Father!' It is that very Spirit bearing witness with our spirit that we are children of God, and if children, then heirs, heirs of God and joint heirs with Christ...'* (Romans 8.15-17).

Those are the facts. The following three short extracts illustrate what it was like to encounter him in the flesh.

'He took her by the hand and said to her, *'Talitha cum',* which means, *'Little girl, get up!'* And immediately the girl got up and began to walk about (she was twelve years of age). At this they were overcome with amazement. He strictly ordered them that no one should know this, and told them to give her something to eat.' (Mark 5.41-43)

You can hear Jesus' trenchant tone of voice, when he was warned that Herod the ruler of Galilee wanted to kill him: *"Go and tell that fox, 'Listen, I am casting out demons and performing cures today and tomorrow, and on the third day I finish my work.'"* (Luke 13.32).

On his last night on earth Yeshua prayed: *"Abba, Father, for you all things are possible; remove this cup from me; yet, not what I want, but what you want."* (Mark 14.36)

WHY DID JESUS DIE – ACCORDING TO JESUS?

One incontrovertible fact about Jesus is that on the night he was betrayed, he took bread and said, *"This is my body".* He then took a cup of wine and said, *"This is my blood of the covenant, which is poured out for many,"* or *"This is the new covenant in my blood."* The words are in the earliest New Testament documents, Mark and 1 Corinthians.

How could he have said such things? My father, a good agnostic Jew, found them a disturbing reference to cannibalism. What must the twelve disciples have thought?

The words, *'This is my body',* is a clear reference to Jesus' approaching death. In other words, Jesus walked towards the cross with his eyes open.

The words he said over the wine are more puzzling, *"This is the blood of the covenant,"* or *"This is the (new) covenant in my blood."*

It is clear that the use of the word blood implies sacrifice. Back in the Upper City of Jerusalem on at Passover there was only one possible reference which these words could refer to, the Temple sacrifices that had been carried out that day. But sacrifice for what?

Philo of Alexandria, a Jewish philosopher and a contemporary of Jesus, discussed sacrifice in terms of three categories: communion sacrifices, whole burnt offerings (where we get the word holocaust from), and sin-offerings.

- Communion-sacrifices (Leviticus 3 & 7) were an expression of fellowship, a communal feast with God as the host.

- Whole burnt-offerings (Leviticus 1) were sacrifices of praise and thanksgiving, in which the whole animal was dedicated to God.

- Sin-offerings (Leviticus 4 - 7) cleansed the offerer from any ritual defilement caused by unintentional breaking of any of God's regulations, not intentional sinning.

The Passover sacrifices were 'communion sacrifices', creating a fellowship between the worshipers as well as between them and God.

Note: Matthew, a later gospel, adds the words: *"which is poured out for many for the forgiveness of sins."* The likelihood is that they were not spoken by Jesus. But they gave rise to the theology that Jesus' death was an atoning sacrifice, releasing us from our sins, providing the church with a built-in predisposition to guilt.

Perhaps the best equivalence to Jesus' words is the sacrifice conducted by Moses at the foot of Mount Sinai: *'Moses took half of the blood and put it in basins, and half of the blood he dashed against the altar. Then he took the book of the covenant, and read it in the hearing of the people; and they said, 'All that the Lord has spoken we will do, and we will be obedient.' Moses took the blood and dashed it on the people, and said, 'See the blood of the covenant that the Lord has made with you in accordance with all these words.'* (Exodus 24.6-8)

In other words, Jesus died a sacrificial death to create a new covenant people of God: 'for many', i.e. the world. This is what the worldwide church bears witness to. Every time we receive the bread and wine of communion, instead of feeling guilty, we can be grateful for being included into God's new community, the community that remembers Jesus.

WHOSE SON?

INTRODUCTION

'It is not for God to take a son unto Him.
Glory be to Him!
When He decrees a thing,
He but says to it
'Be,' and it is.
(Surah Maryam 35, interpretation by A J Arberry)

This verse from the Qur'an follows on immediately from the account of the virginal conception of Isa/Jesus by God's Spirit. The way Christians talk of Jesus as the Son of God has been a stumbling block in the relations with Jews and Muslims, as well as with sympathetic agnostics like my Jewish father. The question is, does it have to be such a stumbling block? If we go back to New Testament times, especially to the time when the Jesus community was entirely composed of Jews, what did 'Son of God' mean? Or even, whose son was he?

NEW TESTAMENT WITNESS

Here are some of titles Jesus was given the New Testament:

Son of Abraham. The first verse of the New Testament, Matthew 1.1 describes Jesus as 'son of Abraham', making it crystal clear that 'Jesus was not a Christian, he was a Jew.' (Albert Schweitzer)

Son of David, also appearing in Matthew 1.1. This refers to the whole history of the kingdom of Judah. It amounts to a claim

that Jesus was authentically the Messiah, God's anointed, as in the royal psalm 110 v.1:
>'The LORD says to my lord,
>'Sit at my right hand
>Until I make your enemies your footstool.'

It is how St Paul starts when describing his faith in *"the gospel concerning his son, who was descended from David according to the flesh..."*. (Romans 1.3). And it is how Bartimaeus the blind beggar caught Jesus' attention: *"Jesus, son of David, have mercy on me!"* (Mark 10.48)

Son of Mary. According to Mark, the earliest gospel, this was how Jesus was referred to in his home town: *"Is not this the carpenter, the son of Mary...?"* (Mark 6.3). This may refer to the dubious rumours about his birth. (Matthew is very uncomfortable with this and so changes it to, *"Is not this the carpenter's son? Is not his mother called Mary?"* (Matthew 13.55)

Son of Joseph. John's gospel always refers to Jesus as: *'Jesus son of Joseph from Nazareth.'* (John 1.45)

Son of Man. This was how Jesus almost always referred to himself. But what did he mean? Shelves of books have been written on this question. There are basically three options: 'Me, myself and I', to quote the Jim Carrey film; or me as a member of the human race; or me as the person whom God has appointed as his agent in the final judgment:
>*I saw one like a son of man*
>*coming with the clouds of heaven.*
>*And he came to the Ancient One*
>*and was presented before him.*

> *To him was given dominion*
> *and glory and kingship...*
> (Daniel 7.13-14)

Even excellent New Testament theologians like Jeremias and Vermes disagreed vociferously about this. Perhaps Jesus wanted the meaning to stay ambiguous.

Son of God.

The Old Testament/Hebrew Scriptures mention three types of 'son of God', namely

    (**a**) heavenly or angelic beings (Job 1);
    (**b**) the people of Israel (Exodus 4.22);
    (**c**) kings of Israel (2 Samuel 7.14).

Later it came to mean a righteous man:

> *Be a father to orphans,*
> *and be like a husband to their mother;*
> *you will then be like a son of the Most High,*
> *and he will love you more than does your mother.*
> (Ecclesiasticus/Sirach 4.10)

Surprisingly, it hardly occurs at all in the gospels. In the first three gospels the high priest asks Jesus *"Are you the messiah, the son of the Blessed One?"* (Mark 14.63, Matthew 26.63). And in Luke 1.37 the angel says, *"He will be called the son of the Most High".*

Note: Greek was written entirely in capital letters up to the 6th century CE, so where English translations put a capital 'S' for son, that is simply an editorial decision. And Greek has no indefinite article, 'a'.

The Gospel of John
'Son of God' is one of John's favourite expressions, but mostly in the mouths of other people:
John the Baptist declares: *"I myself have seen and have testified that this is the Son of God."* (1.33).
Those who do not believe are condemned already, because they have not believed in the name of the only Son of God. (3.18)

Martha, sister of Lazarus, says: *"I believe that you are the Messiah, the Son of God, the one coming into the world."* (11.27)

We don't know when John's gospel was written. Estimates range from 70 to110 CE.

The Church in Acts
Luke gives us a fascinating picture of the original community of Jesus' followers in the Acts of the Apostles, written, I think, about 60 CE. Here are some of the phrases which Luke reports that the original apostles and their followers used:
'A *man accredited by God; the Messiah (Christ - the Anointed); the holy and righteous one; the author of life; (God's) holy servant; leader and saviour; the righteous one; the son of man; Lord Jesus; lord of all;*
(Acts. 2.22, 2.31, 3.14, 3.15, 4.27, 5.31, 7.52, 7.56, 7.59, 10.36).

Only once is the phrase 'Son of God' used:
'Immediately Saul began to proclaim Jesus in the synagogues, saying, 'He is the Son of God.' (9.20). This is clarified two verses later. *'(Saul) confounded the Jews who lived in Damascus by proving that Jesus was the Messiah.'* (9.22)

So 'Son of God' was simply another way of alluding to the calling of Jesus as Messiah. This is the thought behind Paul's summary of the Christian gospel in Romans 1.3-4:

'the gospel concerning his Son, who was descended from David according to the flesh and was declared to be Son of God with power according to the spirit of holiness by resurrection from the dead, Jesus Christ our Lord.'

So what did the first Christians believe? That depends on the nature of time.

A QUESTION OF TIME

Where is Christ now?
The experience of meeting Jesus after he was raised from the dead revolutionised the disciples' whole view of what was happening. Although they could not see it, it was clear that Jesus was now *'exalted at the right hand of God'* (Acts 2.33). There he was waiting for 'the day on which (God) will have the world judged in righteousness by a man he has appointed,' as Paul told the citizens of Athens (Acts 17.31). This was the fervent hope of all the writers of the New Testament. As Peter wrote, "The end of all things is near." (1 Peter 4.7). But the thought behind this is of Jesus as the awaited Messiah rather than son of God.

Where was Christ then?
As hope of the imminent return of Christ began to get harder to hold on to, so attention changed to the other source of Jesus' authority, namely what went on before Jesus was born. Again, everything here had to be a statement of faith, not sight.

He was seen as fulfilling all the prophecies of the Hebrew Bible. But more impressively, he was seen as God's agent in the creation of the world:

'He is the image of the invisible God, the firstborn of all creation; for in him all things in heaven and on earth were created, things visible and invisible, whether thrones or dominions or rulers or powers—all things have been created through him and for him. He himself is before all things, and in him all things hold together.' (Colossians 1.15-17)

'In the beginning was the Word, and the Word was with God, and the Word was God. He was in the beginning with God. All things came into being through him, and without him not one thing came into being. What has come into being in him was life, and the life was the light of all people.' (John 1.1-4)
"Before Abraham was, I am." (John 8.57)

It is passages like these, rather than any titles given to Jesus by the early church, that we see the seeds of the Church's developing doctrine of Jesus as the eternal Son of God. So what were the steps of this development, and what were the consequences?

CHURCH STRUGGLES

The First Split

There is an early tradition that during the Jewish rebellion of 66-70 CE, Jewish Christians fled to the city of Pella the other side of the Jordan. From them originated the sect of Ebionites or Nazarenes, who were Jewish Christians. They proclaimed Jesus as the Messiah but denied his divinity. They kept the written Jewish law, were vegetarians and opposed animal sacrifice. Jerome c.400 wrote: *"They pretend to be both Jews and Christians, they are neither."*

If both sides had been a bit more tolerant and accepting, perhaps the Gentile church would have learned something from their Jewish brothers and sisters. And perhaps the ghastly history of Christian anti-semitism might have been avoided.

The Second Split

The following was written by Bishop Ignatius of Antioch to Christians in Ephesus during his journey to martyrdom in Rome, perhaps in around 110 CE:

'There is one Physician who is possessed both of flesh and spirit; both made and not made; God existing in flesh; true life in death; both of Mary and of God; first passible and then impassible, even Jesus Christ our Lord.' (Letter to the Ephesians, ch. 7)

Note: 'Passible' means being able to be affected by external events, able to suffer. 'Impassible' means not being able to be so affected or changed. It was the classic way that Greek culture thought of God).

Christian thought was moulded by the Gospel of John, particularly the reference to the pre-existent Jesus as the 'Logos', meaning Word or Message. So Justin Martyr (100-165) spoke of previous poets and philosophers as sharing in *'the seed of the Word'.*

It was only when Christianity finally became a legally recognised religion in 315 that a split developed between those who said the Son of God was an aspect of God from within his eternal nature (of one substance) or whether he was God's first creative act (of like substance) - *"There was when he was not."*

At the Council of Nicaea, convened by the emperor Constantine in 325, the former view won, but the latter view, called Arianism after its author Arius, continued to be the majority opinion until the Council of Constantinople in 381. By then Arian missionaries had converted the Germanic tribes who then took over most of the Western Roman Empire. The Franks adopted the Orthodox position in 496, the Vandals (North Africa) in 587, and the Lombards (Italy) only in 653.

The Third Split
Once it had been decided that Jesus/Word was *'God from God, Light from Light, True God from True God, begotten not made...'* (the Nicene Creed), the question then arose of how to understand the actual Jesus of Nazareth. Was he God impersonating a human person within an irrelevant body? Or was God himself suffering? Or was he a human/divine mixture?

The debate was inflamed by the ambitions of the respective patriarchs of Alexandria in Egypt, and Antioch in Syria. It focussed on the question whether Mary should be called 'Mother of God' (literally God-bearer) which Cyril of Alexandria championed, or 'Mother of Christ' as Nestorius of Antioch argued. At the 'robber' Council of Ephesus in 431 Clement won and Nestorius was excommunicated. However, Nestorian missions to the east thrived, even reaching China. The resultant split between the church within the Roman Empire and the 'Church of the East' has continued to this day.

The Fourth Split
Twenty years after Ephesus, in 451, the Council of Chalcedon debated whether Christ had two natures (God and Man) or one nature (God/Man). Rome and Constantinople acknowledged the first, Alexandria the second. The result was that the majority church in Egypt was out of communion with the rest of the church and has remained so to this day, along with the

other Oriental Orthodox churches such as the West Syriac, Armenian, Ethiopian and South Indian churches. Even though twenty five years ago the respective churches accepted that the disagreement was only over a linguistic mistake, they are still out of communion with western churches.

The Fifth Split

Up to 589 the Church's creeds had said that the Holy Spirit *'proceeds from the Father, who together with the Father and the Son is worshipped and glorified.'* But some Western Christians felt that was demeaning to Christ so in that year the Third Council of Toledo added 'and the Son - Filioque' - to the phrase 'proceeds from the Father'. This was finally adopted by the Church in Rome over 400 years later and led in the late 11th century to a permanent split between the Roman Catholic and Orthodox churches. What a shame!

SOME REFLECTIONS

A Godward Word

Words can do two main things. They can describe, and they can express a relationship. When I use 'Son of God' to describe Jesus, the meaning runs through my fingers. Do I mean a righteous man, or someone who had an incredible close relationship with God, or the creator of the universe? When I use it in prayer, as in the Orthodox prayer, *"Lord Jesus Christ, Son of God, have mercy on me, a sinner"* I am lifting up my heart to God, and feel that I am doing something valid. Perhaps what we need is less discussion and more prayer.

What Makes a Christian?

In 1984 David Jenkins, Professor of Theology at Leeds, was chosen to be the next Bishop of Durham. The Church Times reported him as agreeing with a young man who asked: "Am I a Christian if I can't believe in Jesus as the Son of God, but if I do believe in him as a great moral teacher?" I thought that was a bit reductionist and had a letter about it published in the paper. Just in time for a revised article where the paper printed the actual question asked: *"Am I a Christian if I can't believe in Jesus as the Son of God, but I do believe in him passionately as a great moral teacher and as someone who is leading me to God?"* To which Jenkins replied, *"Yes, yes."*

Do you agree?

THE ONLY WAY?

FAITH IN A WORLD OF FAITHS

THE DILEMMA

The British comedy duo Pete and Dud (Peter Cook and Dudley Moore) once had a discussion over the question of other religions. Dud explained the problem:

"You might be a perfickly good Buddhist and believe in Buddha and all that, and when you get to the pearly gates, there's St Peter saying 'Oh no, you were wrong. You go down to the other place.' Or altern'tively, you might be a good Christian and go to church and all that, and when you get upstairs, what do you find? There's Buddha laffing all over his face and sends you back as a worm."

It really puts the issue of faith in a world of faiths in a nutshell. Is our eternal destiny actually like the Lottery with only one right answer?

THE CLASSIC CHRISTIAN RESPONSE

The traditional Christian answer is that Christ is the only way to God. The classic quotation for this is John 14.6: *Jesus said to him, "I am the way, and the truth, and the life. No one comes to the Father except through me."* Indeed this is the final verse for the normal reading in funeral services, leaving the family with the uneasy question, 'Is s/he now lost?'

There is a real problem with ending the reading at this point. John 14.6 comes in the middle of a paragraph, which actually ends one verse later:

"If you know me, you will know my Father also. From now on you do know him and have seen him." In other words, the point is not to close the gate on anyone who doesn't 'get it', but rather the positive purpose of focussing on who Jesus is. I think Queen Elizabeth II agreed with me, because the reading she chose for her funeral using the same passage, continued right up to verse 9: "Whoever has seen me has seen the Father."

The other test verse is from the Acts of the Apostles 4.12. *"There is salvation in no one else, for there is no other name under heaven given among mortals by which we must be saved."* But who are 'we'? Peter is speaking in front of the Sanhedrin, the supreme governing body for Jews. At this time the nascent Christian community was entirely Jewish. So 'we' here means 'we Jews' or 'Israel', and 'saved' could equally be translated as 'healed'.

AN ALTERNATIVE MODEL

A popular approach to the issue of different religions is the Hindu approach. A well-known example is of six blind men describing an elephant: one holding the tail, says 'An elephant is like a rope'. One, holding a leg said 'An elephant is like a tree.' One holding the trunk says, 'An elephant is like a snake.'

Another image is that of religions being like different rivers but all ending up in the sea. The problem with this approach is that it says that differences do not matter, which is just as sweeping a generalisation as saying 'Jesus is the only way'.

My experience of other faiths, both in the two months in India and back in the UK, is that I was constantly being surprised by similarities and dissimilarities, rather like a layer cake or a large club sandwich. Or rather, there are resonances and dissonances, which can occur at surprising points with different religions. Here are some examples I have found with other faiths:

RESONANCES AND DISSONANCES

Judaism

Judaism is a very practical faith. There is no creed other than 'The Lord your God is One'. Jewish life consists of doing the commandments – all 613 of them. Faith is essentially trusting obedience.

The basic conflict between Christianity and Judaism is neatly summed up in the Letter of James: *Was not our ancestor Abraham justified by works when he offered his son Isaac on the altar? You see that faith was active along with his works, and faith was brought to completion by the works. Thus the scripture was fulfilled that says, 'Abraham believed God, and it was reckoned to him as righteousness', and he was called the friend of God. You see that a person is justified by works and not by faith alone.* (James 2.21-24)

No wonder Martin Luther (1483-1546) called it *"a right straw epistle."*

On the other hand, I treasure the brief saying by Rabbi Lionel Blue in 'To Heaven with Scribes and Pharisees', *"Prayer is when God speaks to us."*

Hinduism

Hinduism is a kind of encyclopaedia of religions, and very visual. There are enormous temples and millions of wayside shrines. Reverence for life is seen in the multitude of cows and monkeys wandering city streets in India.

There are three main paths or yogas towards nirvana or spiritual enlightenment: the path of knowledge, the path of action and the path of 'bhakti' or 'devotion'. A key scripture, part of the epic poem Mahabharata is the Bhagavad Gita (Song of God). Here is a verse: *'For the salvation of those who are good, for the destruction of evil in men, for the fulfilment of the kingdom of righteousness, I come to this world in the ages that pass.'* In this tradition one could well sing the hymn 'Amazing grace' and not need to change a word.

Another verse expressing Hindu spirituality is, *'Kill desire, that powerful enemy of the soul.'*

A caution: There are two main streams of thought in India, Advaita or monist, and Dvaita or dualist. The former says that everything is fundamentally one with the One, and that all distinctions of body or mind will be swallowed up as a raindrop is absorbed by the ocean. This is how the saying of Jesus is understood, "I and the Father are One." I had a discussion with a young man who referred to a local mountain Arunachala as God. *"How can a mountain be God?"* I asked. *"Why not?"* he replied.

The Dvaita or dualist school of thought affirms that there is something permanent and real. Our worship and actions are not insignificant. A Catholic priest I spoke to in Chennai thought that Christianity could be expressed as modified dualism.

The most famous Hindu of the last century was Mahatma Gandhi, who exemplified the open attitude of Hinduism to other faiths. In the ashrams he set up there are regular readings from Indian scriptures, the Bible and the Qur'an. And yet the rise of neo-Hindu nationalism has resulted in vicious mob attacks on Moslems and Christians. With Hinduism, the best attitude is just to embrace the mystery.

Buddhism

Buddhism was created 2,500 years ago when an Indian prince, Siddhartha Gautama, sought spiritual enlightenment and found it not in religious rituals or excessive austerities but through reflecting on the Four Noble Truths of the human condition. These, put crudely, are:

- life is suffering;
- cessation from suffering comes through renunciation of desire;
- the Noble Eightfold Path is the means by which one can attain liberation from suffering and desire.
- Practising mindfulness or meditation is central to this path.

Buddhism is non-theistic. It neither affirms nor denies the existence of divinity; different schools of Buddhism take different approaches. Rather it is a practical programme with a strong psychological component. It is thus very different from Christianity, Islam, Judaism and much of Hinduism. As such it is rapidly becoming the go-to religion of the Western world. But when I read the Dhammapada, the oldest Buddhist scripture, I was struck by how close it was to the teachings of Jesus:

'"He insulted me, he hurt me, he defeated me, he robbed me." Those who think not such thoughts will be free from hate.

For hate is not conquered by hate; hate is conquered by love.'
(Dhammapada 1.4-5)

Islam

Islam was created when an Arab merchant called Mohammed received a series of spoken revelations from 610 CE, affirming that there is only one God, and that worship of idols and subsidiary gods was forbidden. For Muslims the Qur'an is the actual words of God in Arabic, which is why it can never by translated as such, only interpreted in different languages. Muhammad Suheyl Umar of SOAS, the School of Oriental and African Studies, wrote:

"(In Islam) the Word did not become flesh, it became book. The recitation of the Qur'an has been, throughout life, my chief means of concentration upon God... My reading thus becomes the equivalent of a long drawn-out invocation of the name 'Allah'."

There is real resonance between this and the Eastern Orthodox practice of continually saying the Jesus prayer: 'O Lord Jesus Christ, Son of the Living God, have mercy on me a sinner'.

Twice I have taken part in the prayers in the mosque, once in Madurai, India and once in Sutton, London. I was struck by the worshippers reverence and seriousness; it was a real school of prayer. Here is the first surah (or chapter) of the Qur'an, called 'The Opening'. It is recited at all prayer times, the equivalent to the Lord's Prayer.

In the name of God, the Merciful, the Compassionate
Praise belongs to God, the Lord of all Being,
The All-merciful, the All-compassionate,

> *the Master of the Day of Doom.*
> *Thee only we serve: to Thee alone we pray for help.*
> *Guide us in the straight path,*
> *the path of those whom Thou hast blessed*
> *not of those against whom Thou art wrathful,*
> *nor of those who are astray.*
>   (Interpretation by Arthur J Arberry, OUP, 1964)

Jesus is highly honoured in the Qur'an. One difficulty is that the Qur'an is interpreted in main-stream Islam as teaching that Jesus was not crucified on Good Friday, but that his death and resurrection are yet to come.

On the other hand, when I was vicar at Hackbridge and Beddington Corner, I frequently included a passage from the Qur'an about the birth of Jesus, Surah Maryam, 19.16-34. If you don't believe that Jesus was conceived by Mary as a virgin through the Holy Spirit, you are not a Muslim. As one of my neighbours said to me in the street, *"I'm a Muslim, and I LOVE Jesus!"*

Another Look at the Bible

Are there any Biblical resources which could help us recognise helpful resonances with other faiths? I believe so.

In his letter to the Christian community at Colossae, Paul describes the Messiah Jesus: *'He is the image of the invisible God, the firstborn of all creation; for in him all things in heaven and on earth were created, things visible and invisible, whether thrones or dominions or rulers or powers — all things have been created through him and for him. He himself is before all things, and in him all things hold together.'* This seems a long way from the radical northern rabbi we meet in the gospels. What can have been the background of Paul's thinking? Was it perhaps a reflection on the role of God's Wisdom as in Proverbs 8.22-31?

> *The Lord created me at the beginning of his work,*
> *the first of his acts of long ago.*
> *Ages ago I was set up,*
> *at the first, before the beginning of the earth...*
> *I was daily his delight,*
> *rejoicing before him always,*
> *rejoicing in his inhabited world and delighting in the human race.*

Can we see Jesus as the embodiment of God's eternal wisdom? Or as the Gospel of John puts it in terms of communication and light:

'In the beginning was the Word, and the Word was with God, and the Word was God. He was in the beginning with God. All things came into being through him, and without him not one thing came into being. What has come into being in him was life, and the life was the light of all people.... The true light, which enlightens everyone, was coming into the world.' (John 1.1-4, 9)

If this is a useful way of looking at the world of faiths, it makes sense of what Queen Elizabeth said about the Anglican Church in February 2012: *"The role of (our Established Church) is not to defend Anglicanism to the exclusion of other religions. Instead, the Church has a duty to protect the free practice of all faiths in this country."*

Towards a True Kinship of Faiths

This is the title of a book recommended to me by an inmate in one of His Majesty's Prisons. It expresses years of the Dalai Lama's work and reflection on bringing peace between faiths. The book describes his meetings with 'my friend the bishop, my friend the rabbi, my friend the swami, my friend the imam etc.'

He sees all faiths as centred on the value of compassion. But unlike the Hindu parables mentioned at the beginning, he does not advocate an amalgamation of them all into one feel-good soup. The life of each the world's faiths is rooted in their specific beliefs and stories; they are what create faith for individual believers.

What we need is both fidelity to the givenness of our own religion, as well as respect for other faiths.

Respect can be accorded by recognising that each has provided a spiritual path for millions of people, and all teach the values of compassion and forgiveness. There is no contemporary religion in the world which would dispute the injunction to love God (according to their understanding) and to love our fellow men and women as ourselves.

WHAT'S THE PROBLEM?

As we look around at the world - both the world outside us and the world within us, we may find ourselves confronting not one problem but two: the problem of sin and the puzzle of good and evil.

THE PROBLEM OF SIN

Does it Mean Anything?

When Calvin Coolidge, President of the United States 1923-1929, returned from church one Sunday morning, his wife asked him what the minister had preached about.

"*Sin*", the President said briefly.

"*What did he say?*"

"*He were agin it,*" was the laconic reply.

'Sin' is a slippery word, which gives colour to statements but not content. If you google quotes on sin, it comes up with things like:

"There ain't no sin and there ain't no virtue. There's just stuff people do." - John Steinbeck, the Grapes of Wrath

"Sin, young man, is when you treat people like things. Including yourself. That's what sin is." (Terry Pratchett, Carpe Jugulum)

"The only sin is the sin of being born" (Samuel Beckett)

In March 2023 I asked three young women in West London what the word conveyed to them. Here are their replies;

"*It's a very very general word about doing something wrong.*"

"*It's used by Christians and Muslims.*"

"*I never use it.*"

Sin and the Church

However, the Church talks a lot about sin. The result is some pretty bad news. Here is what one of the most popular saints, St Francis of Assisi, said:

"We should all realise that no matter where or how a man dies, if he is in the state of mortal sin and does not repent, when he could have done so and did not, the Devil tears his soul from his body with such anguish and distress that only a person who has experienced it can appreciate it."

A key component of sin is disobedience to the commandments of God. But this is tricky. Today's world believe that there are no universal stories and no universal rules. Even good church-going Christians don't take seriously commands they don't like, not working on a Sunday, the Christian sabbath (Exodus 20.8-11); or giving away all one's possessions. (Luke 14.33)

In his short theological explosive bomb 'Honest to God' (1963) Bishop John Robinson denied any final authority to rules or laws, including those written in the Bible. Everything had to be judged in terms of the situation, so-called situation ethics:

"Nothing can of itself always be labelled as 'wrong'... This 'new morality' is, of course, none other than the old morality, just as the new commandment is the old, yet ever fresh, commandment of love. It is what St Augustine dared to say with his 'dilige et quod vis fac', 'Love, and what you will, do.'... Whatever the pointers of the law to the demands of love, there can for the Christian be no 'packaged' moral judgements – for persons are more important than 'standards.'"

What can replace rules as a definition of sin? Great theologians like St Augustine and Martin Luther used the expression *'the heart curved in on itself,'* This tells me that we are all travelling in a spiral, in one of two directions, either moving outward towards greater openness to God and others, or moving in ever-decreasing circles to the point of non-existence.

Sin is a portmanteau word used to cover many words in the Bible. One thesaurus gives sixty one words as English alternatives to 'sinfulness'. The most common Hebrew word is 'khata' meaning to go astray or to miss the mark. The most common Greek word in the New Testament is 'hamartia' which means the same but is used in the Bible as a comprehensive expression of everything against God. When I take a service as an Anglican priest, I always use the words 'failure and rebellion' instead of 'sin'. It makes more sense to me.

The Snake and the Apple

From the beginning of the Church, Christians believed that sin originated in the act of disobedience when Adam and Eve ate some fruit from the tree of the knowledge of good and evil, (not necessarily an apple). As a result they were expelled from the Garden of Eden and had to cope with weeds and painful childbirth. Fundamentalist Christians believe that this is actual history.

I was leading a Bible discussion on Genesis 3 in my vicarage in Hackbridge, doing the normal mealy-mouthed vicar thing, *"Of course no one is sure whether this actually happened or not,"* when my six year old step-son piped up, *"Oh that's easy. It's a parable."* And of course he was right.

Michael Ramsey, when he was Archbishop of Canterbury, visited the USA while there was a big dispute within the Episcopal Church about original sin. As soon as he set foot on the tarmac of JFK airport, a journalist rushed up with the question,
"Archbishop, do you believe in original sin?"
He replied,
"Believe in it? I've seen it."

A neat reply. But only useful if we drill down to actual attitudes and behaviours which can stand in the way of human flourishing.

The Seven Deadly Sins

Round about 2005. The Sun newspaper switched its support away from New Labour with a stinging issue headlined 'BLAIR'S 7 DEADLY SINS'.

On an inside page it helpfully told us that the famous list of sins was created by a 4th century monk Evagrius of Pontus (345-399), who started as a successful cleric in the imperial court of Constantinople and ended as an ascetic monk in the Egyptian desert.

He reduced the number of sins recognised by the monks of Egypt from nine to eight, and two hundred years later Pope Gregory the Great reduced them to seven. Here they are:

- Pride (vainglory, vanity)
- Greed
- Lust (fornication)
- Envy

- Gluttony
- Wrath (anger/hatred)
- Sloth

A sin that got dropped was melancholy/despair/ being apathetic.

They are still a useful checklist to work out how we are doing in our daily life and relationships. Whether avoiding them is the pathway to eternal bliss is beyond my pay grade.

Wisdom from the East

The Eastern religions, Hinduism, Buddhism etc., see the human predicament differently. For them the two great stumbling blocks are desire and wrath. As the Bhagavad Gita says,

'It is greedy desire and wrath, born of passion, the great evil, the sum of destruction: this is the enemy of the soul... Be a warrior and kill desire, the powerful enemy of the soul.' (3.37, 43)

The oldest Buddhist writing, the Dhammapada, has this inspiring verse:

'Hate is not conquered by hate. Hate is conquered by love. This is a law eternal.' (1.5)

Gen Z

Gen Z, generation Z, also called iGen, are those who have been born after 1995. They have no knowledge of a world without the internet. This shapes a radically different view of morality from that of previous generations.

The following quotation is taken from 'iGen' by Jean M Twenge (2017). It is written from the American situation, but is readily applicable to the western world in general.

"In a society where young people hear, 'If it feels good, do it' and 'Believe in yourself', religion seems almost counter-cultural." (P. 138)

"iGen'ers are just less willing to label anything as 'wrong' - it's all up to the individual." (p. 205)

Tolerance

A crucial value is tolerance. Kacey Musgrave, 28, a country singer, said *"I believe that people should do what they want with their own bodies."* The vast majority of iGen'ers see no reason why two people of the same sex should not marry and are supportive of transgender rights people. But anyone who asserts something different can face a 'cancel culture', where social media is used to deny a platform for anyone who goes against the prevailing opinion.

Emotional safety

A key value for iGen'ers is safety. Not just from physical harm but also from emotional harm or even emotional discomfort. In March 2016 someone had written 'Trump 2016' in chalk on the pavement at Emory University.

"Some students said the messages made them feel unsafe, and protesters shouted at the college administrators, 'You are not listening! Come speak to us, we are in pain!'" Two out of three SDSU students agreed that *"If negative racial incidents occur on a college campus, the president of the university needs to apologise even if he/she did not take part in the incidents."*

A consequence has been increasing restriction on free speech. Three out of four college students agreed with the statement, *"If many students disagree with the views of someone who has been invited to speak on campus, the students should create a 'safe space' to come to during the speech."* A direct outcome of the stress on emotional safety is the habit of 'disinviting' speakers whose views some students find upsetting. In 2015 over 40% of new American students thought that extremist speakers should be banned. Actual disinvitations have included former Secretary of State, Condoleeza Rice, and the managing director of the International Monetary Fund, Christine Lagarde.

Sex and relationships

Here are some phrases about relationships and sex:

'At the end of the day your 20s are the years where you do you. Be selfish, have fun and explore the world.'
'You don't need someone else to make you happy – you should make yourself happy.'
By 2014 more 18 to 34 year olds were living with their parents than with a spouse or romantic partner.

The ideal sexual experience is to be emotionless, and drunk. One college website offered advice on 'How to Avoid Catching Feelings':
"Go into it with the attitude that you're not going to develop feelings towards this person. Don't tell them your life story. Don't cuddle.
For the love of God this is a must.... If needed make a barrier of pillows between you. Hey, desperate times call for desperate measures."

The normalisation of pornography has actually contributed to less sex. One 17 year old who first saw porn when he was nine said, *"Pornography, especially on the internet, has desensitised teens into not enjoying or wanting sex or intimacy."* (p. 212iGen). This is borne out by statistics on teenage pregnancy.

Phrases that have triple or quadrupled in books between 1970 and 2008 are: *'Don't need anyone.' 'Never compromise.' 'I love me.'* (p.214-215)

A Conclusion

The history of sin has moved through several stages:
- from implicit belief in the reliability of the Bible in laying down rules for living as interpreted by the Church;
- to widespread literacy and common ownership of the Bible through the invention of printing, and the setting-up of the Ten Commandments as normative for all Christians;
- to a wider debate on the truth of Christianity and the Bible and its replacement by a natural as opposed to a supernatural basis for morality;
- to the current internet-formed generation where all that counts is personal authenticity.

Does the idea enshrined in 'sin' only make sense within the framework of an active faith in God?

WHAT'S OUR PROBLEM?
THE PUZZLE OF GOOD AND EVIL

THE WISE AND THE WICKED

The Bible is quite clear that there are two ways to live your life, the way of wisdom and the way of wickedness. The books of Psalms and Proverbs in the Old Testament, (or in Jesus' words) the Law and the Prophets, make this plain:

> 'The Lord watches over the way of the righteous
> But the way of the wicked will perish.' (Psalm 1.6)
> 'The righteousness of the blameless keeps their ways straight,
> but the wicked fall by their own wickedness.' (Proverbs 11.5)

The problem is that life is not so simple. I remember how shocked I was at the beginning of the film 'Untergang/Downfall', about the last days of Hitler. It started in 1943 with Hitler interviewing some girls for the job of his secretarial assistant. He was genuinely charming and kind.

Himmler was the head of the Nazi SS, ran the German concentration camps and was chief architect of the 'Final Solution' which killed six million Jews as well as three million Poles, half a million gypsies, homosexuals and others. Yet he wrote affectionate letters home to his wife and daughter, (as well as to his mistress and her children), in one of which he wrote, *"We have to be bad so our children can be good."* How strange to hold such contrary opinions in one's own head.

In the fourth volume of G K Chesterton's Father Brown stories, the priest tells how he was able to solve all those mysterious murders:

"You see, I had murdered them all myself... I had planned out each of the crimes very carefully. I had thought out exactly how a thing like that could be done, and in what style or state of mind a man could really do it. And when I was quite sure that I felt exactly like the murderer myself, of course I knew who it was."

The journalist Andrew Brown wrote in the Church Times in 2023, *"Original sin seems to me the one entirely realistic Christian doctrine, and a thing anyone can verify from their own experience. Perhaps this is a matter of temperament; perhaps it is the natural consequence of years spent studying church politics. But I doubt these explanations. Once you make allowance for the non-existence of Adam and the non-occurrence of the fall, the fact of original sin is undeniable."*

OUR BEASTLY INHERITANCE

Though the story of the Fall in Genesis is not historical, in my opinion, it is nevertheless a fact that original sin comes from our past.

Charles Darwin's 'The Origin of the Species' was a violent shock to our great-great-grandparents' view of themselves. Suddenly we were no longer 'the crown of all creation' (to quote the Church of England's 2000 liturgy), but part of the animal kingdom. In fact, in 1990 Pope John Paul II reversed a century of Catholic teaching when he said, *"the animals possess a soul and men must love and feel solidarity with our smaller brethren.... They are the fruit of the creative action of the Holy Spirit and merit respect... and they are as near to God as (humans) are."*

If, because of loss of faith, we could not comfort ourselves with the notion that, unlike animals, we had immortal souls, we could at least differentiate ourselves from the beasts by asserting that we are the only species intelligent enough to use tools. But in 1960 Jane Goodall started her observation of chimpanzees at Gombe, Tanzania. She witnessed acts of compassion, caring and peace-making. She also reported one chimpanzee using grass stems to get termites out of a termite mound. A scientific uproar ensued. 'Man the Toolmaker' was no longer unique.

Sadly, nor was 'Man the Violent'. From 1974 to 1977 Jane witnessed a gruesome war between the main chimpanzee community and a smaller one that had moved away. Unprovoked and vicious attacks by males and females including cannibalism took place until the smaller community had been exterminated.

'So here we are, the human ape, half sinner, half saint, with two opposing tendencies inherited from our ancient past pulling us now towards violence, now toward compassion and love.'
(Goodall - Reason for Hope p. 143)

Our Brain

- In the 1960's the American neuroscientist Paul D. MacLean publicised the triune brain theory. He proposed that there were three brains within our human brain:

- The primal or reptilian brain, centred in the basal ganglia, is devoted to the four 'Fs' - fighting, fleeing, freezing and f......g. This actually predates the evolution of reptiles and may have started developing 500 million years ago;

- The ancient mammalian brain or the limbic system, including the amygdala and hippocampus, is in the centre of the brain and deal with emotions, behaviour and long-term memory;

- The neo-cortex - six layers of neurones, found only in mammals. Human beings have a much larger percentage of the brain as neo-cortex, twice the proportion of that of chimpanzees. It is assumed that the neo-cortex increased in response to pressures for greater cooperation and competition among our early ancestors. With the increase in size of this latest part of the brain, there was greater voluntary inhibitory control of social behaviours resulting in increased social harmony. It also is the instrument for conceptual thought. It is because of our neo-cortex that I am writing this book and you are reading it.

In her book 'The Secret Dowry of Eve, Women's Role in the Development of Consciousness,' Glynda-Lee Hoffmann distinguishes the **prefrontal cortex** as uniquely different from the rest of the neocortex. The prefrontal cortex, as with its agenda of integration, is the part of the brain that can get the other parts to work together for the good of the individual. Hoffmann claims that in many humans the reptilian cortex, (agenda: territory and reproduction; in humans that translates to power and sex), is out of control, and the amygdala stokes the fear that leads to more bad behaviour. The prefrontal cortex, she believes, is the key to our future if we can harness its power. However, our neo-cortex – the most human part of ourselves, is not the prime determinant of our behaviour.

Our Inner Chimp

In 2012 Stephen Peters, an academic psychiatrist working in elite sports, wrote a popular psychology book, 'The Chimp Paradox'. He writes that our brain can be thought of as being comprised of three elements, the human brain (basically the neo-cortex), the chimp brain (centred on the limbic system), and the computer brain (centred in the parietal lobe).

The human brain is our thinking brain, who we are as persons. This is the same between men and women, though it seems that female brains are by and large more skilled at language, male brains at maths and spatial awareness.

The chimp brain is our instinctual brain, using emotion to react to the threats it perceives coming for outside. It works about five time as fast as the human brain. The most important thing about the chimp brain is that its habitual state is one of anxiety.

The computer brain carries out all the things we do automatically – breathing, making coffee, riding a bike – carries automatic programmes and acts as our reference library. It works about four times faster than the chimp brain, i.e. twenty time faster than the human brain.

OUR INSTINCTUAL DRIVES

Homo sapiens has been around for about 300,000 years. 95% of that time we were hunter-gatherers. Hard-wired into our 'chimp' brains are the ways we coped with a dangerous environment for thousands of years. Our survival as a species depended on three attitudes: follow the leader; my country, right or wrong; and there is nothing like a dame.

Follow the leader

Imagine you are part of a group of hunters hoping to kill a mammoth and not get killed by a sabre-tooth tiger. It's an anxious-making situation and the group needs to act in concert or each member will be picked of one by one. So there is a leader, probably the strongest in the group. Survival depends on doing what he says. There is little room for independent thought.

Scroll forwards several thousand years. In Germany Hitler proclaims that "He who would save a people can only think heroically". People submerge their doubts and enthusiastically follow his lead – or else they keep silent. Putin's popular approval rate in Russia is over 75% (as at April 2023). It is the patriotic, the honourable thing to do to 'follow the leader'. So ordinary people get seduced into becoming killers and torturers by regimes like Hitler and the Gestapo, Pinochet's regime in Chile, the Argentina junta and the Russian FSB today. The alternative is to use our human brain, our neo-cortex, to think for ourselves – but that could well be dangerous.

My country right or wrong

Each kinship group of our hunter ancestors would have had their territory, as the great apes do today. Survival depended on defending it against the depredations of neighbours, particularly if they were of a slightly different species. If the numbers of our group became too many for our existing territory, or we thought that was happening, then survival depended on taking over the territory of our neighbours. Genocide was the natural result, whether the extermination of our Neanderthal cousins or the wiping out of the Canaanites. The policy of the Assyrian empire of merely relocating a population to a different part of the empire was a dramatic improvement in human behaviour.

An example of how easy it is to make humans commit genocide is seen in Rwanda. Between January 1993 and March 1994 half a million machetes were imported into the country. In August

1993 a new radio station came on the air, Radio-Television Libre des Milles Collines (RTLM). It started by playing Congolese dance music almost non-stop and became very popular. At the start of 1994 it started saying that the country faced an internal threat. Tutsis were regularly referred to as cockroaches. Children also became a target: "A cockroach cannot give birth to a butterfly." On 6th April 1994 the President was killed by a rocket attack on his airplane. Instantly the genocide plans were put into effect. "Do your work. Clean your neighbourhood of brush. Cut the tall trees (i.e. Tutsis)." Between 7th April and 15th July between 500,000 and 660,000 Tutsis were killed, many by their neighbours and fellow-villagers.

There is nothing like a dame

Human beings are unusual. We are part of that 5% of mammalian species which are largely monogamous. Our nearest relatives who are monogamous are marmosets and tamarins; certainly not chimpanzees. And we are almost the only one to have no mating season. So presumably in our hunter-gatherer days, any male finding a female alone would attempt to impregnate her, as his contribution to the survival of the species.

However, because human children take so long to reach maturity, it was also essential to have a parental drive, giving long-term protection and care to the female and her offspring.

Anything that broke that bond would provoke a violent reaction:

He who commits adultery has no sense;
he who does it destroys himself.
For jealousy arouses a husband's fury,
and he shows no restraint when he takes revenge.

*He will accept no compensation,
and refuses a bribe no matter how great.*
   (Proverbs 6.32, 34-35)

Once again, our two parts of the brain have different agendas.

What's the point of it all?

In his remarkable book 'The Devils of Loudun' (1952), Aldous Huxley reflected on the discreditable story of the worldly parish priest, Urbain Grandier, and his destruction by means of the apparent demonic possession of the nuns of the town. Yet throughout he gave the most life-affirming reflections. In chapter three he discussed the human urge of self-transcendence, to go beyond our 'sweating selves'.
'Self-transcendence is by no means invariably upwards. Indeed, in most cases, it is an escape either downwards into a state below that of personality, or else horizontally into something wider than the ego, but not higher, not essentially other.

'We are forever trying to mitigate the effects of the collective Fall into insulated selfhood by another, strictly private, fall into animality and mental derangement, or by some more or less creditable self-dispersion into art or science, into politics, a hobby or a job. Needless to say, these substitutes for upward self-transcendence, these escapes into the subhuman or merely human surrogates for Grace, are unsatisfactory at the best and, at the worst, disastrous.

'The only liberating self-transcendence is through selflessness and docility to inspiration (in other words union with the Son and the Holy Spirit) into the consciousness of that union with the Father in which, without knowing it, we have always lived.
(Chapter III.iii)

SEX AND SOCIETY

RADICAL VIEWS ON MARRIAGE

In 1848 Karl Marx and Frederick Engels published a small explosive book called 'The Communist Manifesto.' It was a stringent attack on the bourgeois society of the time. The key concept was that the way that different societies functioned was entirely dependent on their economic and technological foundations. *"In one word, man's* (it was 1848) *consciousness changes with every change of his material existence, in his social relations and in his social life."* (p. 51) The family is not spared.

"On what foundations is the present family, the bourgeois family, based? On capital, upon private gain… (We find) *its complement in the practical absence of family among the proletariat, and in public prostitution…".* (p. 28)

Political anarchism developed at the same time, promoted especially by Pierre-Joseph Proudhon (1809-1865) and Mikhail Bakunin (1814-1876). They advocated the replacement of the state with stateless societies and voluntary free associations. In the early twentieth century a key concept was free love, with a new emphasis on polyamory, relationship anarchy and queer anarchism.

A CHANGING SOCIETY

Marx was right when he linked social relations to economic and technological forces. We have been in the middle of just such a revolution for three hundred years.

In 1700 most production took place in the home. In Coventry you can see the very large windows on the first floor of working class homes, to allow families to make ribbons for sale to middlemen. The factory system from 1800 enabled much higher and cheaper rates of production, creating a new proletarian class who worked very long hours outside the home, which included women and children. The Factory Acts of 1833, 1844 and 1847 eventually enforced a ten hour day for all workers in 1847.

The home was still central to consumption. In my research for a history of the parish of Hackbridge and Beddington Corner in Surrey, it was clear that a working man could not survive on his own. If his wife died, her place was immediately taken by her sister or other family relation. Then there were no white goods (washing machine etc.), and all food had to be prepared from scratch. Then with the abolition of Resale Price Maintenance in 1964, small family shops gave way to large supermarkets, and previous household tasks were increasingly outsourced to industrial capitalism.

Whereas the home in 1700 had been a joint enterprise of both production and consumption, by 1970, its only remaining societal function was the raising of children. In 1870 Foster's Education Act made schooling the province of the state.

Since men and women are equally competent in most employment tasks, once legislation such as the Employment Protection Act 1975 was passed, there was no barrier against women competing equally in the marketplace.

We could call it the de-sexing of society. Who are the beneficiaries? Clearly women in the developed world. But also, because of a larger pool of possible employees, shareholders.

CHANGING MEDICAL TECHNOLOGIES
Three monumental medical developments overturned millennia of human sexual history.

1   The Pill. The introduction of the first birth control pill in 1960 broke the implicit link between sex and conception. In the 1970s the morning-after pill was developed.

2   IVF or in vitro fertilisation (test tube baby). The first successful birth following IVF treatment was of Louise Brown in 1978. It is used by couples wishing to conceive but who have been unable to. It is also used by lesbian couples.

3   Surrogacy. Surrogacy is where a woman lends her womb to a couple, straight or gay, who want to have a child but cannot. Major tech companies in California, offer employees half the cost of surrogate fees so their careers are not impacted.

CHANGING LAWS
1. Divorce. Prior to 1867 the only way to get divorced in England and Wales was by annulment in the Ecclesiastical Courts or by a private members bill in Parliament, both forbiddingly expensive. In the 1930s the grounds for divorce were broadened to include adultery by either party, as well as cruelty, desertion and insanity. In 2020 the only grounds for divorce became if either party maintained that the marriage had irretrievably broken down.

2. Homosexuality. For 2,000 years the Church preached that homosexuality was immoral, but it was not illegal until 1533 when Parliament passed the Buggery Act. Homosexuality was only decriminalised in 1967 by the Sexual Offences Act, with the strong support of Michael Ramsey, Archbishop of

Canterbury. Since 2000 LGBT rights have been increasingly strengthened. In 2005 same-sex couples were able to enter into civil partnerships with the right to adopt children. Same-sex marriage was legalised in 2014. In a 2019 poll, 86% of the UK agreed that homosexuality should be accepted by society. In the 2021 census 3.2% of people in England and Wales identified themselves as lesbian, gay, bisexual or other and 262,000 as trans-gender; but this is probably an under-reporting. YouGov estimates the real figure to be 5-7%.

SEX - A LONG STORY

Sex has been around a very long time. Some two billion years ago simple organisms started reproducing through the amalgamation of differing DNAs instead of simply through cloning. Around 500 million years ago early Cambrian fish engaged in external fertilisation – male fish sent sperm into a cloudy mass of ova. Around 235 million years ago our ancient, rather tiny, ancestors developed breasts/mammaries with which to feed their young – hence 'mammal'. Between 125 and 60 million years ago, mammalian external penises made their appearance along with clitorises. Since then external stimulation for self-pleasure has characterised many species, from lions to porcupines.

Homosexuality has been around for some time. In 1911 the Antarctic explorer George Murray Levick reported on his observation of homosexual behaviour in Adelie penguins. His 'depraved' report was judged too scandalous to be released.

About 10 million years ago mammals started giving live birth, which necessitated a much longer period of caring and protecting the young. Parental care was born.

Our closest relatives in terms of DNA are the primates, i.e. gorillas, orang-utans, bonobos and chimpanzees, with DNAs of between 96 to 98.7% similarity. But there are very wide differences in sexual structures and practices. 'New World' monkeys, such as titi monkeys, are monogamous. 'Old World' monkeys such as baboons and chimpanzees have sex with as many females that they can, with or without consent. It is the main marker of social dominance in the group. Practices include polygyny, polyandry, polygamy (multiple women, multiple men, multiple anyone) with sexual violence thrown in. Infanticide and rape of juveniles by males is common. Definitely not the Garden of Eden.

THE BEGINNING OF LOVE

Finally, 1.9 million years ago, along come Adam and Eve, or more prosaically Homo Erectus. At last a primate/human species that not merely walks around on two legs, but practises monogamy! And invents fatherhood. This new type of savannah-dweller with a bigger than normal brain and so a bigger than normal head made childbirth difficult and painful, and because of the length of time before a human child could fend for itself in the wild, it needed parents to look after it for years. Feelings of security and dependence grew into love, encouraged by sexual consummation which probably started to take fifteen minutes, a far cry from the seven seconds for our chimpanzee cousins. Millennia of poetry bear witness to our human devotion to love. As the 'Song of Songs 1.14-15 has it:

She   *My beloved is to me a cluster of henna blossoms in the vineyards of En-gedi.*

He   *Ah, you are beautiful, my love;*
ah, you are beautiful;
your eyes are doves.

THE FLY IN THE OINTMENT

Sadly, as Alcoholics Anonymous found out, a new location, occupation or relationship does not make our past selves disappear. Wherever we go, we take them with us. And that is what happened to Homo Erectus, Home Sapiens, and you and me. The male-male aggression which marks out primate competition for mates is still a daily occurrence. The male-female sexual violence, seen particularly in chimpanzees, is just as present and toxic in our own societies. There is even some approval in the Bible, as in Judges 21, or in classical literature, as in the rape of the Sabine Women. 'Playing away' is the stuff of films, songs and novels. And when not acted out they can still be present in fantasies. As C S Lewis says (as the senior devil Screwtape) in the Screwtape Letters, *"You will find, if you look carefully into any human heart, that he is haunted by at least two imaginary women - a terrestrial and an infernal Venus. There is one type... readily mixed with charity...There is another type which he desires brutally, and desires to desire brutally..."* (Letter XX)

LOVE ON THE FARM

About 12,000 years ago humans changed from being hunter-gatherers living in small kinship groups to agricultural workers. The steady availability of food brought about a large increase in of population, the creation of villages and eventually small city states.

The farm workers/peasants were monogamous, but the heads of the hierarchies usually had multiple women in their households, a mix of wives and concubines. Here is a tally from the early Hebrew Scriptures:

Abraham	1 wife	1 concubine
Jacob	2 wives	2 concubines
David	8 wives	
Solomon	700 wives	300 concubines

There is a touching account in 1 Samuel 1.8 of an infertile wife, Hannah, who was unable to provide her husband with a child, unlike the other wife, Peninah. Therefore Hannah wept and would not eat. Her husband Elkanah said to her, *"Hannah, why do you weep? Why do you not eat? Why is your heart sad? Am I not more to you than ten sons?"*

SOCIETY'S RESPONSES

Every society tries to keep a workable balance on the scales between good behaviour and bad behaviour, whether through a light touch of a finger or the crashing down of a fist.

In the new agricultural society formal sexual relations became closely tied to land and property, with inheritance usually being through the male line. Marriage typically became a property contract, vigorously defended and when infringed, stringently punished. For example, in Islam sex outside marriage merits a flogging; adultery (sex with a married woman) is punishable by stoning both parties to death.

Around 5,500 years ago warfare created a soldier class, together with slavery of the defeated, including sexual slavery. Here is an example of Hebrew warfare under the leadership of Moses: *'Kill every male among the little ones, and kill every woman who has known a man by sleeping with him. But all the young girls who have not known a man by sleeping with him, keep alive for yourselves.'* (Numbers 31.17-18)

HOMOSEXUALITY

Ancient societies in Mesopotamia, Egypt, India and China seem to have had a relaxed attitude towards homosexuality. The Code of Hammurabi (c.1750 BCE) even makes provision for women to marry women. There is no evidence of homosexuality being frowned on in ancient Egypt or in China before 600 - 1200 CE. In India the Kama Sutra (c.400 BCE) details some homosexual practices, but around 200 BCE these became punishable by a fine and after the Muslim conquest in 1200 by imprisonment or death. In 19th century China homosexuality became punishable by death, as it still is today in Iran and Saudi Arabia. As a result of the Roman empire's adoption of Christianity, homosexuality became outlawed in Europe from late antiquity until the mid-twentieth century.

The key statement for the Church is by Paul in Romans 1. 26-27: *'For this reason (idolatry) God gave them up to degrading passions. Their women exchanged natural intercourse for unnatural, and in the same way also the men, giving up natural intercourse with women, were consumed with passion for one another. Men committed shameless acts with men and received in their own persons the due penalty for their error.'*

Paul is here rehearsing common accusations which Jews made against the surrounding Gentile culture. He probably had in mind two things, temple prostitution and the permitted infatuation of older men with young beautiful boys, as in Plato's Symposium. In Corinth *'the Temple of Aphrodite was so rich that it owned a thousand temple-slaves, courtesans, whom both men and women had dedicated to the goddess'.* (Strabo 63 BCE - 24 CE). In the Roman temple in Bulla Regia, modern-day Tunisia, a woman was buried with the inscription: *'Adulteress.*

Prostitute. Seized, because I fled from Bulla Regia.' She may have been a woman forced into sacred prostitution as a punishment for adultery. It had nothing to do with a committed same-sex couple exercising *'compassion, kindness, humility, meekness, and patience.'* (Colossians 3.12)

THE FUTURE IS THE PAST

For 250,000 years humans have amalgamated the procreation and nurturing of children within an economic and social framework of the family as the main producer of food and survival. Husband (which originally was another word for farmer) and wife were a joint enterprise. For example, making bread was a laborious process of sowing, reaping, grinding and baking. All that is now incorporated in the weekly shop in the nearest superstore or in one's online ordering. Are human relationships going back then to those of Homo Erectus, but in much greater comfort? (Unless of course one is living in a war zone). The provision of goods and services now legally takes no account of one's sex, gender, sexual preferences or lifestyle choices. How should the Church adapt to this new situation?

WHAT SHOULD THE CHURCH DO?

For over a thousand years the church had little to do with marriage. Early church fathers suggested that the parents and/or a priest might say a prayer of blessing over the couple, but that was an optional extra. In 866 the newly converted Emperor of the Bulgarians wrote to Pope Nicholas I asking about the essence of Christian marriage. The Pope replied, *"The consent of the partners is the essential element of Christian marriage."* (866). Three hundred years later Pope Alexander III (1100-1181) said that mutual consent makes the marriage, but it is perfected and made absolutely indissoluble through consummation. Around 1200 marriage was upgraded to a sacrament. The venue moved from a blessing held in the family home to a full service in the church sanctuary. Eventually the Catholic Church taught that, unless a marriage was conducted in church, it was not a marriage. This is not the Church of England's position, nor that of other Protestant churches; wherever and however the ceremony takes place, if it is legal, it is valid.

On the other hand, since the French Revolution most European and Latin American countries only recognise marriages that have been conducted in a civil ceremony. A religious ceremony is an optional add-on.

Perhaps the Church should stop trying to act as a sort of policeman and just accept what their state or society legislate as marriage. That would leave it free to fulfil its primary function of pastoral care and prayer.

WHAT SHOULD THE CHURCH SAY?

a) Faithfulness
For over 3,000 years Jews and Christians have tried to obey the commandment 'Do not commit adultery' (Exodus 20.14). And Jesus agreed with it: "From the beginning of creation, "God made them male and female. For this reason a man shall leave his father and mother and be joined to his wife and the two shall become one flesh. So they are no longer two, but one flesh. Therefore what God has joined together, let no one separate." (Mark 10.6-9)

However, in 1 Corinthians 7,12-15, Paul gives his personal opinion about divorce: *"To the rest I say — I and not the Lord — that if any believer has a wife who is an unbeliever, and she consents to live with him, he should not divorce her. And if any woman has a husband who is an unbeliever, and he consents to live with her, she should not divorce him... But if the unbelieving partner separates, let it be so; in such a case the brother or sister is not bound."*

In 1604 separation and remarriage was classified as bigamy and a felony. 1857 saw the first English law allowing divorce on the grounds of adultery. However the Church of England was firmly opposed to it and barred people who had divorced and remarried from receiving holy communion until 1978. In 2002 remarriage after divorce was finally allowed by General Synod.

b) Equality
"In the Lord woman is not independent of man or man independent of woman. For just as woman came from man, so man comes through woman; but all things come from God." (1 Corinthians 11.11-12)

Paul has a generally bad press concerning women, yet he is the one to emphasise the radical equality of men and women in the place where it counts most, in the bedroom.
"The husband should give to his wife her conjugal rights, and likewise the wife to her husband. 4For the wife does not have authority over her own body, but the husband does; likewise the husband does not have authority over his own body, but the wife does."
(1 Corinthians 7.3-4)

c) Kindness (1 Corinthians 13.4)
Paul describes what should characterise relationships in general. *"Clothe yourselves with compassion, kindness, humility, meekness, and patience. Bear with one another and, if anyone has a complaint against another, forgive each other; just as the Lord has forgiven you, so you also must forgive. Above all, clothe yourselves with love, which binds everything together in perfect harmony."* (Colossians 3.12-14)
"Love is kind." (1 Corinthians 13.4)

Perhaps the Church, instead laying down societal rules, should be preaching to all and sundry three gospel principles:

>Be faithful
>Show respect
>Be kind.

A HISTORY OF HELL

The Four Last Things

For over 1500 years the four weeks before Christmas were marked by the church as a time of penitence and were used to reflect on the Four Last Things namely, Death, Judgment, Heaven and Hell.

They are all now squeezed into the first Sunday of Advent, but it does not mean that their ghosts don't still haunt our nightmares.

Hell in the world's religions

Hell is everywhere: Christianity, Islam, Hinduism and Buddhism. Here are some descriptions:

Christianity:

"An ever-burning Gehenna will burn up the condemned... Souls with their bodies will be reserved in infinite tortures of suffering."
(St Cyprian, Letter to Demetrius 24, c.250 CE)

Islam:

"Those who deny (their Lord), for them will be cut out a garment of fire. Over their heads will be poured out boiling water. With it will be scalded what is within their bodies, as well as (their) skins."
(Qur'an 22:19-22).

Hinduism:

Naraka or Yamaloka are the two main names for hell where sinners are tormented after death. There are twenty eight separate hells for different sins. For instance, in some descriptions Vahnijawa is the hell of fiery flames reserved for potters, hunters and shepherds. The classic belief about re-incarnation is that one gets another shot at Nirvana when a new aeon comes around. That could mean waiting in hell for 4.32 billion years.

Buddhism.
Buddhist teaching is that one is born into a Naraka or hell, a freezing one or a fiery one, as a result of one's accumulated actions. One remains there for hundreds of millions of years.

Judaism.
Liberal Judaism has no teaching about the afterlife. The promise of the future relies on one's physical descendants and on the life of the community. Orthodox Judaism sees hell or Gehinnom as a waiting room for the purification of souls. Most rabbis teach that one stays there for no more than 12 months.

What do people think?
No one talks about hell or judgement nowadays.. But this does not mean that they have stopped being part of people's mental furniture entirely. I recently conducted a small experiment. I asked ten people chosen entirely at random on the underground and at a cafe near Piccadilly Circus if they thought that hell existed. Here are the results:
Yes: 1; Probably: 2; Possibly: 4; No: 3.

Unlike Elon Musk's ambition to fly to Mars, there is no way that anyone can go on a reconnaissance mission to hell and report back. The best we can do is look at how the idea of hell developed in the Judaeo-Christian tradition.

The Old Testament

For most of the 1200 years or more during which the Hebrew Scriptures arose, there was scarcely any idea of the afterlife. The best they could guess was a dark underworld where the dead had a grey shadowy existence, if you can call it an existence.

In death there is no remembrance of you;
in Sheol who can give you praise? (Psalm 6.5)
But there is a problem.
If God is just and if death is the end,
what about the manifest unfairness of life?
As for me, my feet had almost stumbled;
my steps had nearly slipped.
For I was envious of the arrogant;
I saw the prosperity of the wicked.
For they have no pain;
their bodies are sound and sleek.
Therefore pride is their necklace;
violence covers them like a garment.
Therefore the people turn and praise them,
and find no fault in them.
And they say, 'How can God know?
Is there knowledge in the Most High?'
(Psalm 73.2-6, 10)

The book of Job has 40 chapters discussing unmerited suffering, with only a couple of verses, Job 19.25-27, giving any sense of hope that might transcend death.

Martyrdom and Hope

By 325 BCE Alexander the Great had conquered the whole of the Middle East. By 312 BCE the former Persian empire was a Greek state ruled by a general Seleucus I who founded the Seleucid empire. A hundred and forty years later a new king Antiochus Epiphanes sacked the temple at Jerusalem and tried to eliminate the Jewish religion. This led to a revolt led by the Maccabee family. The sufferings of this time are mentioned in the New Testament Letter to the Hebrews in the chapter about faith:

"(Some) suffered mocking and flogging, and even chains and imprisonment. They were stoned to death, they were sawn in two, they were killed by the sword; they went about in skins of sheep and goats, destitute, persecuted, tormented — of whom the world was not worthy. They wandered in deserts and mountains, and in caves and holes in the ground."
(Hebrews 11.36-38)

It surely was not just for God to provide no future for his faithful witnesses and to ignore the crimes of their tormentors. Several writings came about which were treasured by the later Christian church such as 1 Enoch, 4 Ezra, the four books of Maccabees and the Psalms of Solomon. These were either written in Greek, or rapidly translated into Greek. Here are some examples:

2 and 4 Maccabees tells the story of seven brothers who were tortured to death for keeping the Jewish law. As they died two of them said to the king: *"You accursed wretch, you dismiss us from this present life, but the King of the universe will raise us up to an everlasting renewal of life, because we have died for his laws."*

"One cannot but choose to die at the hands of mortals and to cherish the hope God gives of being raised again by him. But for you there will be no resurrection to life!"
(2 Maccabees 7.9, 14, c.120 BCE)

"The destruction of the sinner is for ever, but those who fear the Lord will rise to everlasting life."
(Psalms of Solomon 3.11-12, c.100 BCE)

The fate of the wicked is seen as purely negative, they will not inherit life. 4 Maccabees, written about the same time, has a grimmer ending:

"Because of your bloodthirstiness towards us, you will deservedly undergo from the divine justice eternal torment by fire."
(4 Maccabees 9.8, c.100 BCE)

Jewish Opinions

What did Jews believe at the time of Jesus? It depended on who you asked. Josephus in his 'Antiquities of the Jews', c.100 CE, explained the ideas of the various groups.

Sadducees, the Temple hierarchy, did not believe in the persistence of souls after death, nor in penalties or rewards in the underworld.

Pharisees held a variety of beliefs about life after death, ranging from the resurrection of the dead a to some form of reincarnation, as well as the punishment of the wicked. What they did believe was that the faithfull would be re-embodied at the general resurection.

Essenes believed in the immortality of the soul.

So Judaism in Jesus' time embraced the three main options: annihilation, resurrection and immortality. But none of them necessarily included the concept of eternal torment for the wicked.

What was Jesus' position?

Jesus made his position about the afterlife crystal clear when the Sadducees tried to trip him up. *'When they rise from the dead, they neither marry nor are given in marriage, but are like angels in heaven.'* (Mark 12.25)

But this was not for everyone. *"Enter through the narrow gate; for the gate is wide and the road is easy that leads to destruction, and there are many who take it."*
(Matthew 7.13)

So what happens to those who don't qualify for resurrection to life?

"If your eye causes you to stumble, tear it out; it is better for you to enter the kingdom of God with one eye than to have two eyes and to be thrown into hell, where their worm never dies, and the fire is never quenched." (Mark 9.47)

This could just as well mean destruction rather than torment. The destiny of the wicked is Gehenna, the God-forsaken valley outside Jerusalem which in the past had been a place of child sacrifice. The unquenchable fire was an image of total destruction, clearly painful, but not of everlasting torture.

"Do not fear those who kill the body but cannot kill the soul; rather fear him who can destroy both soul and body in Gehenna."
(Matthew 10.28)

Paul saw wrath and anguish waiting for those who do not obey God, but these are strictly limited:

"Then comes the end, when (Christ) hands over the kingdom to God the Father, after he has destroyed every ruler and every authority and power. For he must reign until he has put all his enemies under his feet. The last enemy to be destroyed is death." (1 Corinthians 15.24-26)

The only description of fiery torment comes in Jesus' parable of the rich man and Lazarus in Luke 16.19-31. The point of the story is not to teach about the afterlife, but to give another warning about money. As Jesus said in the Beatitudes in Luke, *"Blessed are you poor, woe to you rich!"*
(Luke 6.2 0, 24)

(Note: In the traditional wording of the Apostles' Creed we say "he descended into hell". The word in Greek is not Gehenna, the place of punishment, but the neutral word Hades, the abode of the dead).

The invention of hell

According to early tradition Jesus at the cross said *"Father, forgive them, they do not know what they are doing."* When the first Christian martyr, Stephen, was stoned to death, his last words were, *"Lord, do not hold this sin against them."* (Luke 23.34, Acts 7.60).

From the second century on the martyrs were not so forgiving:

"You threaten me with a fire that burns for a season, and after a little while is quenched; but you are ignorant of the fire of everlasting punishment that is prepared for the wicked."
(Martyrdom of Polycarp, c.155 CE)

By 400 CE the Church had been fully accepted within the Roman Empire. A popular book of that time, 'The Apocalypse of Paul', gave detailed descriptions of heaven and hell. But now hell was full of Christians who had not come up to scratch. Christians who leave church services to engage in idle disputes would stand in a river of boiling fire up to their knees. Slanderers of other Christians would be in it up to their lips. Theologians who write bad theology are enclosed in a deep well with an unbearable stench.

The greatest western theologian, Augustine of Hippo (354-430) affirmed that the pains of hell would be proportional to the sins of which they were the punishment. This would come about at the general resurrection at the last judgement. *Until that time "souls will be kept in hidden places of rest and punishment depending on what each soul deserves."* (Enchiridion 109)

Lightening the load

It was a popular idea that the prayers of living Christians could help the dead even in the afterlife. Augustine said: *"This idea I do not contradict, because possibly it's true."* He taught that purifying of souls before the final judgment was possible for members of the church but not for those outside. 870 years later the Catholic Church finally accepted the idea:

"If they die truly repentant in charity before they have made satisfaction by worthy fruits of penance for (sins) committed and omitted, their souls are cleansed after death by purgatorical or purifying punishments. And to relieve punishments of this kind, the offerings of the living faithful are of advantage..."
(2nd Council of Lyons 1274)

At the Reformation, the Protestant churches abandoned the idea of purgatory: *"The Romish Doctrine concerning Purgatory, Pardons, Worshipping, and Adoration, as well of Images as of Reliques, and also invocation of Saints, is a fond thing vainly invented, and grounded upon no warranty of Scripture, but rather repugnant to the Word of God."* (Articles of Religion, Article XXII, 1562)

A more modern approach was taken by Josef Ratzinger, the future Pope Benedict XVI: *"Purgatory is not, as Tertullian thought, some kind of supra-worldly concentration camp where man is forced to undergo punishment in a more or less arbitrary fashion. Rather it is the inwardly necessary process of transformation in which a person becomes capable of Christ, capable of God, and thus capable of unity with the whole communion of saints."*
(Eschatology: Death and Eternal Life, 2007)

The roots of Hell

There is something in us that enjoys fear-fulfilment as much as wish-fulfilment. We all enjoy movies about *"big planes crashing, big ships sinking, big buildings burning"*, to quote the introduction to the film 'The Big Bus'. Just look at all of today's dystopian novels. It is not difficult to see why hell has held such a grip on human imagination. All the 'Doom' paintings in mediaeval churches as well the (wildly popular) sadistic paintings of Hieronymous Bosch bear witness to this.

The Swiss psychiatrist Carl Jung proposed that underneath our personal consciousness and subconsciousness there is an inherited collective unconscious – universal psychic structures that underlie all human experience and behaviour – with basic thought patterns such as mother, father, child, journey etc. To each 'good' archetype there is corresponding shadow archetype. It is through these archetypes that we unconsciously make sense of our lives. If one archetype is a place of blessedness (the Elysian Fields, heaven etc.), the corresponding shadow archetype is hell, Gehenna, the world after a nuclear catastrophe. It is no surprise that the idea of a place of eternal or quasi-eternal torment should be so long-lasting.

The end of Hell

For the Western world, hell died in the trenches of the First World War. Every year we still pause to remember all those who have died in war, particularly the 744,000 British soldiers who died 1914-1919 out of a total of 15-22 million. Every year we hear the words:

They shall grow not old, as we that are left grow old;
Age shall not weary them, nor the years condemn.
At the going down of the sun and in the morning
We will remember them.

It is impossible to suggest that a majority of those young men are now enduring eternal torments.

Simon wrote: *"The contribution (of Auschwitz) to the doctrine of hell is a clear-cut refusal to grant perpetuity horror and nothingness."*

For God to emulate the Nazis by creating effectively an eternal Auschwitz for the wicked was impossible. The only just end for those who created that hell on earth was annihilation.

Jesus seems to have agreed.

DEATH ETC.
THE PSYCHIC REALM

*From ghoulies and ghosties and long-leggedy beasties
and things that go bump in the night,
Good Lord deliver us.*
(Traditional Scottish prayer)

As we think about death and what if anything might come after, we need neither blind belief nor blind unbelief. We need to look at the evidence, even if the evidence is going to be anecdotal. And we need to start by considering various phenomena which happen here and now.

Ghosts

Ghosts are usually inert apparitions from the past. I knew a girl who went to look at an empty house which her family was thinking of buying. In one room she saw a woman playing the piano. She did not mention this, but was interested to note that when they moved in, her parents put the piano in the same position.

A lady I knew in Earls Court once saw a lady in an old-fashioned dress posting a letter in a post box in Barkston Gardens.

There is the famous ghost of the battle of Edgehill 1642, the first battle of the English Civil war. It is the only ghost recorded in the British Public Record Office under the heading *'A Great Wonder in Heaven, showing the late apparitions and prestigious Noises of the War and Battles, seen at Edgehill, near Kineton'*. The apparitions were noisy, terrifying and recognisable,, but after three months, when the dead had been given Christian burial, the sightings mostly stopped; though some are still witnessed around the anniversary of the battle, 23rd October.

These apparitions seem to be something like photographs of the past caught in time.

More active ghosts

A young couple I knew in Kingston-upon-Thames had an elderly male ghost in their Edwardian house. He was sometimes heard going up the stairs. When the wife was on her own, reading a book on the sofa, he would sit companionably next to her and cough occasionally. It did not faze them at all!

A more disturbing ghost was in a 1920s house. It once sheered off the base of a decorated glass tumbler while the woman was holding it. (I had it on my window shelf for a number of years). My guess is that it was annoyed by her smoking in the kitchen.

Poltergeists

When I came up for interview at Merton College Oxford, I read in a local paper of a mischievous ghost in a local Co-op store which kept moving packets of bicarbonate of soda through the air to the sugar counter. At one such occurrence, the cashier fainted, so the manager called in the local vicar to conduct an exorcism. At the conclusion of the service there was a blue flash from one of the neon lights and the disturbances ceased.

Poltergeist behaviour, I understand, is usually the product of excess mental energy from someone present, often a teenager.

My rule of thumb is that the more obvious the phenomenon, the less there is to worry about.

Spirit infestation

In Kingston two young women came to see me about a very unpleasant atmosphere in their flat, which they attributed to a room downstairs which had been painted black. I went with a church member and we had a simple service of Compline or Night Prayer, during which my colleague felt something unpleasant leave. As Dom Robert Petitpierre, a monk who was officially allowed to conduct exorcisms in London, said, *"It's quite simple really, you say your prayers and the Lord deals with it."*

Psychic Studies

Near South Kensington tube station is the College of Psychic Studies, formed in 1884. There you can get workshops and courses in mediumship, chakras, dowsing, tarot, shamanism, palmistry, astrology, witchcraft and psychic development.

Of course, the trouble is that you do not know what you are getting into. In his book 'The Devils of Loudun' Aldous Huxley has this warning:

"If they ignore the call to union with the Son through works, if they forget that the final end of human life is the liberating and transfiguring knowledge of the Father... there will be a mere merging with spirit, with every Tom, Dick and Harry of a psychic world, most of whose inhabitants are no nearer enlightenment than we are, while some may actually be more impenetrable to the Light than the most opaque of incarnate beings." (p.84)

Dawkins' view

Richard Dawkins, guru of the New Atheists, has a chapter in his excellent book 'Unweaving the Rainbow' called 'Hoodwink'd with Faery Fancy'. He is particularly scornful of the way television and newspapers take the authenticity of psychic practitioners for granted. His targets are astrology, faith healing, telepathy and reports of miracles like levitation. Even where reports are possible, as in alien visitors from space, the alternative explanations of fraud or illusion are more probable. He closes the chapter with this sweeping but undiscussed assertion:

"There are no (fairies but) also no devils, no hellfire, no wicked witches, no ghosts, no haunted houses, no demonic possession…" (p. 142)

'That's pretty dogmatic.'

DEATH ETC.
THE REALM OF LIGHT

To die, to sleep. To sleep, perchance to dream;
for in that sleep of death what dreams may come
must give us pause.

(Hamlet, Shakespeare)

Medical death

In 1981 50 states of the United States adopted the Uniform Determination of Death Act. This stated that *"an individual who has sustained either (1) irreversible cessation of circulatory and respiratory functions, or (2) irreversible cessation of all functions of the entire brain, including the brain stem, is dead."*

Is that the end of the story?

Death in Hinduism

The most ancient traditions of what happens after death come from India. Here is how the Encyclopedia Britannica describes the Hindu view of the process of death.

'The Hindu concept of the soul is central to an understanding of most Hindu practices related to death.

'Immediately after death, the soul is not clothed in a physical *body but in a vaporous thumb-sized structure ('llinga sarīra'). This is immediately seized by two servants of Yama, the god of death, who carry it to their master for a preliminary identity check. Afterward, the soul is promptly returned to the abode of the deceased, where it hovers around the doorstep.*

It is important that the cremation be completed by the time of the soul's return, to prevent it from re-entering the body.... (Various rituals are held to create a new body for the soul).... The soul of the deceased then leaves this world for its yearlong and perilous journey to Yama's kingdom. If the rituals had not been performed, the 'preta' (soul) could have become a malignant spirit, repeatedly turning up to frighten the living. For the deceased, things would have been worse: the 'preta' would have been left wandering. (A similar fate befalls the soul of a person who commits suicide.)

'After a year, the soul in its more substantial physical body, reaches Yama's seat of judgment, where it is sentenced to a strictly limited term in heaven or hell according to its deserts. This completed, it moves into another body, whose form depends on the individual's 'karma'. It could be a plant, a cockroach, a canine intestinal parasite, a mouse, or a human being.'

Spirit visible

So what really happens when we die? There are some clues.

In the 1920's Sir William Fletcher Bennett FRS wrote a book, published posthumously, called Death-Bed Visions. In it are the words of a church dean; while he and his wife were present at the deathbed of their son, they both noticed *'something rise as if it were from his face like a delicate veil or mist, and slowly pass away... We were deeply impressed and remarked, "How wonderful! Surely that must be the departure of his spirit."'*

In the book 'At Heaven's Door', a woman Stephanie, who had accompanied her husband to 'the other side' three days before he died, finally told his oncologist:

'He hesitated and then he got up, and he went over and closed his door. He came back and he sat down and he said, "I will never share this with anyone else, but I will tell you. When I was an intern, and I was doing my ER rotation, we lost someone one day. I actually saw their body rise, the form lift out of his body."'

Peter, a neighbour of mine, told me of his experience as a small boy of eight. He was eating grapes and happened to throw one on to the bars of an electric fire. He thought he had harmed it and seized one of the bars. It was painful, he thought he had given himself an electric shock and screamed inwardly. *"Suddenly I found himself in a rather quiet peaceful place. I remember the sense of looking down on this child in pain, and knowing it was me. I didn't feel any pain, and looked down in a rather detached way. When I came back to myself, I was not in pain, but I recall smelling the burning on my hand so I knew what had happened."*

The following story was found in a book of legal deeds and documents at a Rare Book Auctions, Lichfield in October 2024. The handwritten account comes with letters between two clergymen, one from Cresswell, Northumberland, the other from Malpas, Cheshire, together with the testimony of a servant.
(Evening Standard 17/10/24)

In the early hours of 29 March 1785 Francis Eid was in his young daughter's bedroom at Seighford Hall near Stafford. He experienced 'a puff of air' across his face and saw 'a sort of cloud or vapour', which took on the appearance and voice of his mother. At the time she was residing at Pit Place in Surrey. The apparition said: *"My child, be not grieved. I am dead but happy."* Two days later he received a letter informing him that his mother had passed away. The realisation caused him to 'faint away' at the shock.

Near death experiences (NDEs)

In 1975 the American psychiatrist Raymon A Moody published 'Life after Life' in which he coined the term 'near-death experience'. In it he told of those who were clinically dead for a short time and who had revived. They had had remarkably similar experiences: being out of one's body, the sensation of traveling through a tunnel, meeting dead relatives, and encountering a bright light. The book sold 14 million copies.

I have known three people with that experience. One was a lady in Beddington Corner who had gone through the windshield of her car. Another, in Kingston-upon-Thames, had been a soldier in the Second World War and was caught in a shell-burst. His first reaction to the comrade who saved his life was of irritation; being on the other side was much more pleasant. The third was crushed by a fork-lift truck, on grass, and experienced a long tunnel with a bright light.

A scientific approach

In June 2020 Scientific American published a sympathetic but sceptical article by Christof Koch entitled 'Tales of the Dying Brain', or 'What Near-Death Experiences Reveal about the Brain'.

Thousands of survivors of traumatic episodes tell of leaving their damaged bodies behind and encountering a realm beyond everyday existence. These experiences can lead to permanent transformation of their lives. Most memories fade over time, but NDEs continue to be recalled with unusual intensity.

A young Ernest Hemingway, badly injured by an exploding shell on a World War I battlefield, wrote in a letter home that *"dying is a very simple thing. I've looked at death, and really I know. If I should have died it would have been very easy for me. Quite the easiest thing I ever did."*

Though most NDEs are positive, some bring distress. Feelings can include loss of control, or sadness, of empty space or occasionally hell. A clinical social worker observed, *"All the people I know who have had negative spiritual experiences have become Bible-based Christians."* (Missouri Medicine Nov-Dec 2014)

The Scientific American article goes on: *"The underlying neurological sequence of events in a near-death experience is difficult to determine with any precision because of the dizzying variety of ways in which the brain can be damaged... Like a town that loses power one neighbourhood at a time, local regions of the brain go offline one after another.*

The mind ... does what it always does: it tells a story shaped by the person's experience, memory and cultural expectations."

And yet earlier in the article the author remarks that *"These experiences have been with us at all times and in all cultures."*

"Neurosurgeons are able to induce... ecstatic feelings by electrically stimulating parts of the cortex called the insula... This brute link between abnormal activity patterns... and subjective experience provides support for a biological, not spiritual origin. The same is likely to be true for NDEs."

Shared death experience (SDE)
But what if the brain is not damaged?

The following three stories are taken from 'At Heaven's Door', a collection of shared death experiences (SDEs) written in 2021 by William J Peters, an end-of-life therapist.

They are accounts of people, mostly women, who have consciously been with someone as they transitioned through death.

1. Cristina was a home health aide in Pittsburgh. When she was five, her mother had a brain tumour. Cristina and her mum became and remained incredibly close. In 2016 the mother suffered a stroke and never regained consciousness. She held her mum after they stopped the life support.

'The last thing I said to her was "Mommy, it's OK. I'm here. God's here." Right when I said that, that's when I felt light. I felt like the whole room was weightless and I was weightless... I saw her go towards this bright light.

I didn't see her face, but I knew it was her. It was the best feeling in the whole world. I have never been so happy in my life. The peace I felt was just incredible...'

She has been hesitant to talk about it. Her mother's doctor told her, *"It was probably just a reflex."*
(p53-56)

2. A more difficult story was told by Jeanne, who had worked in hospice care. In his late eighties her father, a matter-of-fact man,

after heart surgery had a frightening near-death experience. *"I thought I had died, it was all black ... and nobody was there."*

Jeanne's father went into a decline on Sunday when Jeanne was in New York, she booked a flight on Tuesday but he died on Monday night, just when Jeanne felt a strong urge to call him. On the early morning flight she finally had a moment to meditate.
"That's when I saw Dad. It was a young face, him as a young man. His face felt like it was right up close next to mine, and he was terrified." Startled, she opened her eyes… After going to the bathroom she closed her eyes again. *"There was nothing except blackness, and him and me, and the terror he was in. It seemed just like how he had described his NDE, except that I could see a point of light behind him. I could see it, but he couldn't.*

"I realised that he had to get to the light, but I just couldn't get him to turn around so he could see it…. I thought, 'Well, I'm his daughter, he's not listening to me, but if we had a little party here, they can help him.' "Jeanne began to concentrate on summoning a welcoming party. As she saw her father join the gathering and reorientate himself towards the light *"I put myself back in the picture, and I was walking with him and talking with him.*

He's now joyous, and I'm joyous that he's joyous…. Of course now the light's getting larger and larger, and we're walking as this love opens, and we connect. It didn't take long before we were at a round opening with lights streaming out of it… and there were people peering through. It was his aunt Bernice, his sister, his parents."
(p. 84-86)

3. Stephanie's husband was diagnosed with lung cancer in 1999. In the end he was admitted to a hospice room in the hospital and he slipped into a coma. Stephanie did not leave his side. Eventually Stephanie was so exhausted she put her head down.

In that moment it was as if *"we were no longer in that room. We were in that white light, incredibly bright light."* Neither she nor her husband were in their *'human shapes'* and she saw 'two other entities there.' *"There was no pain, no hurt.... It was like you understood the universe. It was peaceful."*

Her husband's shape turned to her along with the two other entities, and they communicated to her: *"You cannot continue on. You must go back." "I knew my husband would be okay. In that split second, I came back and I was in my body".*
Although her husband did not die for three more days, Stephanie believes that he had already passed on and gone on 'to a different dimension'.

Stephanie described her husband as being 'pure energy'. There was no form to him or the other entities, nothing that would identify then as male or female, young or old. *"He didn't look like a human being, and yet I knew that it was him."*
(p.96-98)

Note how this echoes St Paul's insight in 1 Corinthians 15:42-44: *"So it is with the resurrection of the dead. What is sown is perishable, what is raised is imperishable. It is sown in dishonour, it is raised in glory. It is sown in weakness, it is raised in power. It is sown a physical body, it is raised a spiritual body."*

So, was Jesus right when he said, *"When they rise from the dead, they ... are like angels in heaven"* ?

Communication

The only satisfactory example I have come across concerning contact between the dead and the living comes in C S Lewis' book 'A Grief Observed'. This is a series of notes that Lewis wrote to keep himself sane after his wife died. During his lifetime they were published under a pseudonym.

"I said several notebooks ago, that even if I got what seemed like an assurance of H's presence, I wouldn't believe it. Easier said than done. Even now, though, I won't treat anything of that sort as evidence. It's the quality of last night's experience - not what it proves but what it was - that makes it worth putting down. It was quite incredibly unemotional. Just the impression of her mind momentarily facing my own. Mind, not 'soul' as we tend to think of soul. Certainly the reverse of what is called 'soulful'. Much more like getting a telephone call or a wire from her about some practical arrangement. Not that there was any 'message' – just intelligence and attention. No sense of joy or sorrow. No love even, in our ordinary sense. No un-love. I had never in any mood imagined the dead as being so – well, so business-like. Yet there was an extreme and cheerful intimacy... One didn't need emotion.

The intimacy was complete – sharply bracing and restorative too – without it.... A society or common of pure intelligence would not be cold, drab and comfortless... It would, if I have had a glimpse, be – well, I'm almost scared at the adjectives I'd have to use. Brisk? cheerful? keen? alert? intense? wide-awake? Above all, solid. Utterly reliable. Firm. There is no nonsense about the dead."
(A Grief Observed p. 61-63)

An obituary

In January 2025 the Economist published the obituary of Peter Fenwick. He was a British neuropsychologist working at Kings College, Maudsley and John Radcliffe hospitals. His interest was piqued when one of his own patients reported a detailed near death experience. He collected and analysed over three hundred such experiences. These *'fortified his own growing belief in a consciousness that was universal, external and contained many levels of reality.'*

'His field of interest, controversial as it remained, filled him with joy and curiosity. Whatever was to come next, beyond the body, he knew it would be wonderful. He could hardly wait.' (Economist)

Envoi

Perhaps we should leave the last word with Shakespeare's Hamlet:

'There are more things in heaven and earth, Horatio, than are dreamt of in our philosophy.'

TRANSFORMATIONS

INTRODUCTION

It is a simple fact that all through Christian history people have experienced a spiritual change of heart, bringing a new vitality to their lives. Here is a famous example.

"In the evening I went very unwillingly to a society in Aldersgate Street, where one was reading Luther's preface to the Epistle to the Romans. About a quarter before nine, while he was describing the change which God works in the heart through faith in Christ, I felt my heart strangely warmed. I felt I did trust in Christ, Christ alone, for salvation; and an assurance was given me that He had taken away my sins, even mine, and saved me from the law of sin and death."
(From John Wesley's journal for 24th May 1738)

That strange and extremely personal momentary experience had momentous consequences. It transformed John Wesley from a serious and devout Anglican Christian and priest to a powerful evangelist whose preaching converted thousands of working people in Britain, founded the worldwide Methodist Church, and according to some historians, saved England from its own version of the French Revolution.

VARIETIES OF RELIGIOUS EXPERIENCE

In 1901 William James, Harvard Professor of Psychology and Philosophy, gave the Gifford Lectures on Natural Religion in Edinburgh. It was published the following year as 'The Varieties of Religious Experience - a Study In Human Nature'. It went through twenty reprints in just nine years. It is the most comprehensive and fascinating book with multitudes of individual personal experiences. As he says, *"Personal experience (is) the exclusive subject of our study."* (p. 379)
Note: all page numbers refers to this work.

He discusses everything with a professional and respectful attitude. Although he includes Catholic witnesses and those of other faiths, his own viewpoint is as a North American Protestant.

Here are his main headings:
- feelings of objective presence,
- once-born and twice-born people,
    - conversion,
    - saintliness,
    - mysticism.

1. Feelings of objective presence

All but one examples were very positive: *"We were on our sixth day of tramping and in good training ... All at once I experienced a feeling of being raised above myself, I felt the presence of God ... as if his goodness and his power were penetrating me altogether..."* (p. 68)

"I have on a number of occasions felt that I had enjoyed a period of intimate communion with the divine... What I felt on these occasions was a temporary loss of my own identity, accompanied by an illumination which revealed to me a deeper significance than I had been wont to attach to life." (p. 70)

2. Once-born and twice-born

Francis W Newman, writer and activist and brother of the Catholic convert John Henry Newman, wrote, *"God has two families of children on their earth, the once-born and the twice-born."* The once-born have an optimistic view of life. *"They see God, not as a strict Judge .. but as the animating Spirit of a beautiful and harmonious world...".* Their conversion will tend to be gradual, without notable crises, but no less valid for that.

Dramatic experiences of conversion tend to be encountered by those of an underlying pessimistic temperament. As an example of this temperament James quotes a letter originally written in French: *"I awoke morning after morning with a sense of the insecurity of life that I never knew before."* (He had spoken of his experiences working in an insane asylum). *"I remember wondering how other people could live, how I myself had ever lived, so unconscious of that pit of insecurity beneath the surface of life."* (p. 160-161)

3. Conversion

a) Luther
Martin Luther, the originator of the Protestant Reformation in the 16th century, is a classic instance of the conversion of the twice-born:

'Though I lived as a monk without reproach, I felt that I was a sinner before God with an extremely disturbed conscience... I did not love, yes, I hated the righteous God who punishes sinners... At last, by the mercy of God, meditating day and night, I gave heed to the context of the words namely, "In it the righteousness of God is revealed"... There I began to understand that the righteousness of God is that by which the righteous lives by a gift of God, namely by faith. ... Here I felt that I was altogether born again and had entered paradise itself through open gates.'
(Martin Luther, Preface to his collected works 1545)

b) The process of conversion

William James describes conversion as *'the process, gradual or sudden, by which a self, hitherto divided... becomes unified.'* (p. 189)

It typically brings about *'a firmness, stability and equilibrium succeeding a period of storm and stress and inconsistency'.* What happens is a *'process of unification'* whether from unbelief to belief or sometimes from religion to incredulity. In both cases James assumes that a period of *'subconscious incubation'* precedes the crisis. He writes of conversion as *'the striking and sudden unification of a discordant self.'* (p. 483)

E D Starbuck (1866-1947) was an American educational psychologist who pioneered the use of questionnaire surveys to study religion. He found that the effect of conversion brings with it *'a changed attitude towards life, which is fairly constant and permanent, although the feelings fluctuate.'* (p. 258)

The one essential to any act of conversion towards the spiritual life is an act of self-surrender. As Starbuck put it, *'The personal will must be given up.'* (p. 208) An example he quoted was, "I

simply said, 'Lord, I have done all I can; I leave the whole matter with Thee;' and immediately there came to me a great peace."
Carl Hilty (1833-1909) was a Swiss constitutional lawyer and theologian. In 1901 he published the book 'Glück' (Luck or Happiness). In it he wrote, *"the compensation for the loss of that sense of personal independence which we so unwillingly give up, is the disappearance of all fear from one's life and an inexplicable feeling of an inner security."* (p.275)

c) Two types of conversion
Starbuck described two main types of conversion, one being 'escape from sin'; the other being 'spiritual illumination'. The former tends to be associated with large meetings and powerful preachers, from John Wesley to Billy Graham. The latter seems to be the prime mode expected in the Alpha course and the Charismatic movement. Both can be life-changing.

d) Psychology and religion
Psychology and religion both admit that there are forces seemingly outside the conscious individual that bring redemption to his life... Psychology defines these forces as 'subconscious'... Christian theology.... insists that they are direct supernatural operations of the Deity."(p. 211)

Psychology cannot always help, according to the famous psychotherapist C G Jung. Working with an alcoholic Rowland H, Jung said, *"You have the mind of a chronic alcoholic. I have never seen one single case recover where the state of mind exists to the extent that it does in you... (But) once in a while alcoholics have had what are called vital spiritual experiences... I have been trying to produce some such emotional rearrangement within you... but I have never been successful with an alcoholic of your description."* (Alcoholics Anonymous p. 27)

e) An example

There are thousands, possibly millions of accounts to choose from. Here is the experience Sam Follett, an Anglican pastor currently serving at HTB Queen's Gate.

"My father was a vicar. I grew up in a Christian home but thankfully my parents did not pressure me to be a Christian, though I went to church with them and was familiar with it. When I was twelve, I went to an event for youth groups in St Albans. It was actually held in my father's church. There was some worship and a talk, which left the impression that God was interested in a personal relationship with us. Then we were asked to go off on our own with just a candle. I prayed in my head, 'If you're real and if you are actually interested in a relationship with me, please let me know.' And he did. I sensed a warmth which began in my heart and spread all over my body, bringing a sense of peace. I knew that I was loved. I had the conviction that you had to be different, that's what turning to Christ meant. Self-confidence and knowing that I was known replaced previous insecurity and feeling misunderstood. I had vision and purpose, and a desire to serve."

This happened when Sam was twelve. It is noteworthy how untheological, how personal the experience was, and how long-lasting its effects.

4. Saintliness

Saintliness, or sanctification, is the expected consequence of conversion. William James opens his chapter on saintliness by saying that *'the best fruits of religious experience are the best things that history has to show.'* (p. 259)

Of course, we will always be subject to the two basic imperatives of human nature, the urge to grab/get, and the impulse to give. That tension will be with us to the end of our lives. But the experience of conversion makes giving the prime value of our lives.

It is powerfully expressed in St Paul's letter to Christians in Galatia (c.55 CE):

"Live by the Spirit, I say, and do not gratify the desires of the flesh. (Paul basically means the ego). *For what the flesh desires is opposed to the Spirit, and what the Spirit desires is opposed to the flesh... Now the works of the flesh are obvious: fornication, impurity, licentiousness, idolatry, sorcery, enmities, strife, jealousy, anger, quarrels, dissensions, factions, envy, drunkenness, carousing, and things like these.... By contrast, the fruit of the Spirit is love, joy, peace, patience, kindness, generosity, faithfulness, gentleness, and self-control... If we live by the Spirit, let us also be guided by the Spirit."*
(Galatians 5.16-25 NRSV, edited)

5. Mysticism

a) Four marks
What are 'mystical states of consciousness'? William James talks about *'consciousness of illumination'* as being the essential property of them. (p. 408n). *'We feel them as reconciling, unifying states.'* (p. 416) He proposes four marks which can justify an experience as being mystical.

Ineffability. The person talking about such experiences may say that they defy expression. They are *'more like states of feeling than states of the intellect'.*

Noetic quality. To those that experience them they also seem to be states of knowledge.

Transiency. Such states cannot be sustained for long... Half an hour or at most an hour or two seems to be the limit beyond which they fade into the light of common day.

Passivity. Once the characteristic sort of consciousness has set in, the (person) feels as if his own will were in abeyance, and indeed sometimes as if he were grasped and held by a superior power.
(pp. 380-381)

b) Cosmic consciousness
Such experiences are instances of a sort of 'cosmic consciousness' which overtakes some people.

"An officer in our police force told me that many times when off duty, and on his way home in the evening, there comes to him such a vivid and vital realisation of his oneness with this Infinite Power, and this Spirit of Infinite Peace so takes hold of and so fills him, that it seems as if his feet could hardly keep to the pavement, so buoyant and so exhilarated does he become by reason of this inflowing tide." (p. 393)

"I had a long drive in a hansom to my lodging.... All at once, without warning of any kind, I found myself wrapped in flame-coloured cloud... There came upon me a sense of exultation, of immense joyousness... I saw that the universe is not composed of dead matter, but is, on the contrary, a living Presence... I saw

that all men are immortal,.. that all things work together for the good of each and all..."
(p. 399, quoting Bucke: 'Cosmic Consciousness')

c) Other religions
Similar experiences are encountered in other faiths.
The Hindu Swami Vivekananda (1863-1902) wrote, *"All the different steps in yoga are intended to bring us scientifically to the superconscious state or samadhi.."*

Buddhists have the special word 'dhyana' for higher stages of contemplation. These continue until one reaches *'the end of both idea and perception...'*

In Islam it is Sufism which expresses the mystical tradition. The 11th century (CE) Persian philosopher Al-Ghazzali wrote: *"The Science of the Sufis aims at detaching the heart from all that is not God, and at giving to it the sole occupation of the meditation of the divine being."* (p. 402)

d) What kind of truth?
Are such mystical states convincing evidence of a super-sensory realm? William James makes three points:

1 *"Mystical states ... usually are absolutely authoritative over the individuals to whom they come"*
2 *"Those who stand outside (have no duty) to accept the revelations uncritically."*
3 *"Non-mystical or rational consciousness, based upon the understanding and the senses alone, (are shown to be) only one kind of consciousness. (Mystical experiences) open out the possibility of other orders of truth."*
(p. 422-423)

SUMMING IT UP

What does this discussion about conversion and mystical experiences signify in today's world?

In May 2023 I met Sabine, a pastor in east London, at St Mellitus' College. We walked to Earls Court station talking about the questions that were in people's mind in the past like, *'Is is true?'* She commented that young people came into her church with one simple question, *'What's in it for me?'* This sounds merely selfish. But it actually expresses a quest for something personal, something that can change their lives. The message of conversion and mystical experience relates directly to this desire. Perhaps this is what will survive of the church after the current crisis.

CONCLUSION
CRISIS? WHAT CRISIS?

The Lobster

If you want to cook a live lobster, it's important not to throw it into boiling water. It will struggle desperately to escape. If you put it into a pan of cold water and slowly increase the heat, the lobster will go to sleep, stay stunned and die. Is this what is happening to the Church? The institutions continue to operate with somewhat reduced numbers, looking for any green shoots of growth that might indicate a more hopeful future. But the stats are against them.

The R factor

The number of people in the UK who identified themselves as Christian dropped to 46.2% in the 2021 census, a decline of 22% from 2011. This decline was partly mirrored in church attendance. Between 2011 and 2019 adult church attendance in the Church of England also declined from 851,000 in 2010 to 734,000 in 2019, a decline of 12.6%.

The problem is that this has been relentless. The same statistical tool which was used to determine the spread or otherwise of the Covid 19 virus can be used in respect of the Church. John Hayward, a mathematician of the University of South Wales, started a church growth modelling project back in 1995.

If the Reproduction Potential, 'R', is less than one, then losses outweigh conversions and the church eventually dies. If 'R' is greater than one, then conversions outweigh losses and the church grows. For many decades those churches founded before 1900 have had an 'R' of less than one and have been in steady decline. It is churches such as Elim, New Frontiers and Vineyard which have shown steady growth. To put this into perspective, the Church of England has a weekly attendance of about 700,000 compared to 50,000 for Elim churches.

Dr Hayward concludes:
"The Baptists and Brethren should last until the end of the century. Their decline is slow, and there is hope that they could return to growth if they make conversions their priority.

"The Church of England and Catholics should last until the second half of the century. However, they need to take urgent action now. Stemming losses is not enough. None of us can prevent ageing! Whatever their current denominational emphases, they should put all aside to encourage members to make new disciples who can replicate themselves. Praying for an outpouring of the Holy Spirit would not go amiss either.

"Sadly, the immediate future looks bleak for the Church in Wales, Church of Scotland, Episcopalians, and Methodists."

"One thing is clear: if things carry on as they are, the future of Christianity does not lie in the hands of the older denominations. These products of the Reformation and Puritan times have run their course. They have fulfilled God's purposes and are no longer part of his plan. The Church of England will cease to be a national church, and the Churches of Scotland and Wales will disappear by the middle of this century. Instead, God will work through the next cycle of denominations – Pentecostal and Evangelical ones, picking up the pieces left by the extinct historic churches."
('Growth, Decline and Extinction of UK Churches', John Hayward May 2022)

However this does not take into account the difference in absolute numbers. It is not beyond the bounds of possibility that after a period of decline, the historic churches could grow again from a smaller but more enthusiastic base.

Note: Even membership of the Church in the United States has declined, from 70% in 2000 to 47% in 2020.

The age factor
In 2019 people over 70 made up 33.5% of the worshipping population. In 2021 that figure was 36.4%. Even with the advance in medical science, it is clear that even greater conversions are needed if the churches are to grow rather than decline.

The Covid factor
The Covid pandemic of 2020 hit all institutions including the church really hard. The problem is that the churches have had a lower rate of recovery. *"Although weekly in-person attendances at services were up more than one third from 2020 levels, they remained almost one third lower than pre-pandemic levels."* (Church Times, December 2022). The Church Times also commented that whereas church attendances were down 30%, football matches numbers were only down 5%. However, recent figures indicate that the longer term effect of Covid has been to stablise church numbers in the US, France and Britain. GenZ men *"Are particularly keen on God."* The Economist 6/25

The Old Churches

Once denominations fall below a critical level, institution-wide support will cease to be practicable. Churches will have to sink or swim on their own. This will happen either through financial self-sufficiency by growth in numbers, or by retrenchment to smaller sustainable levels, such as through leadership by people in secular employment. In 2020 of the 10,550 priests in the Church of England, over 30% were in secular jobs (like St Paul). There were a further 7,210 retired clergy (grey power). The traditional model of a paid vicar for every parish will no longer be the norm. But large churches such as cathedrals or small self-sustaining community churches could continue and even flourish, appealing to those who appreciate liturgical or contemporary styles of worship. The diversity of the Church of England could turn out to be a crucial strength.

Revitalisation

The Church of England is investing heavily in creating 'resourcing churches'. These are churches which intentionally plant new churches. The first was St Peter's Brighton which grew from 30 in 2009 to more than 1,000 in 2017. By 2022 the Strategic Development Funding of the Church of England had awarded about £45 million to 'resourcing churches'. Will it work in reversing the general decline or will it create a few 'peak' churches which will survive as islands within the encroaching sea?

Disestablishment?

Disestablishment means the cutting of the residual ties between the Church of England and the state, with the consequent reduction in both rights and responsibilities.

It does not take a crystal ball to forecast that within thirty years all the major denominations will face an existential crisis, simply because over a third of existing congregations will be dead. There will be a massive transfer of responsibility for Church of England church buildings to other bodies, whether the National Churches Trust, the Churches Conservation Trust, English Heritage or the Government. There will still be vibrant congregations led by clergy being ordained now, but the parish system is almost certain to break down. Disestablishment hovers as a blessing or a curse. A curse because it will reduce the footprint of the church in the life of the nation, and so by itself is a recipe for further decline; a blessing because it releases us from the role of being official providers of weddings. The consequence of being an official provider of weddings has meant that the Church of England has had to have an official line on same-sex relationships which has become a real quagmire of dissension. If the provision of weddings becomes simply the prerogative of the state, as in most of Europe, then the decision of whether or not to bless any couple, heterosexual, divorced or gay, becomes a matter for the individual conscience of the church minister.

The New Churches

The growth sector is likely be pentecostal and evangelical churches. For instance, the Fellowship of Independent Evangelical Churches has 639 participating churches in Great Britain with 50,000 members. It is linked to Affinity, formerly the British Evangelical Council, which aims to *"encourage strong, meaningful relationships between Bible-centred churches and organisations."* They *"enjoy fellowship with like-minded churches and evangelical agencies worldwide".*

This does not include the World Council of Churches, which they regard as dangerously liberal.

The Evangelical movement is not a unified body. Conservative evangelicalism is different from liberal evangelicalism, open evangelicalism, charismatic evangelicalism and reformed funda-mentalism.

Pentecostalism shares many of the tenets of evangelical churches, with added emphasis on the gifts of the Spirit such as speaking in tongues. With over 700 denominations it is highly decentralised and is probably the fastest growing religious movement in the world with up to 280 million members worldwide. An equal number are in charismatic churches, often denominational churches which have welcomed the Pentecostal experience.

Why are they growing? Perhaps because they tap into one of the core values of 20th and 21st century life, the primacy of individual experience. *"If it feels good, do it."* This is even more engaging if you are in a large group with everyone having the same experience. How these churches will respond to their enthusiasts encountering the inevitable heartaches and tragedies life remains to be seen However, there is no denying that there's a big, disorganised church out there!

Africa Rising

The future of the Church may well lie in Africa. Over half of Africans say they are Christian. In Nigeria the largest churches are Anglican and Roman Catholic with 18 million and 18.9 million respectively.

The largest evangelical church is the Redeemed Christian Church of God with over 5 million in Nigeria alone and 9 million in the world.

Founded in 1952, its main auditorium on the Lagos-Ibadan highway can host over a million people at major events. It has over 50,000 branches globally and 870 churches in Britain. It appeals particularly to young Nigerians and is fully digital. Two thirds of the congregants in Croydon dial in online. Also, there are monthly services in Yoruba: *"People believe that the type of prayer that they pray in Yoruba is more powerful than when they do it in English."* (The Economist 26/10/24)

Church vs. Sect

A woman chaplain in the Lithuanian Lutheran church said in 2022: *"Our institutions may die. Our buildings may die. But our faith will survive."* The question is, what sort of faith? There is a crisis facing the churches beyond the question of numbers. Just what sort of church do we want to be? A church which is able to relate to society as a whole, or a sect which exists simply for and by conversions? Will the church be able to reclaim a voice in the public square, or is our future simply to be having faith-filled conversations within the bubble of the saved?

Faiths in the Public Square

A defining moment for the place of Christianity in Britain was the year 2000. It obviously marked 2000 years (roughly) after the birth of Jesus. But in the Faith Zone of the Millennium Dome exhibition, Christianity was but one of the six pavilions showcasing the major religions practised in the UK. And it never was going to give the Church a special place. The earlier idea had been to have a 'Spirit Zone' - an even more amorphous concept.

In her first Christmas Day broadcast in 1952, Queen Elizabeth asked the people of the Commonwealth *"whatever your religion may be, to pray for me on that day (the coronation)".*

At her Diamond Jubilee in 2012, before representatives of Christian denominations as well as of Baha'i, Buddhist, Hindu, Jain, Jewish, Muslim, Sikh and Zoroastrian communities, the Queen declared, *"(The Church's) role is not to defend Anglicanism to the exclusion of other religions. Instead the Church has a duty to protect the free practice of all faiths in this country."*

Increasingly, the only way that the Church can be heard effectively in the public square is by speaking alongside other religions. So in the aftermath of the riots following the stabbing of three young girls in Southport, a statement was made by the Anglican and Catholic bishops, as well as by Muslim, Jewish, Sikh and Hindu representatives. It is the only way the church can be heard. But what it means for the Church to accept other religions as allies rather than rivals needs a lot of theological work.

There are opportunities. Britain's biggest aircraft maker is Airbus in Flintshire, with 5,000 employees. Andy Liston is the Site Safety Box Facilitator and is also training to be a pastoral assistant in Chester diocese. A Muslim trainee asked Andy for a place to pray, and as a result the company now has a multi-faith prayer room and a prayer garden. Andy said: *"Airbus feels the benefit, as it allows people to bring their whole selves to work."*

A Community of Communities

The most likely future is that organised Christianity is going to give way to disorganised Christianity. That is already seen in the proliferation of Pentecostal churches in Africa and Latin America.

The religious landscape will be transformed into a community of communities, communities of prayer and communities of transformation. The older denominations could become communities of prayer, using the wealth of centuries of liturgical prayer and classical music. They could easily become prayer centres teaching meditation and contemplation. Communities of transformation will centre their lives on leading new people to a vibrant relationship with God. These are of course not mutually exclusive, but the death of the organised church will disclose the hidden tension which has probably always existed within the Christianity.

Leaving a legacy

Does this mean that 2,000 years of Christian worship and spirituality is going to disappear? Canon Ian Mobsby, a Diocesan Missioner in Ontario, Canada, wrote in the Church Times (25/10/24): *"Unchurched people are largely not going to come to a liturgical worship service."* But perhaps there are within the institutional structures of the church treasures of prayer, meditation and contemplation which directly address the bewildering world we live in, practices that are already being rediscovered.

Archie Coates is the vicar of Holy Trinity Brompton (HTB), an evangelical charismatic church in the Church of England. In 2023 he invited as the main speaker to the annual weekend of HTB's family of churches Rich Villodas, lead pastor of New Life

Fellowship, a large multi-racial church in Queens, New York. Archie had invited him simply on the basis of a book he had read, 'The Deeply Formed Life'. The first section is all about monastic spirituality. *"Deep in our souls, we crave space with God that is defined by silence, stillness and solitude."* (p. 8)

At the same time the midweek groups of HTB were all learning how to practise 'lectio divina' – the monastic way of reading the Bible as quiet meditation. It is just the kind of practice which can answer the question which Elias Odunlami voiced at the end of part 2: "I keep chasing tomorrow. How can I live in the now?"

I hope for the day when times of quiet meditation or contemplation will be just as much part of the life of the local church as Sunday worship and Bible study groups. Agatha Christie said about her writing: "All you need is a chair and a table, a typewriter and a bit of peace." To bring a culture of meditative stillness to our churches all we need is a chair, a candle and silence.

Humility

Whatever the shape of the Church in the future, we will have to grapple with the Church's self-understanding which no longer makes sense to 21st century people. The Church will have to learn how to listen to different voices, different ways of understanding, different ways of belief, just as Charles Gore in 'Lux Mundi' did in 1889 and John Robinson in 'Honest to God' in 1963. It will, at last, have to learn the virtue of humility.

BIBLIOGRAPHY

PART 1
CONTINUING CONVERSATIONS

Michael Green - Evangelism in the Early Church

Peter Brown - The World of Late Antiquity

ed. Sherwood Eliot Wirt - The Confessions of St Augustine

Bede - A History of the English Church and People

R H C Davis - A History of Medieval Europe

Anselm of Canterbury - The Major Works (Oxford)

Glenn E Myers - Seeking Spiritual Intimacy

Thomas a Kempis - The Imitation of Christ

ed Carter Lindberg - The European Reformations source book

Graham Tomlin - Luther and his world

ed. John Stacey - John Wesley: Contemporary Perspectives

Harvey Cox - Fire from Heaven

Tom Holland - Dominion

The Oxford History of England - various volumes

PART 2

NEW WORLD/NEW CONSCIOUSNESS

THANKS TO

Bob Pajkowski	AI and Technology
Rev Joe Roberts	Video Games
Chileab Redwood-Sawyer	Synthetic biology
Kevin O'Sullivan -	Climate change, air pollution
James Burdass	Climate change

PART 3

BEING CREDIBLE IN THE POST-MODERN WORLD

BOOKS WHICH HELPED ME THINK
(in order of being mentioned in Part 3)

C S Lewis	The Screwtape Letters
Yuval Hariri	Sapiens
-	Alcoholics Anonymous
Kallistos Ware	The Orthodox Way
	The 39 Articles of Religion (1562)
Nick Page	The Badly Behaved Bible
Andy Roland	Jesus the Troublemaker - his last eight days
Andy Roland	Daily Prayers from the World's Faiths
Dalai Lama	Towards a true kinship of faiths
John Robinson	Honest to God
Jane Goodall	Reason for Hope
Stephen Peters	The Chimp Paradox
Aldous Huxley	The Devils of Loudon
Karl Marx	The Communist Manifesto
David Baker	The Shortest History of Sex
(Church House)	Living in Love and Faith
Bart Ehrman	A History of the Afterlife
Ulrich Simon	A Theology of Auschwitz
William J Peters	At heaven's door
William James	Varieties of Religious Experience

Books of Faith and Belief (in order of first writing)
The Bible - the Hebrew Scriptures
The Upanishads
The Dhammapada
The Bhagavad Gita
The Bible - the Christian Scriptures
The Qur'an

OTHER BOOKS BY ANDY ROLAND

BIBLE IN BRIEF

A methodical introduction to the whole Bible in six months. Each month has a separate topic, like the Prophets, Law Psalms & Wisdom, and Jesus. Each week has a separate topic like David & Solomon and the Gospel of John. Each day gives a chapter to read and one question which people can respond to in the book or on line.

There are archaeological drawings, maps and timelines. At the end of each month is a section 'The Other Side', with contemporary quotes from the surrounding cultures, such as the Babylonian Creation Myth, and sayings of the early rabbis.

"This book does what few others do – it offers a very helpful guide for those looking for a brief overview of the Bible and its story."
   Bishop Graham Tomlin

JESUS THE TROUBLEMAKER
HIS LAST EIGHT DAYS

A historical novel based on the gospels, especially Mark. Jesus is placed fully into his Jewish context and is called Yeshua throughout. The story starts with Yeshua walking towards Yericho and ends with a report by the captain of the Temple Police on the events of Pentecost/Shavu'ot. Dialogues and events are vividly re-imagined and new light is shed on many questions which arise from seeing the story as continuous events.

After each section, notes describe what narrative editorial decisions were made and why. Three maps and 16 illustrations show the context of the story.
At the end there are sections on the reliability of the gospels, on languages and names, on history and politics and on contemporary religious movements.

'*Well! Holy Week has come alive in a new way and will never be the same again.*
The book has finally removed set images and confusions stuck in my mind from so many years and something much more vibrant and alive has replaced them.'
    Sr Hilda Mary CSC, *St Michael's Convent*

'An interesting and challenging book'.
    Rabbi Helen Freeman, *West London Synagogue*

DAILY PRAYERS FROM THE WORLD'S FAITH

The first part is a multi-faith devotional with prayers and reflections from Hinduism, Buddhism, Judaism, Western Christianity, Eastern Christianity, Islam, Sikhism and Alcoholics Anonymous. Leading members of each faith were then consulted about what prayers and reflections to include. The themes covered are Foundations, Welcoming the Day, Thanks, Sorry, Please, At Night, Surrender and Christmas.

The second part describes each faith in just 500 words - Hinduism took 780. Each account is arranged according to the suggestions of a leader of each faith.

'One of the deepest levels of interfaith encounter is reached when we understand how our neighbours and friends of different faiths express themselves in prayer before the One who is absolute in their own tradition.

In this wide-ranging selection of prayers, Andy Roland, writing as a Christian, provides some varied trustworthy stepping stones for Christians who want to set off on that journey of appreciation in respect and humility.'
    Rt Rev Dr Michael Ipgrave, Bishop of Lichfield

'This book would be good for R.E.' **Edward age 12**

JOURNEY THROUGH LENT WITH JESUS

A 50-day devotional walking with Jesus in his last eight days. It starts in the Jordan valley and ends at the empty tomb. Each day has a Bible reading, a quote from 'Jesus the Troublemaker', some factual comments, a personal reflection and a suggestion for action.

'It is very easy to engage with. The style is wonderfully conversational, drawing the audience into the life of 'Yeshua' and his disciples in a very imaginative and challenging way... Your reflections are appropriate for us today, encouraging us to live our faith.' **Rob Gillion, Bishop for the Arts**

DISCOVERING PSALMS AS PRAYER

At a Christian ashram in India Andy encountered the Syrian orthodox tradition of engaging with the psalms. He adopted it was his framework for daily prayer for the next forty years. The book tells the story and how psalms can be used morning, noon and night.

'In 'Discovering Psalms as Prayer' Andy Roland weaves together the wisdom of a faithful, personal pilgrimage with practical guidance for reading the psalms. It will be a gift to those wanting to make that discovery for themselves.'
Rev David Runcorn, author of 'Love means love', 'Spirituality Workbook' and 'Playing in the Dust'.

✝

www.ingramcontent.com/pod-product-compliance
Lightning Source LLC
Chambersburg PA
CBHW061214070526
44584CB00029B/3825